Ana Oncina
CROQUETTE & EMPANADA

CROQUETTE & EMPANADA

Andrews McMeel Publishing
a division of Andrews McMeel Universal
1130 Walnut Street, Kansas City, Missouri 64106

www.andrewsmcmeel.com

Originally published in Spain by Ediciones La Cúpula (www.lacupula.com).

19 20 21 22 23 RLP 10 9 8 7 6 5 4 3 2 1

ISBN: 978-1-4494-9706-4

Library of Congress Control Number: 2018911295

Editor: Patty Rice
Art Director: Holly Swayne
Production Manager: Tamara Haus
Production Editor: Elizabeth A. Garcia

Attention: Schools and Businesses

Andrews McMeel books are available at quantity discounts with bulk purchase for educational, business, or sales promotional use. For information, please e-mail the Andrews McMeel Publishing Special Sales Department: specialsales@amuniversal.com.

CROQUETTE & EMPANADA

Ana Oncina

Andrews McMeel
PUBLISHING®

THANKS TO:

MY FAMILY;
MY FRIENDS, ESPECIALLY TO MARINA FOR HER UNCONDITIONAL SUPPORT;
THE PUBLISHER EDICIONES LA CÚPULA, FOR HAVING CONFIDENCE IN ME;
AND TO ALEX—WITHOUT YOU THESE STORIES WOULD NOT HAVE
BEEN POSSIBLE.

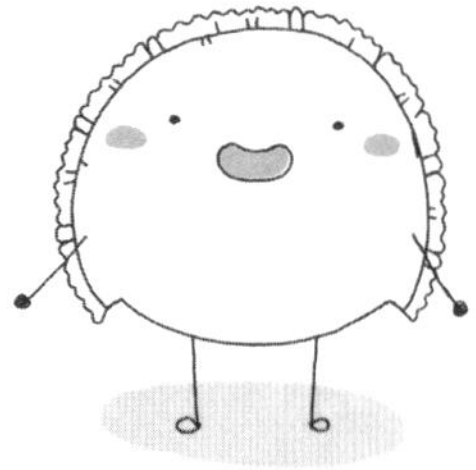

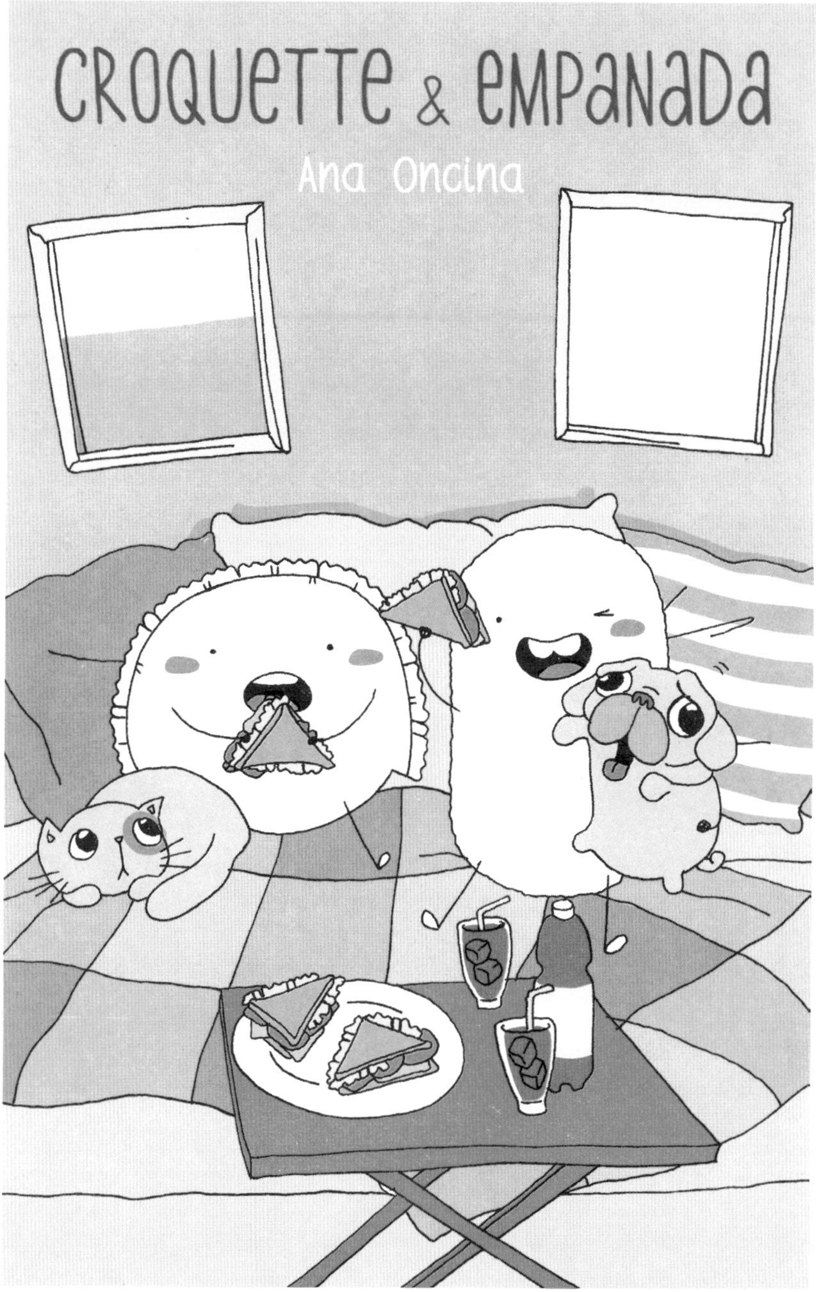
CROQUETTE & EMPANADA
Ana Oncina

- STARTING OUT ON THE RIGHT FOOT -

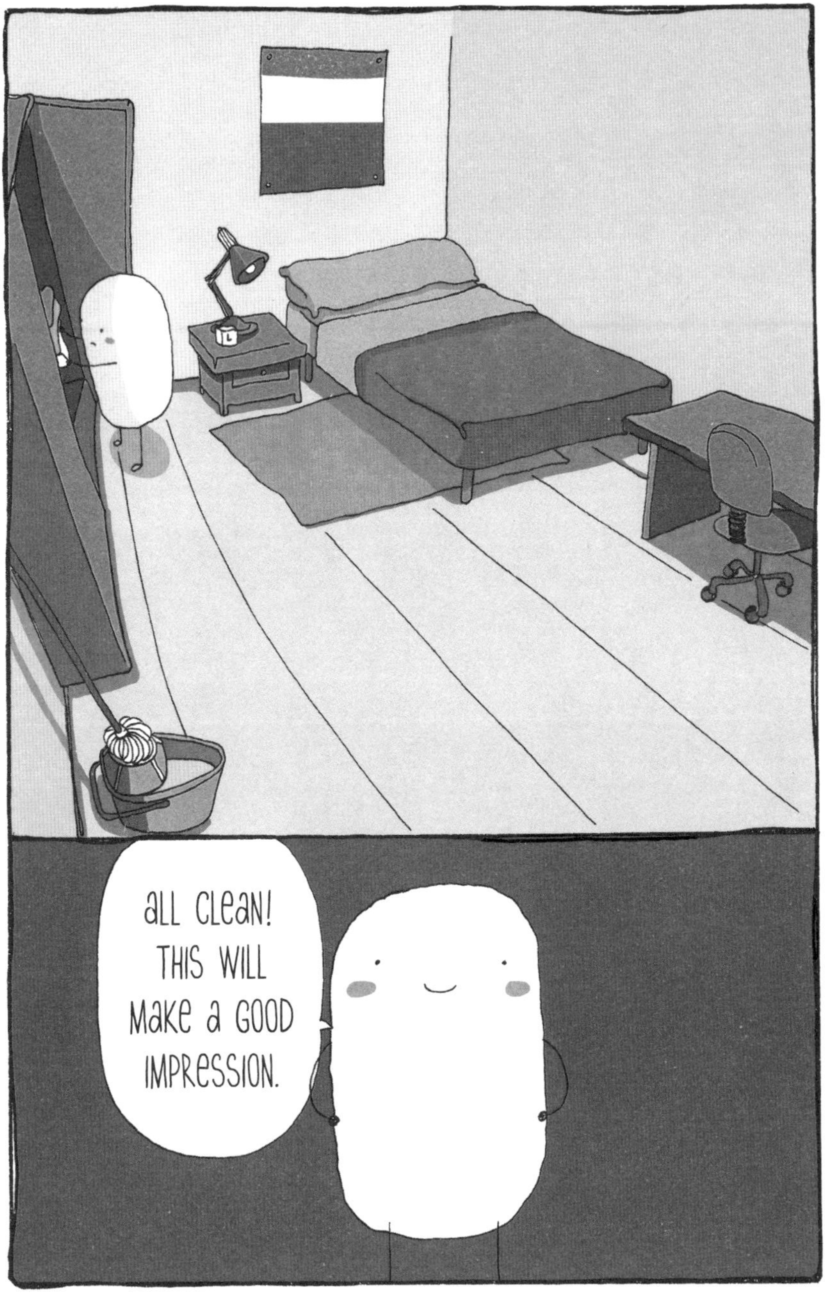
ALL CLEAN! THIS WILL MAKE A GOOD IMPRESSION.

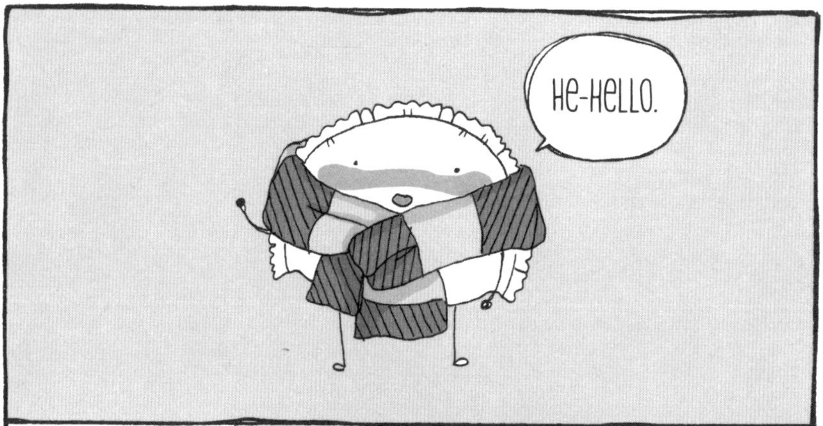
HE-HELLO.

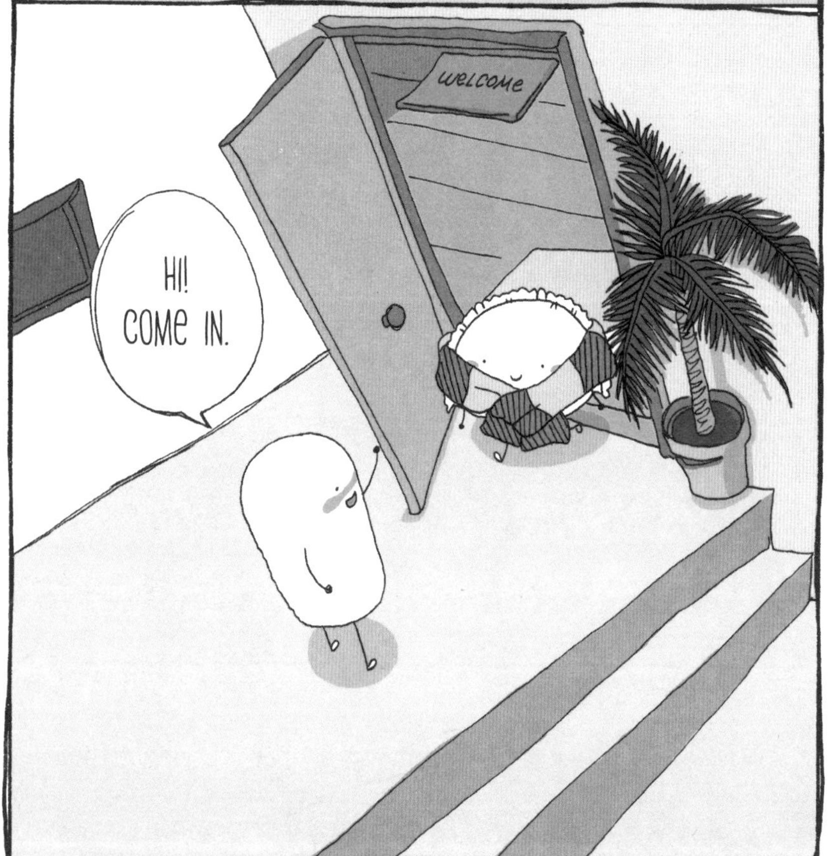
WELCOME
HI! COME IN.

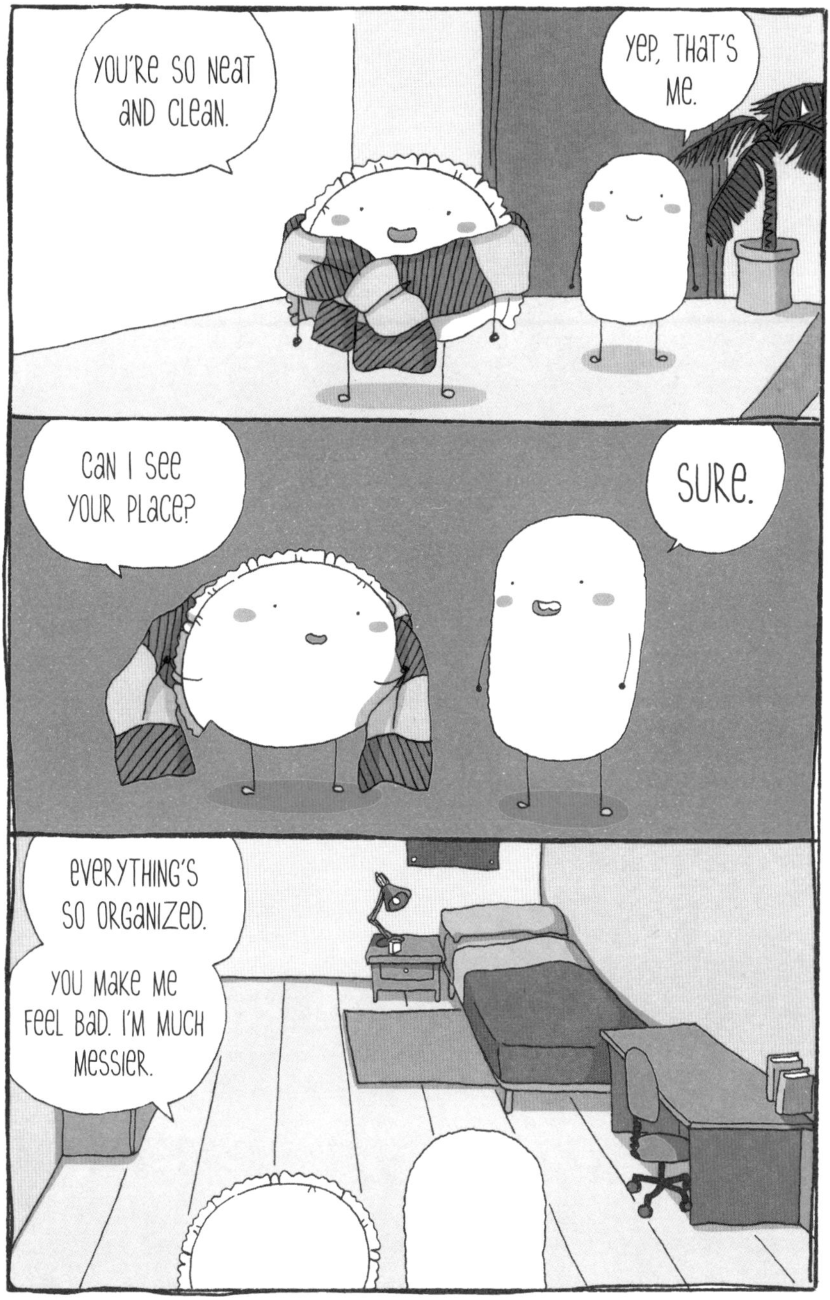
YOU'RE SO NEAT AND CLEAN.
YEP, THAT'S ME.
CAN I SEE YOUR PLACE?
SURE.
EVERYTHING'S SO ORGANIZED.
YOU MAKE ME FEEL BAD. I'M MUCH MESSIER.

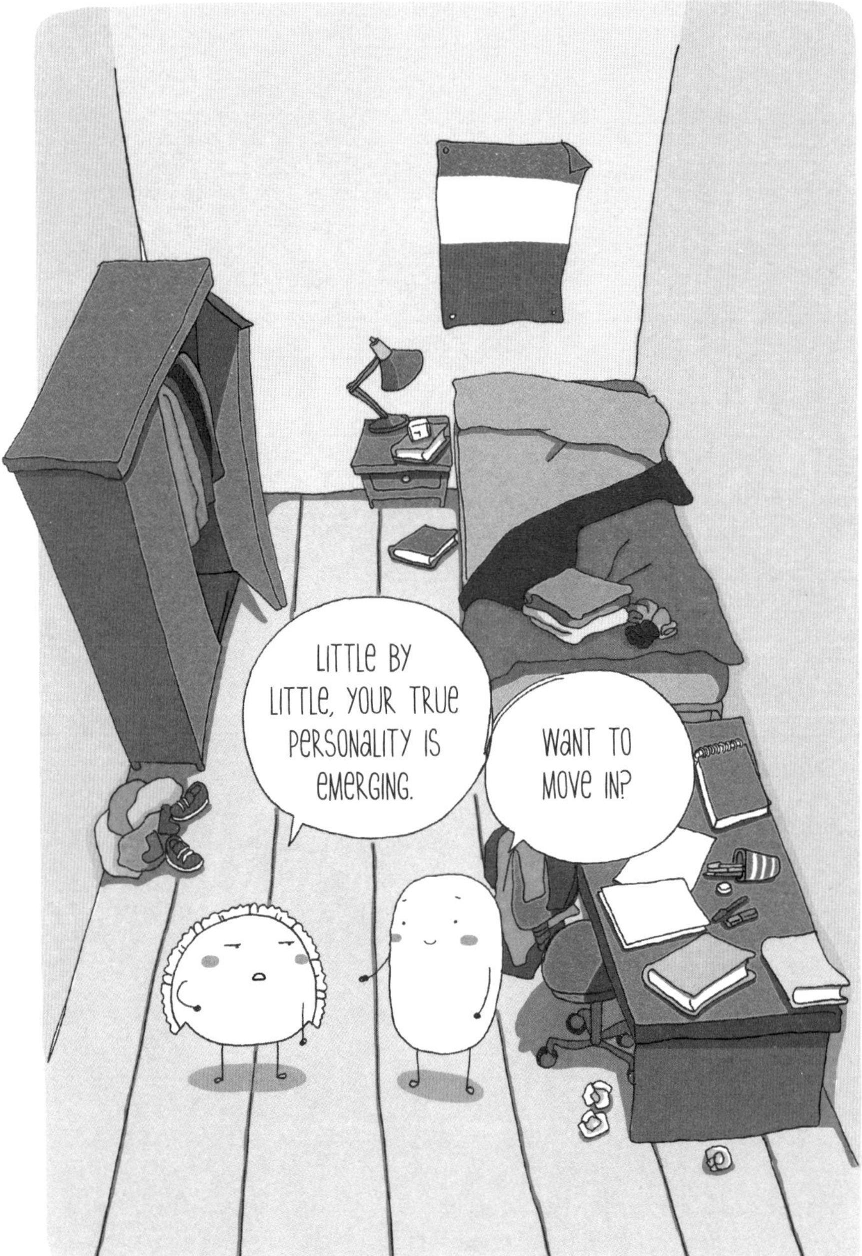
LITTLE BY LITTLE, YOUR TRUE PERSONALITY IS EMERGING.
WANT TO MOVE IN?

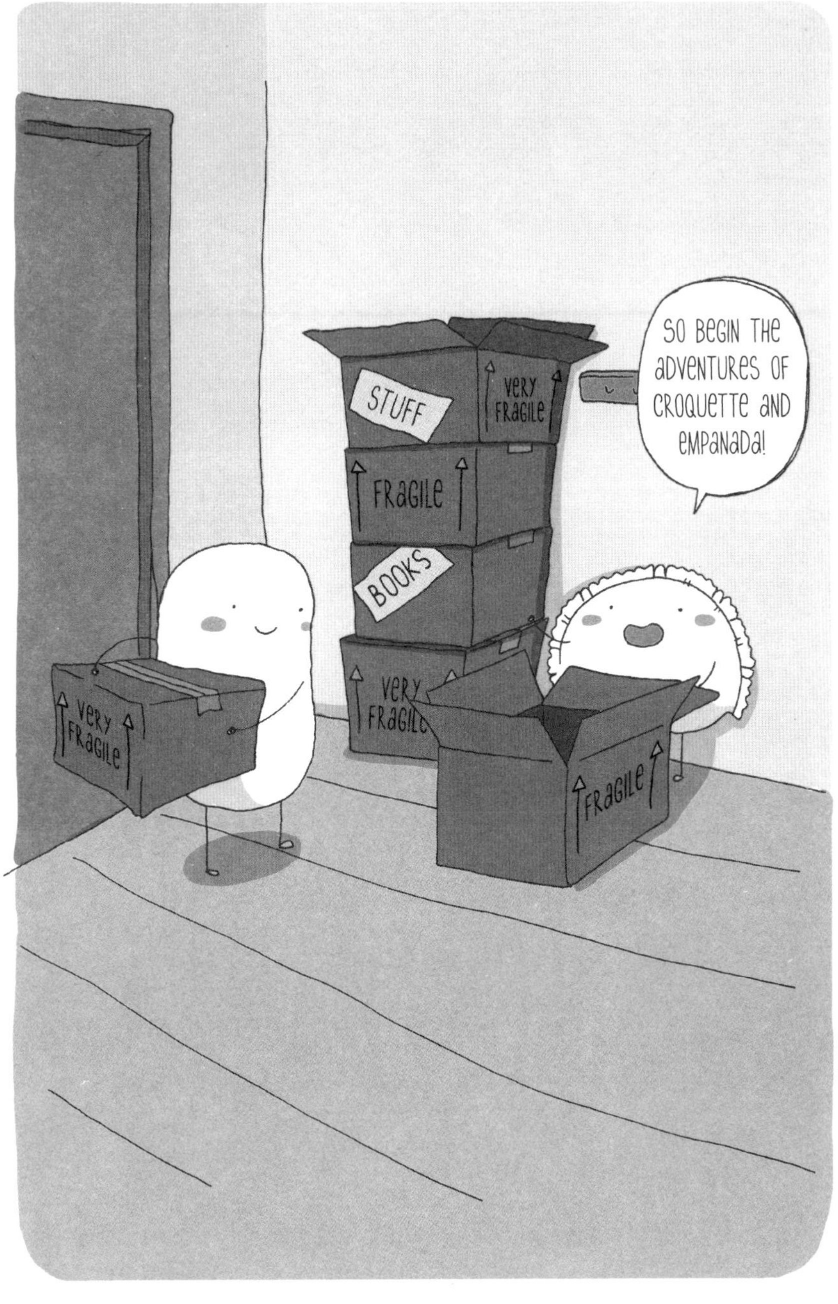
SO BEGIN THE ADVENTURES OF CROQUETTE AND EMPANADA!
STUFF
VERY FRAGILE
FRAGILE
BOOKS
VERY FRAGILE
VERY FRAGILE
FRAGILE

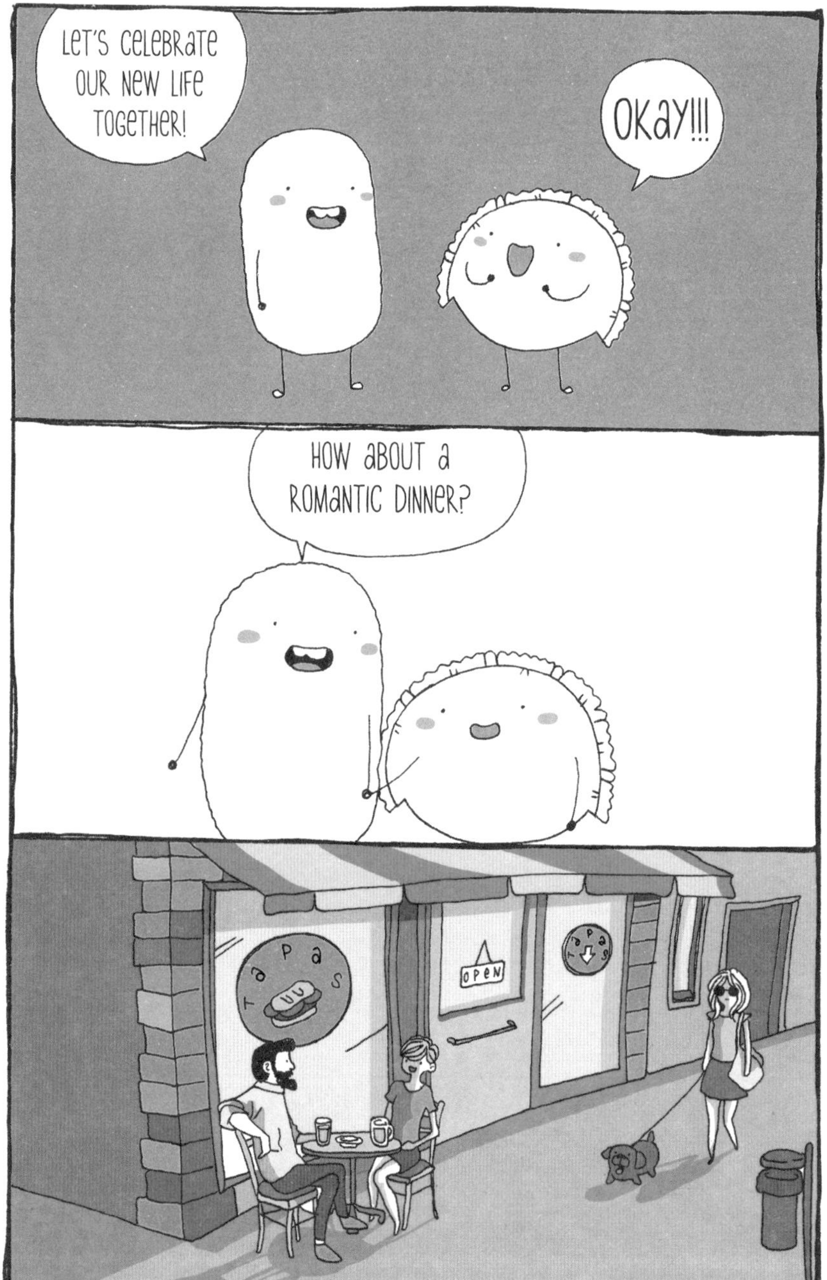
LET'S CELEBRATE OUR NEW LIFE TOGETHER!
OKAY!!!
HOW ABOUT A ROMANTIC DINNER?
Tapas
OPEN
Tapas

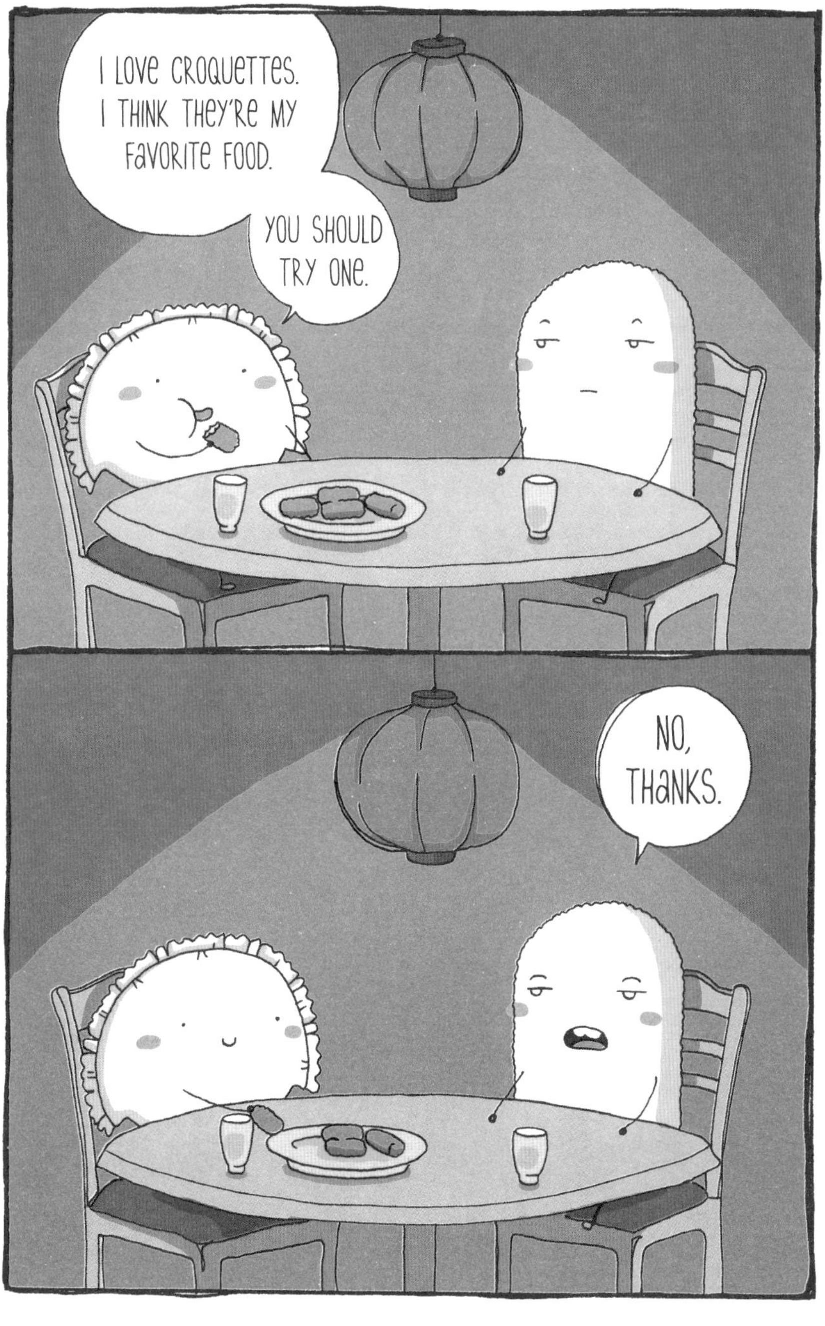
I LOVE CROQUETTES. I THINK THEY'RE MY FAVORITE FOOD.
YOU SHOULD TRY ONE.
NO, THANKS.

- THE COMPLEXITY OF WOMEN -

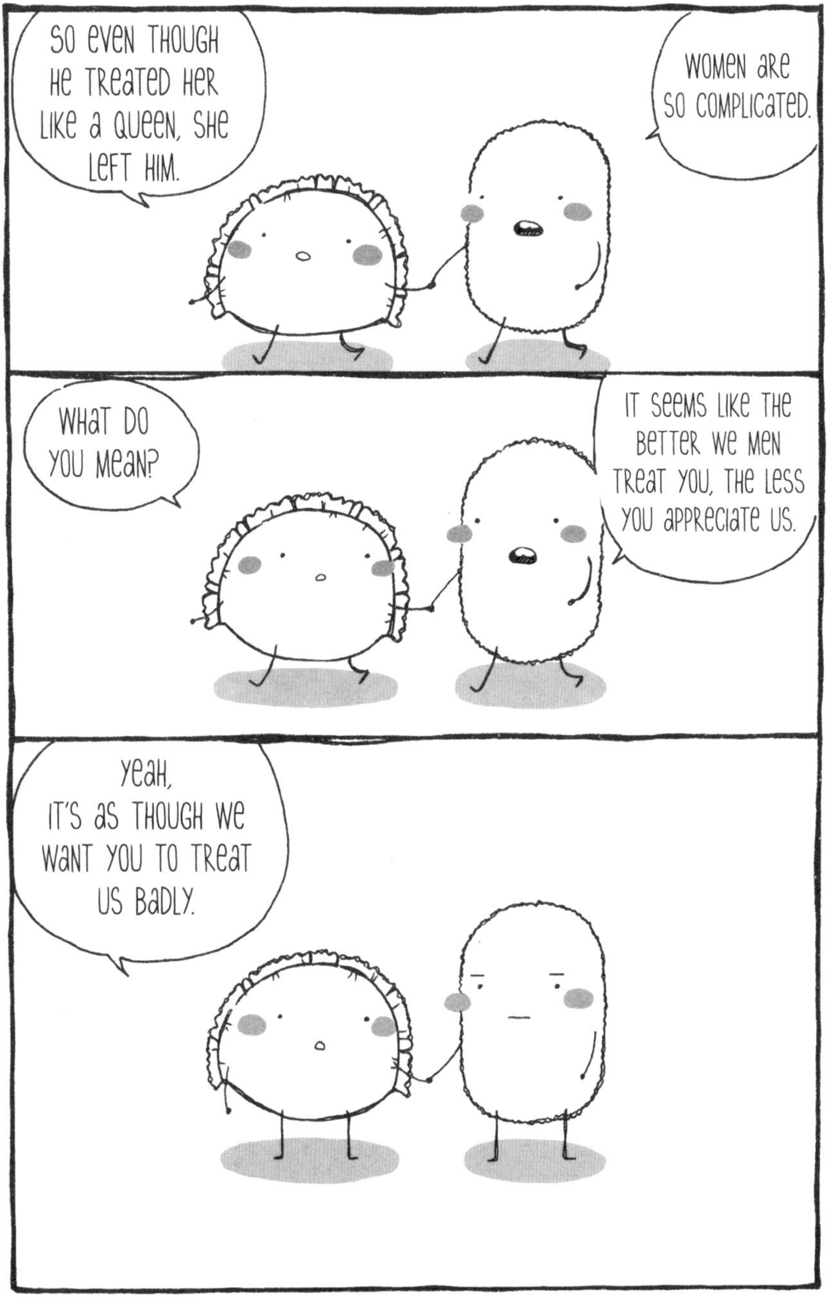
SO EVEN THOUGH HE TREATED HER LIKE A QUEEN, SHE LEFT HIM.
WOMEN ARE SO COMPLICATED.
WHAT DO YOU MEAN?
IT SEEMS LIKE THE BETTER WE MEN TREAT YOU, THE LESS YOU APPRECIATE US.
YEAH, IT'S AS THOUGH WE WANT YOU TO TREAT US BADLY.

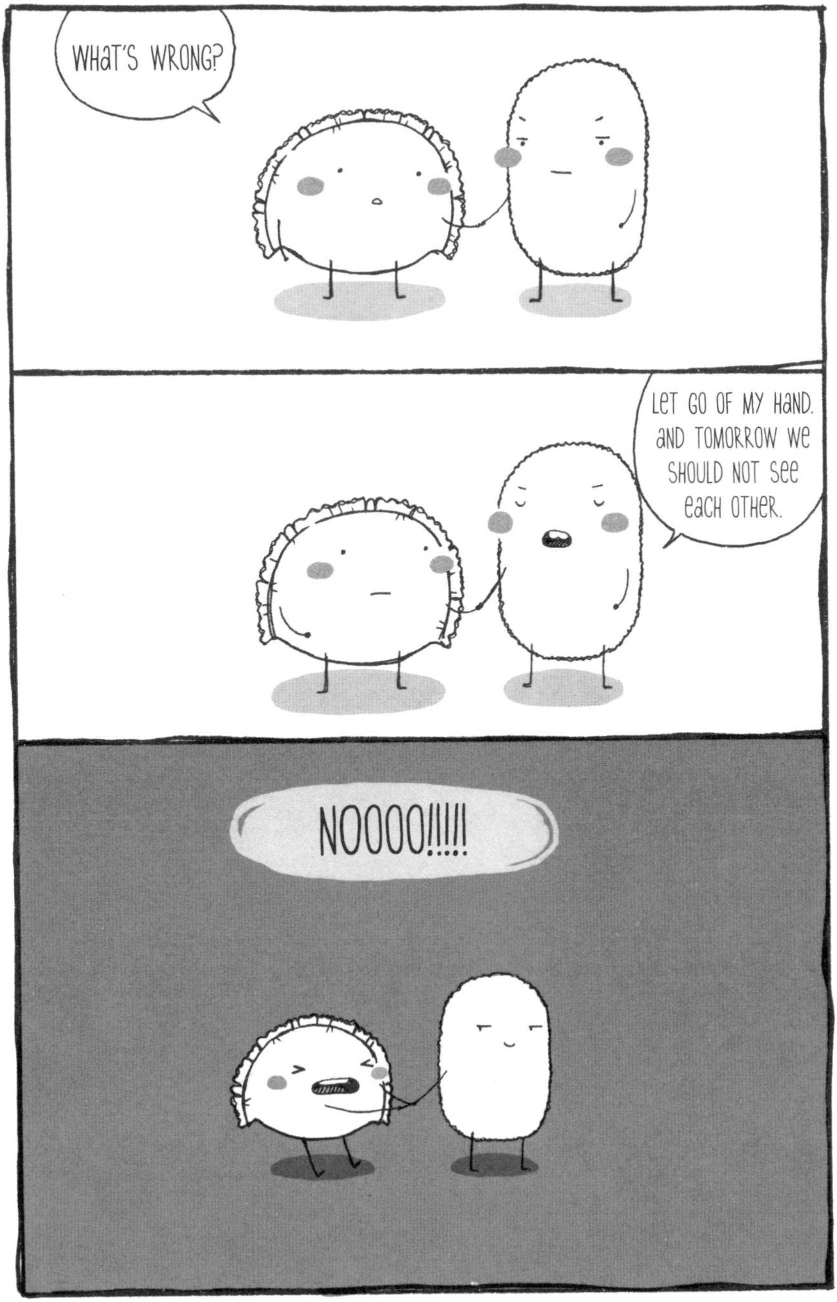
WHAT'S WRONG?
LET GO OF MY HAND. AND TOMORROW WE SHOULD NOT SEE EACH OTHER.
NOOOO!!!!!

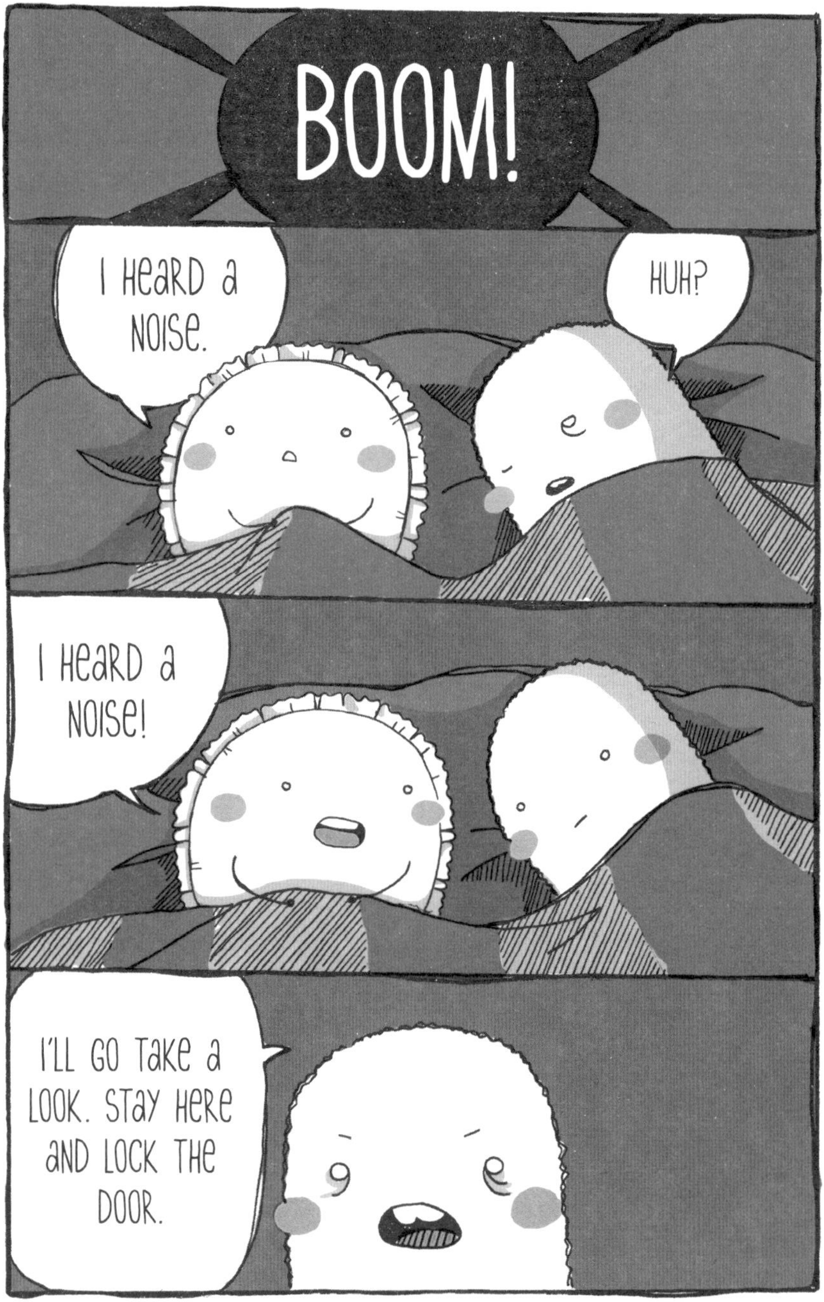
BOOM!
I HEARD A NOISE.
HUH?
I HEARD A NOISE!
I'LL GO TAKE A LOOK. STAY HERE AND LOCK THE DOOR.

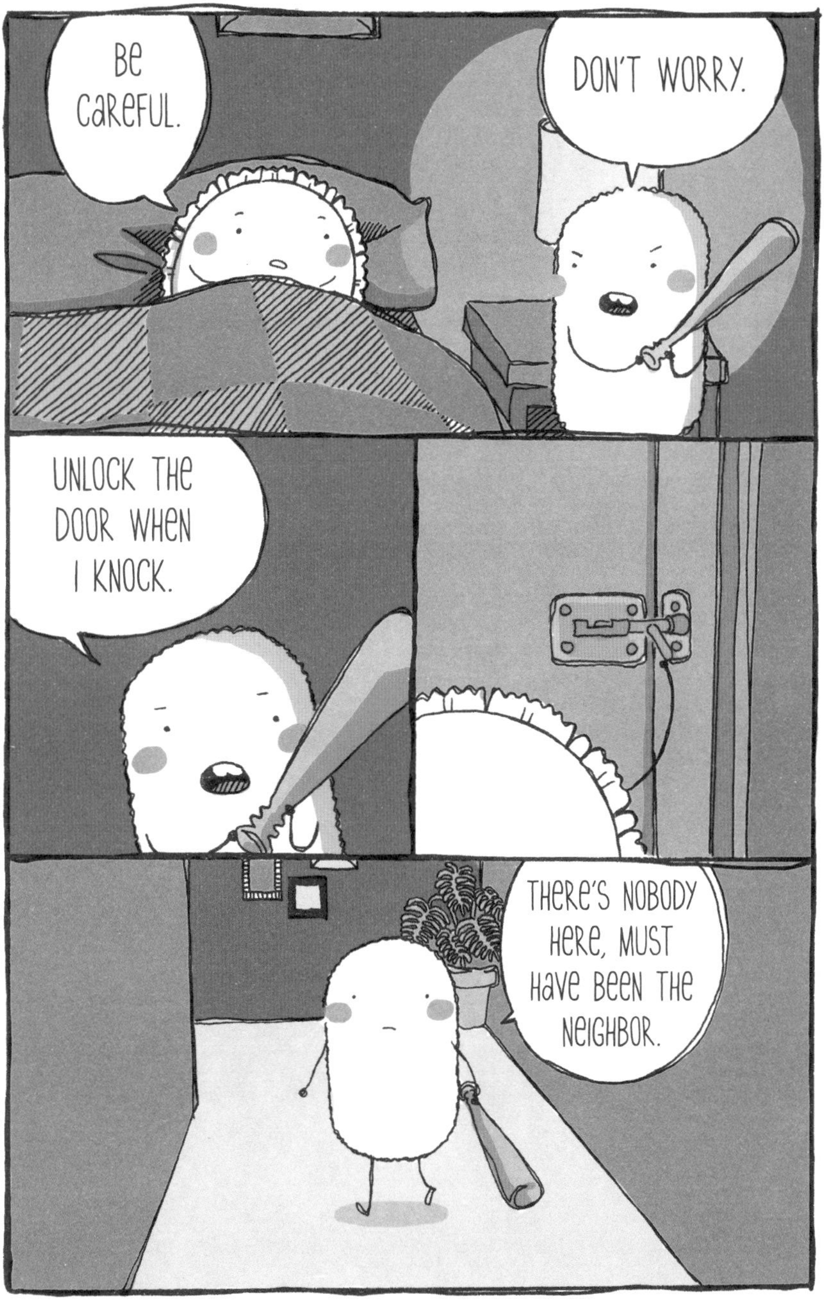
Be careful.
DON'T WORRY.
UNLOCK THE DOOR WHEN I KNOCK.
THERE'S NOBODY HERE, MUST HAVE BEEN THE NEIGHBOR.

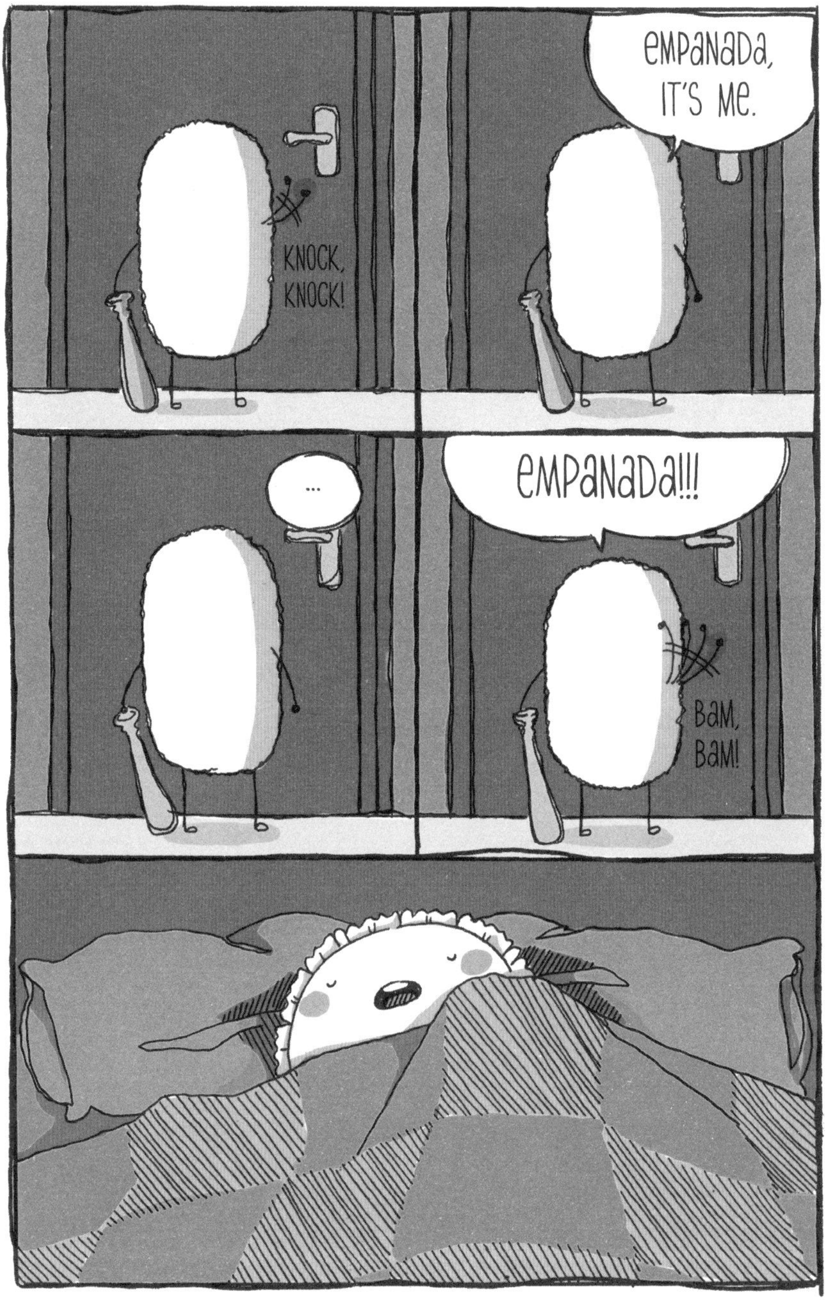
KNOCK, KNOCK!
EMPANADA, IT'S ME.
...
EMPANADA!!!
BAM, BAM!

- URBAN STRESS -

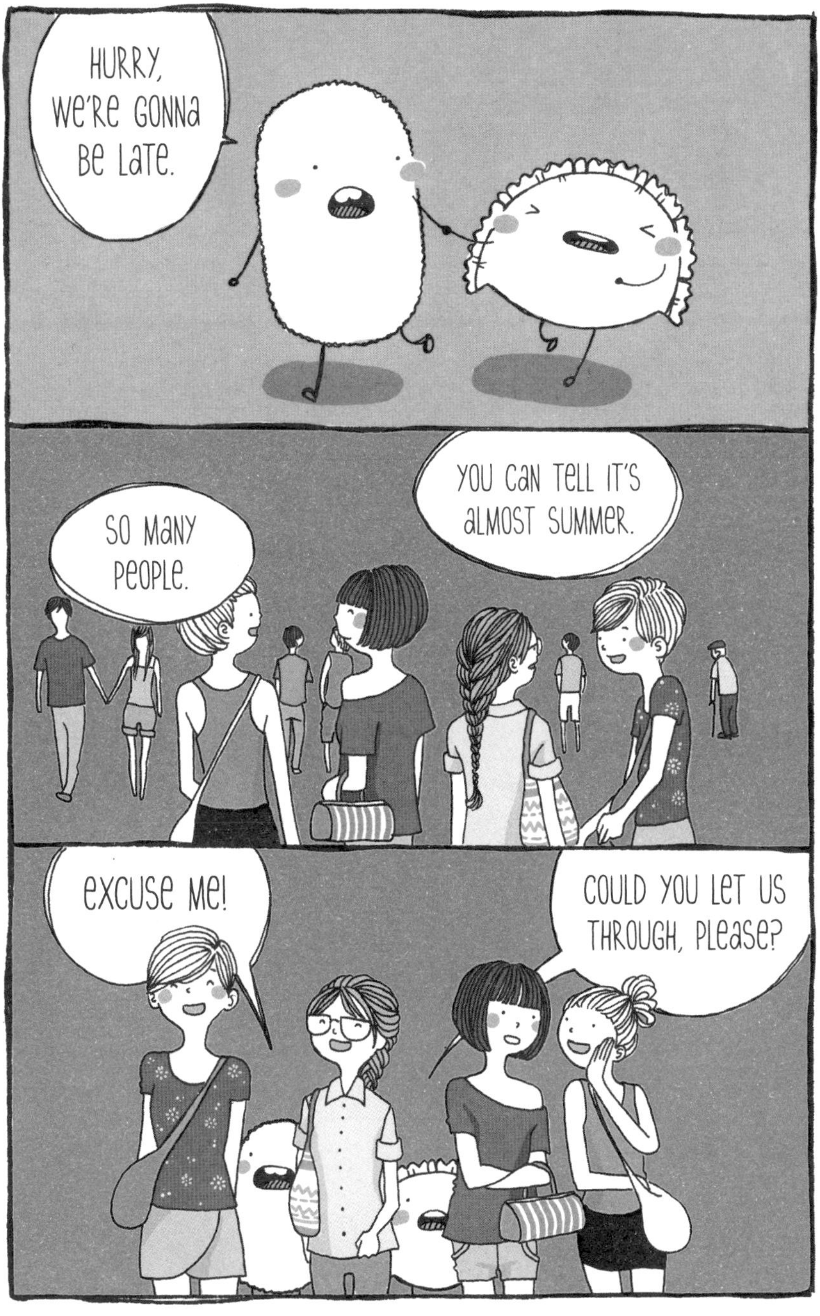
HURRY, WE'RE GONNA BE LATE.
SO MANY PEOPLE.
YOU CAN TELL IT'S ALMOST SUMMER.
EXCUSE ME!
COULD YOU LET US THROUGH, PLEASE?

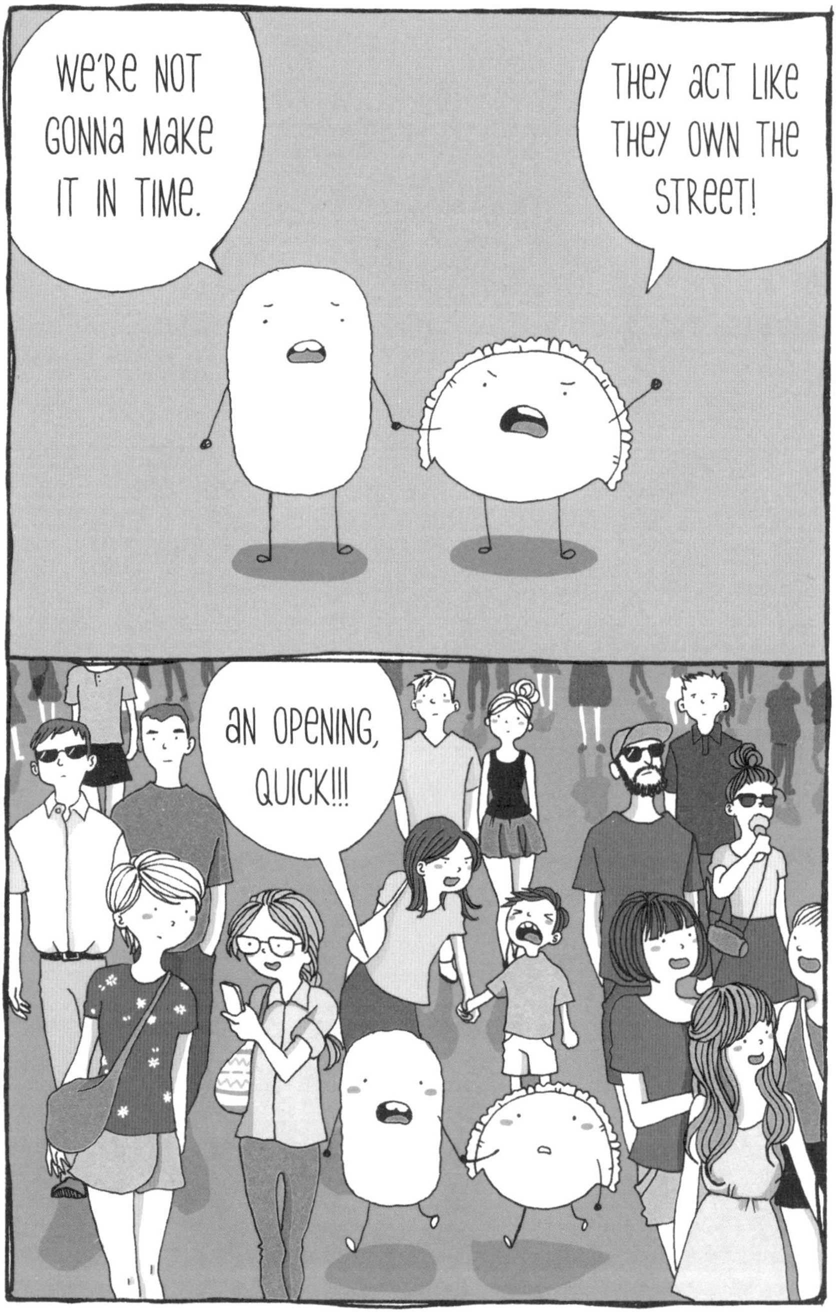
WE'RE NOT GONNA MAKE IT IN TIME.
THEY ACT LIKE THEY OWN THE STREET!
AN OPENING, QUICK!!!

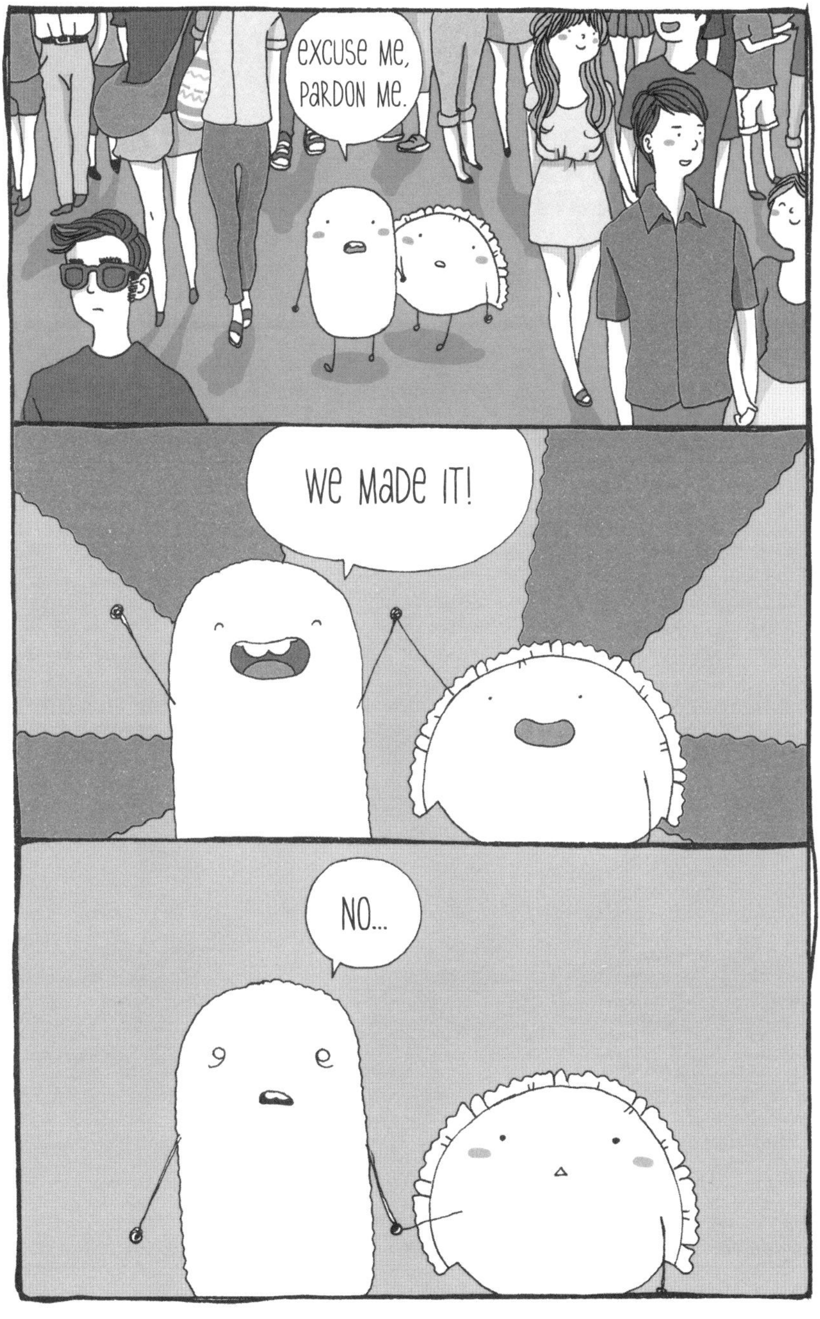
EXCUSE ME, PARDON ME.
WE MADE IT!
NO...

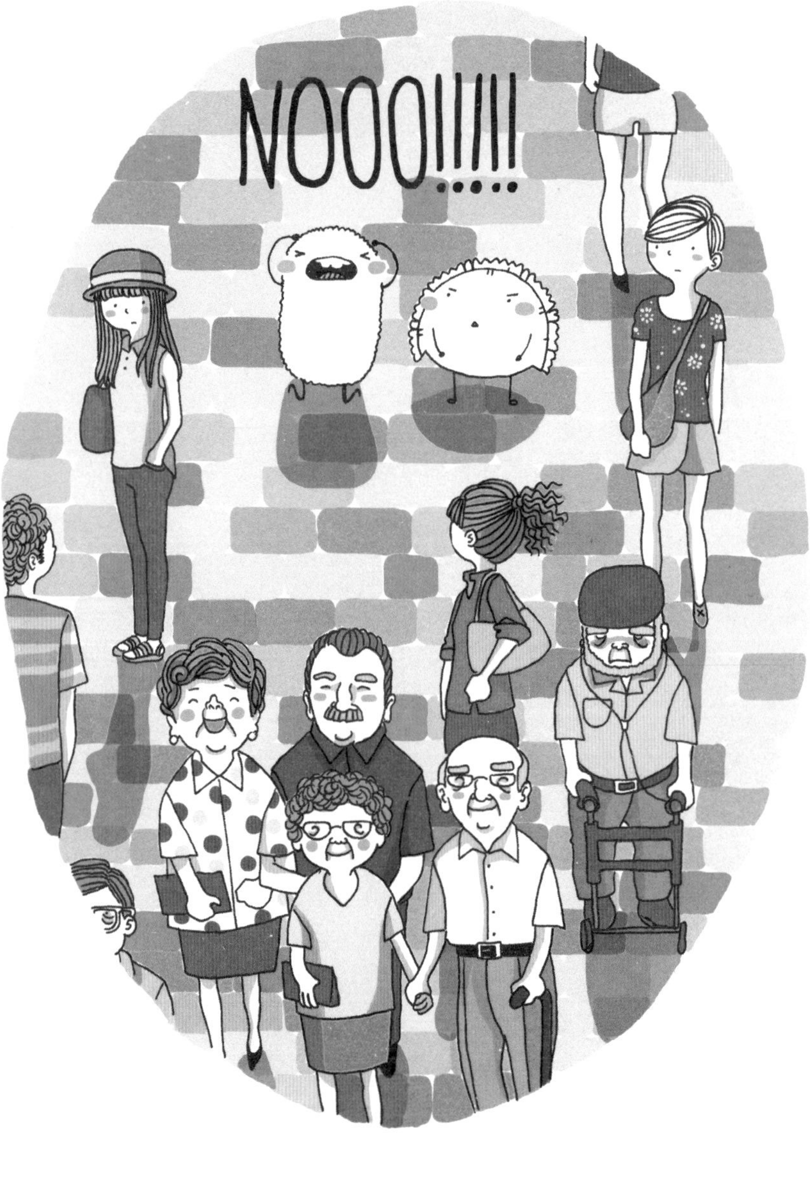
NOOO!!!!!!

- SCARY BEDTIME STORIES -

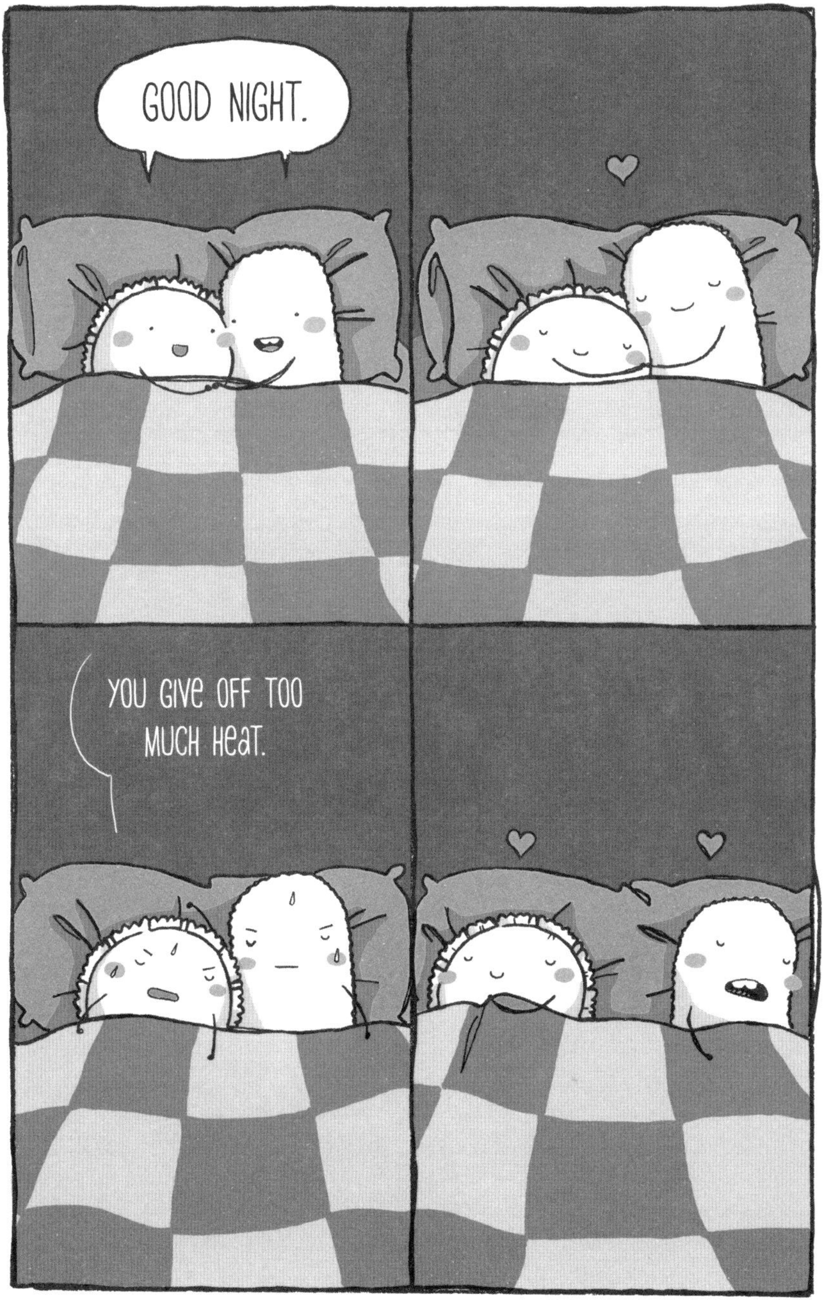
GOOD NIGHT.
YOU GIVE OFF TOO MUCH HEAT.

- MASTER CHEF -

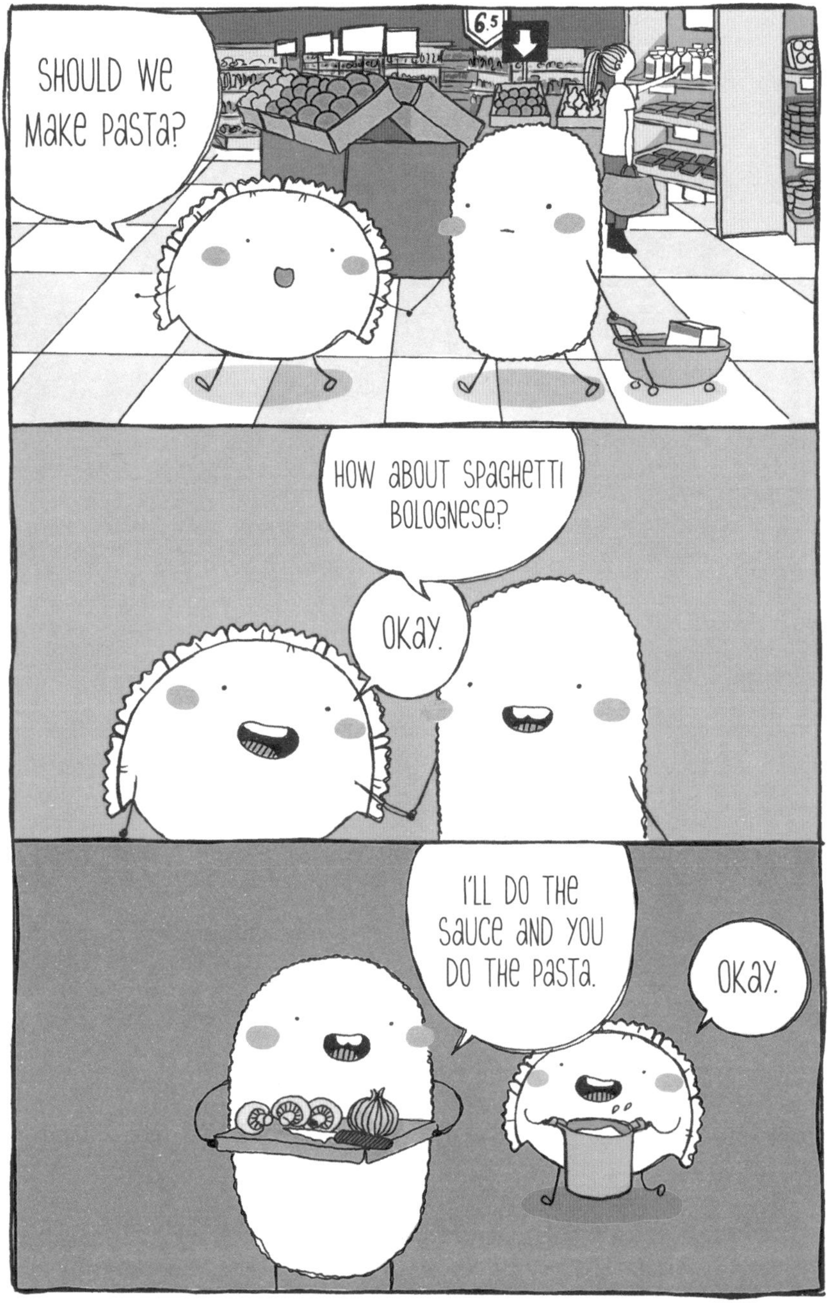
SHOULD WE MAKE PASTA?
HOW ABOUT SPAGHETTI BOLOGNESE?
OKAY.
I'LL DO THE SAUCE AND YOU DO THE PASTA.
OKAY.

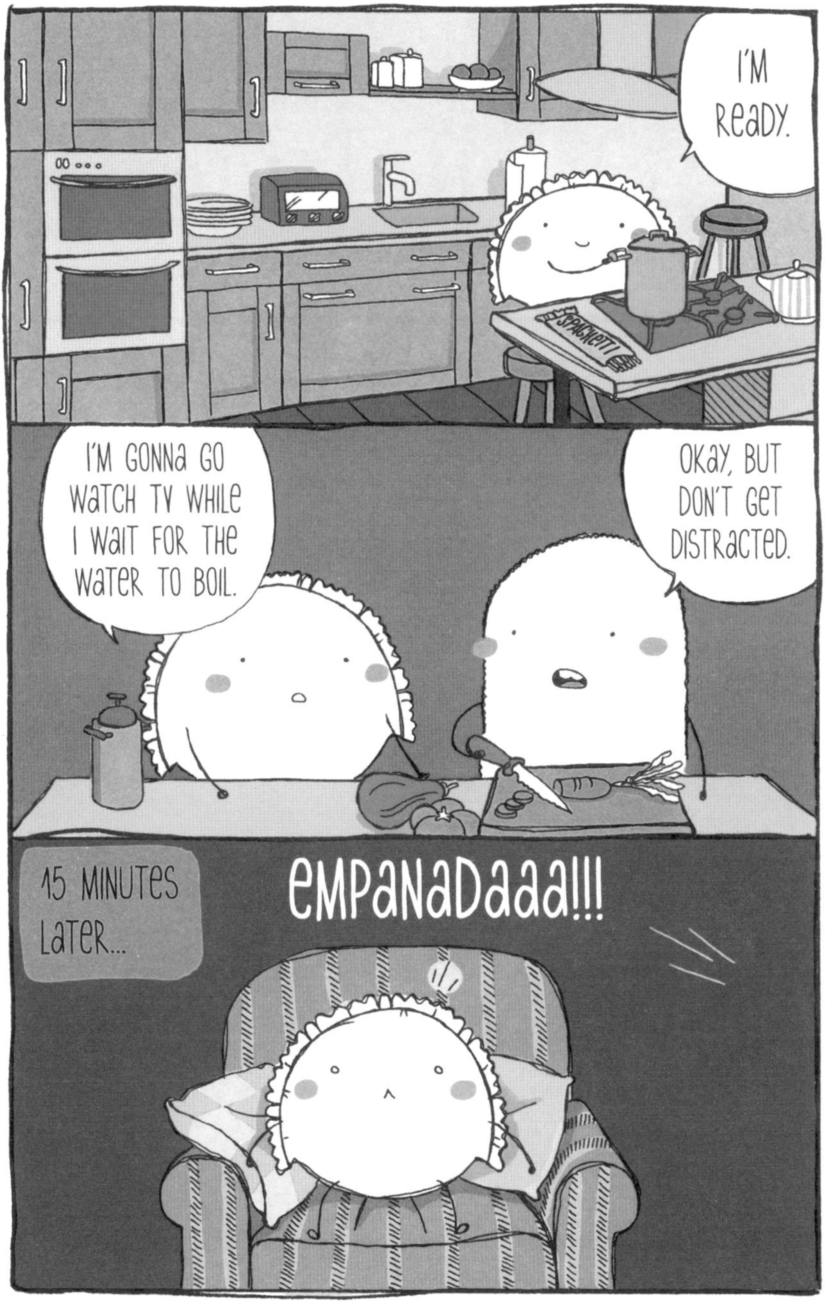

I'M READY.
I'M GONNA GO WATCH TV WHILE I WAIT FOR THE WATER TO BOIL.
OKAY, BUT DON'T GET DISTRACTED.
15 MINUTES LATER...
EMPANADAAA!!!

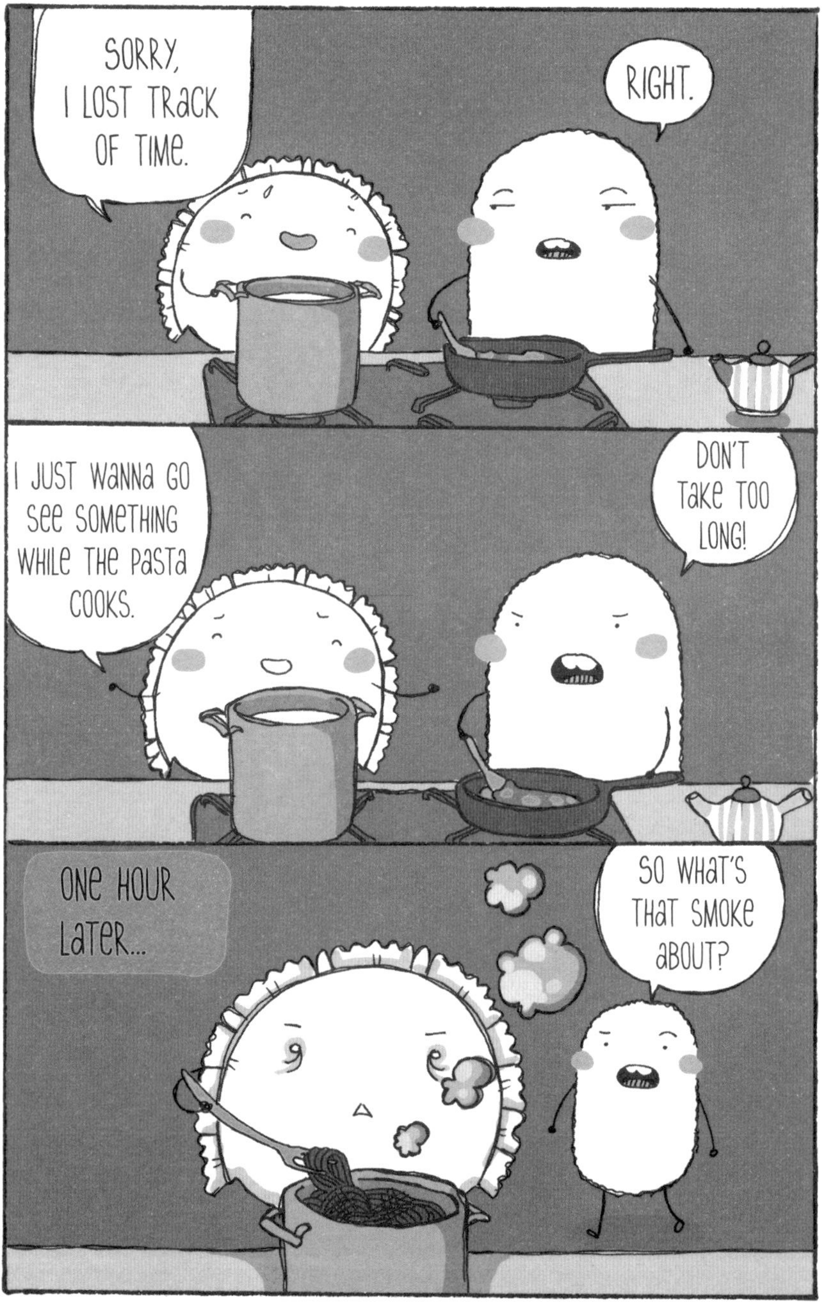
SORRY, I LOST TRACK OF TIME.
RIGHT.
I JUST WANNA GO SEE SOMETHING WHILE THE PASTA COOKS.
DON'T TAKE TOO LONG!
ONE HOUR LATER...
SO WHAT'S THAT SMOKE ABOUT?

- KITTIES -

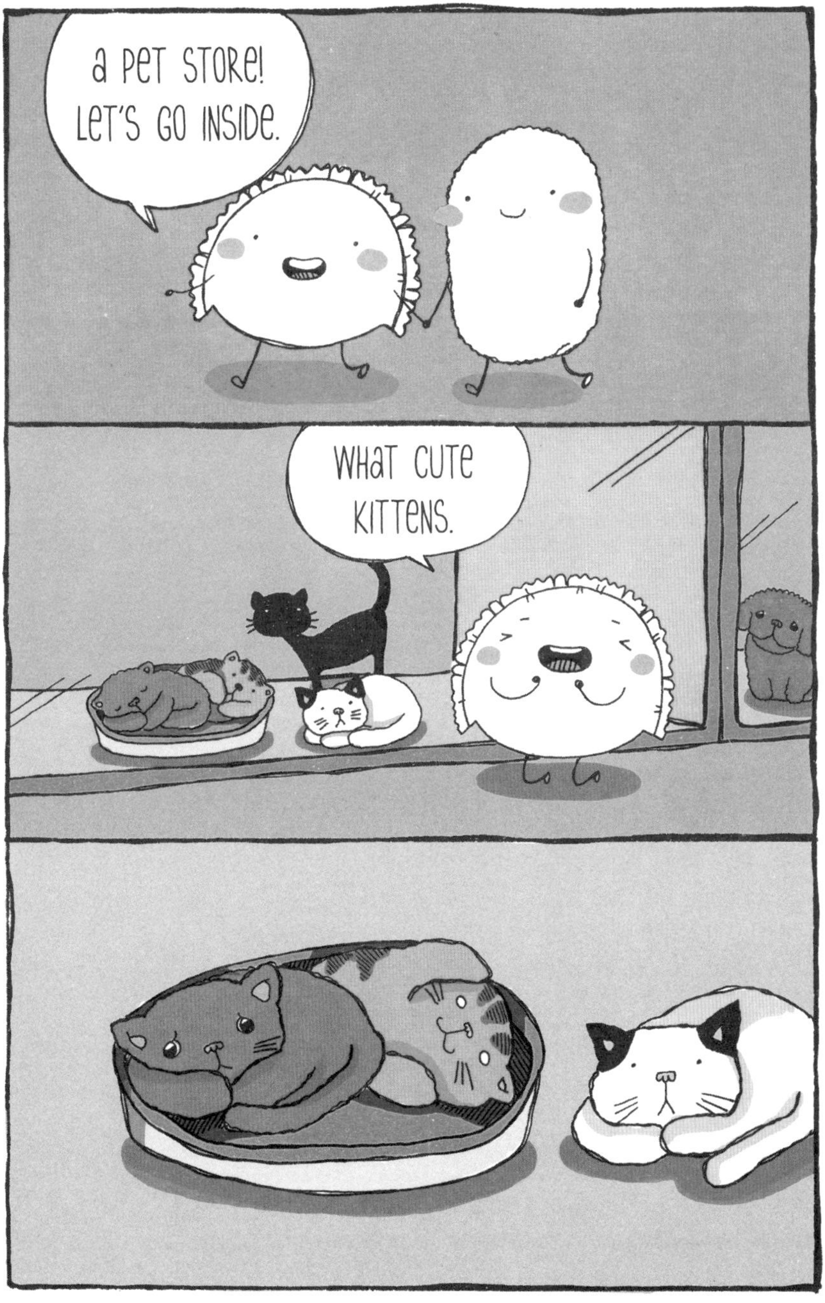
A PET STORE! LET'S GO INSIDE.
WHAT CUTE KITTENS.

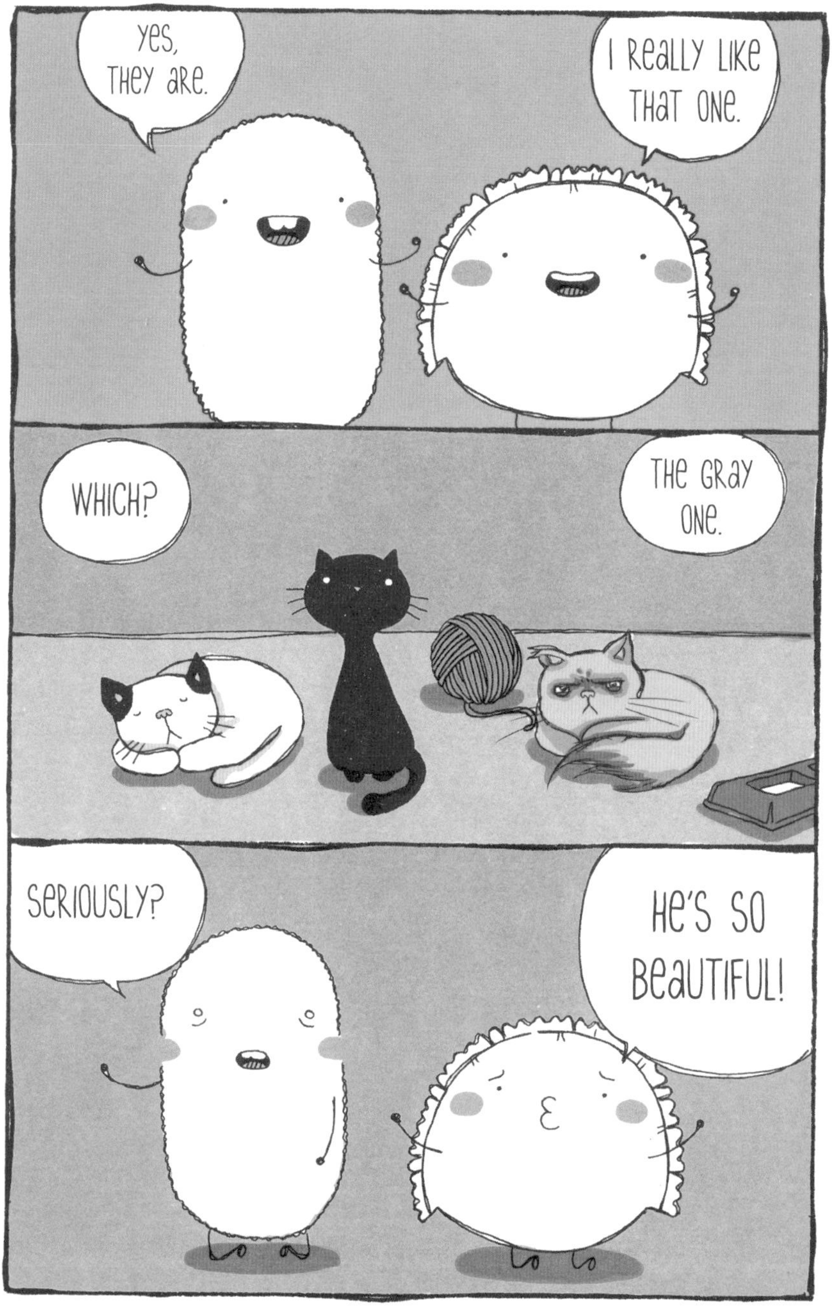
YES, THEY ARE.
I REALLY LIKE THAT ONE.
WHICH?
THE GRAY ONE.
SERIOUSLY?
HE'S SO BEAUTIFUL!

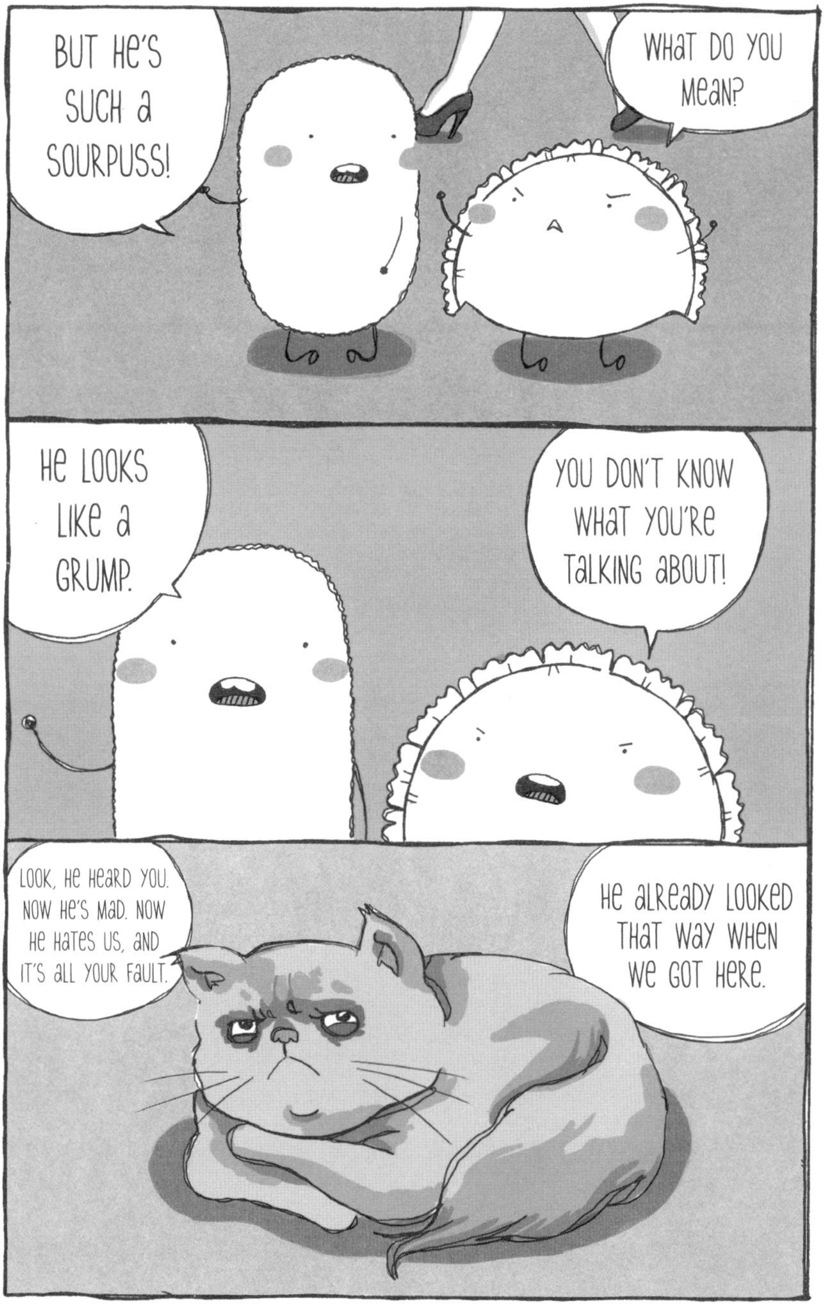
BUT HE'S SUCH A SOURPUSS!
WHAT DO YOU MEAN?
HE LOOKS LIKE A GRUMP.
YOU DON'T KNOW WHAT YOU'RE TALKING ABOUT!
LOOK, HE HEARD YOU. NOW HE'S MAD. NOW HE HATES US, AND IT'S ALL YOUR FAULT.
HE ALREADY LOOKED THAT WAY WHEN WE GOT HERE.

- CROQUETTE ON A ROLL -

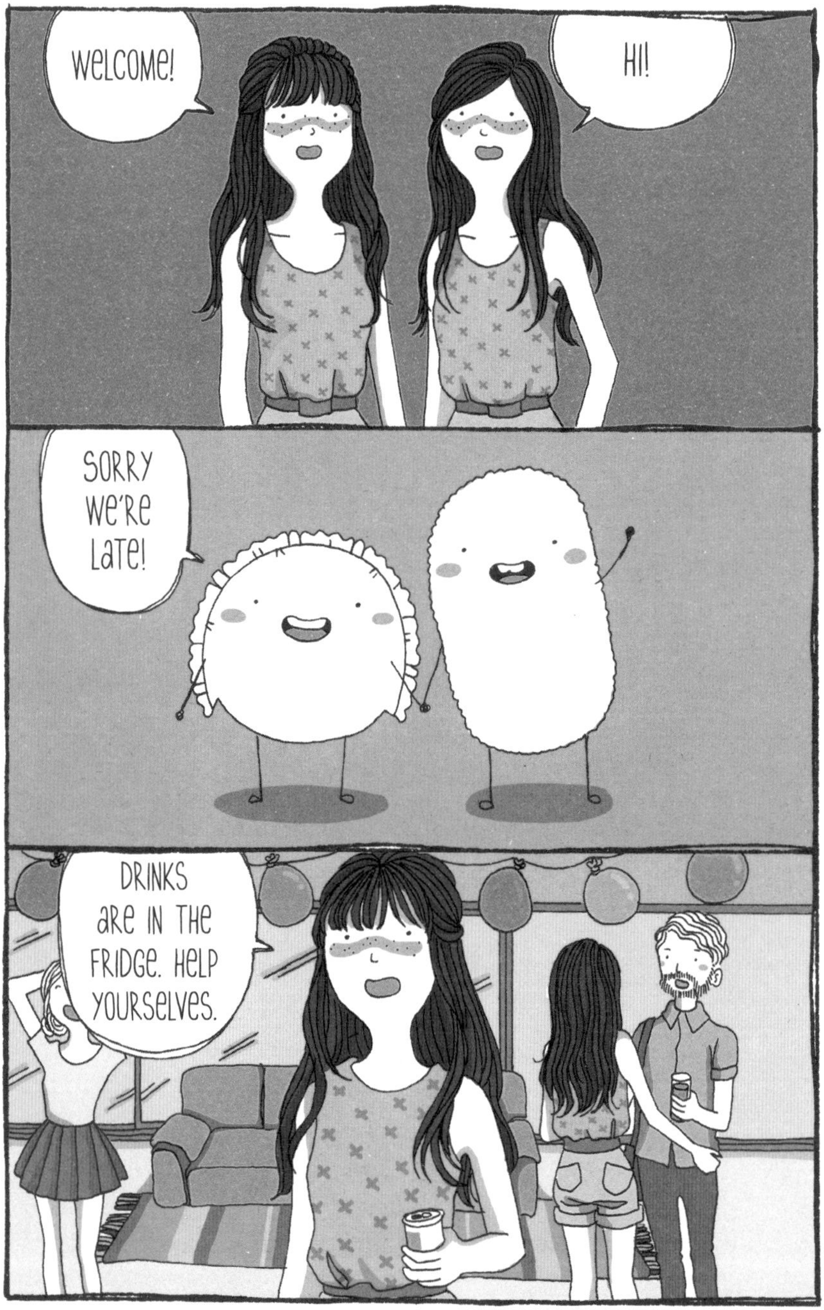
WELCOME!
HI!
SORRY WE'RE LATE!
DRINKS ARE IN THE FRIDGE. HELP YOURSELVES.

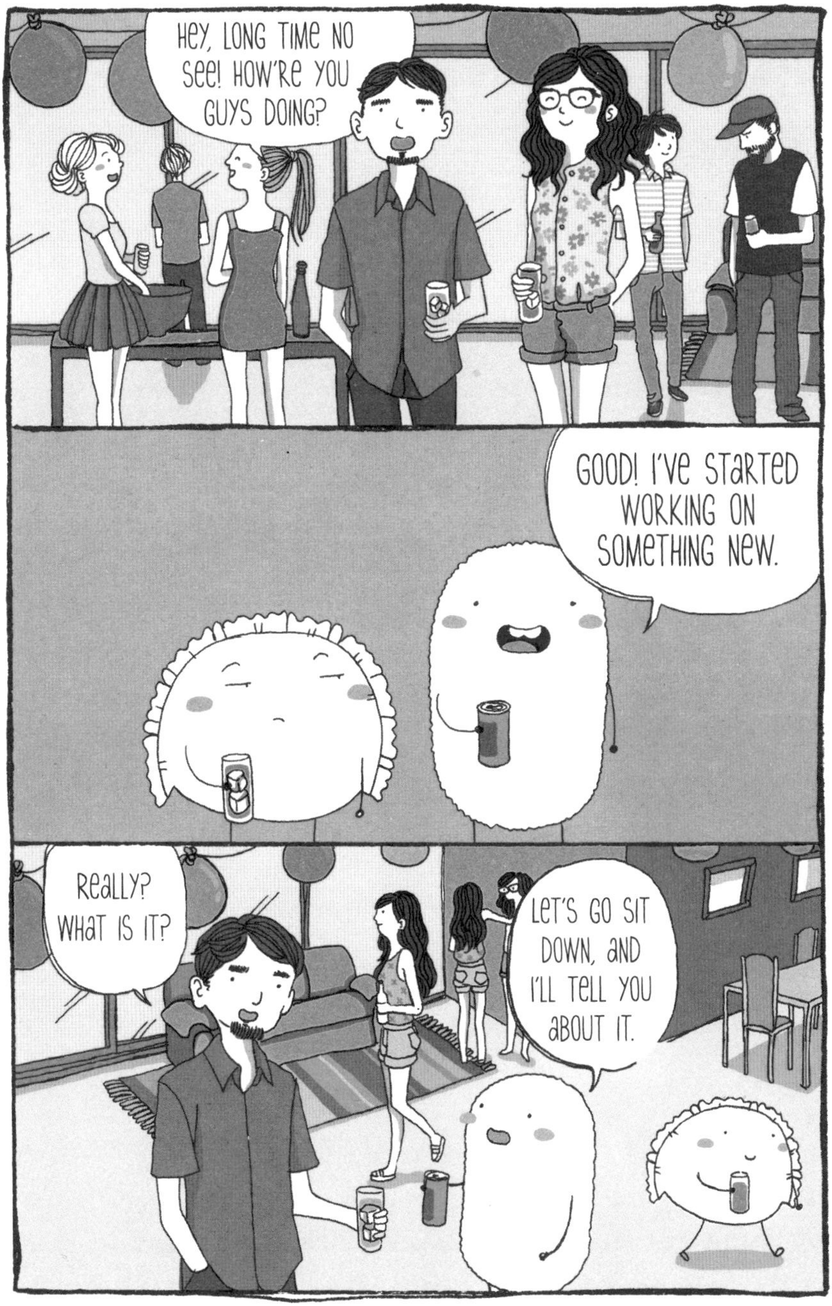

HEY, LONG TIME NO SEE! HOW'RE YOU GUYS DOING?
GOOD! I'VE STARTED WORKING ON SOMETHING NEW.
REALLY? WHAT IS IT?
LET'S GO SIT DOWN, AND I'LL TELL YOU ABOUT IT.

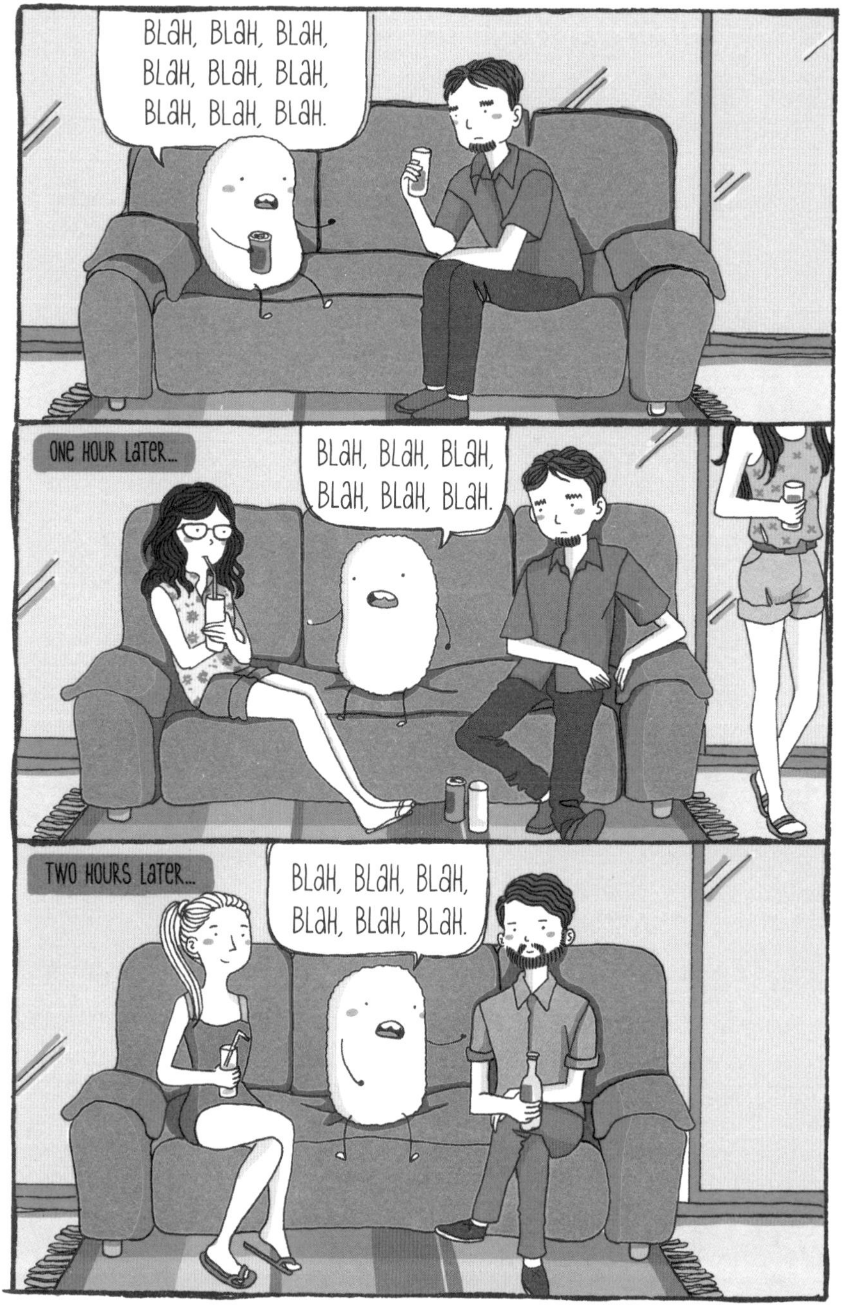
BLAH, BLAH, BLAH,
BLAH, BLAH, BLAH,
BLAH, BLAH, BLAH.
ONE HOUR LATER...
BLAH, BLAH, BLAH,
BLAH, BLAH, BLAH.
TWO HOURS LATER...
BLAH, BLAH, BLAH,
BLAH, BLAH, BLAH.

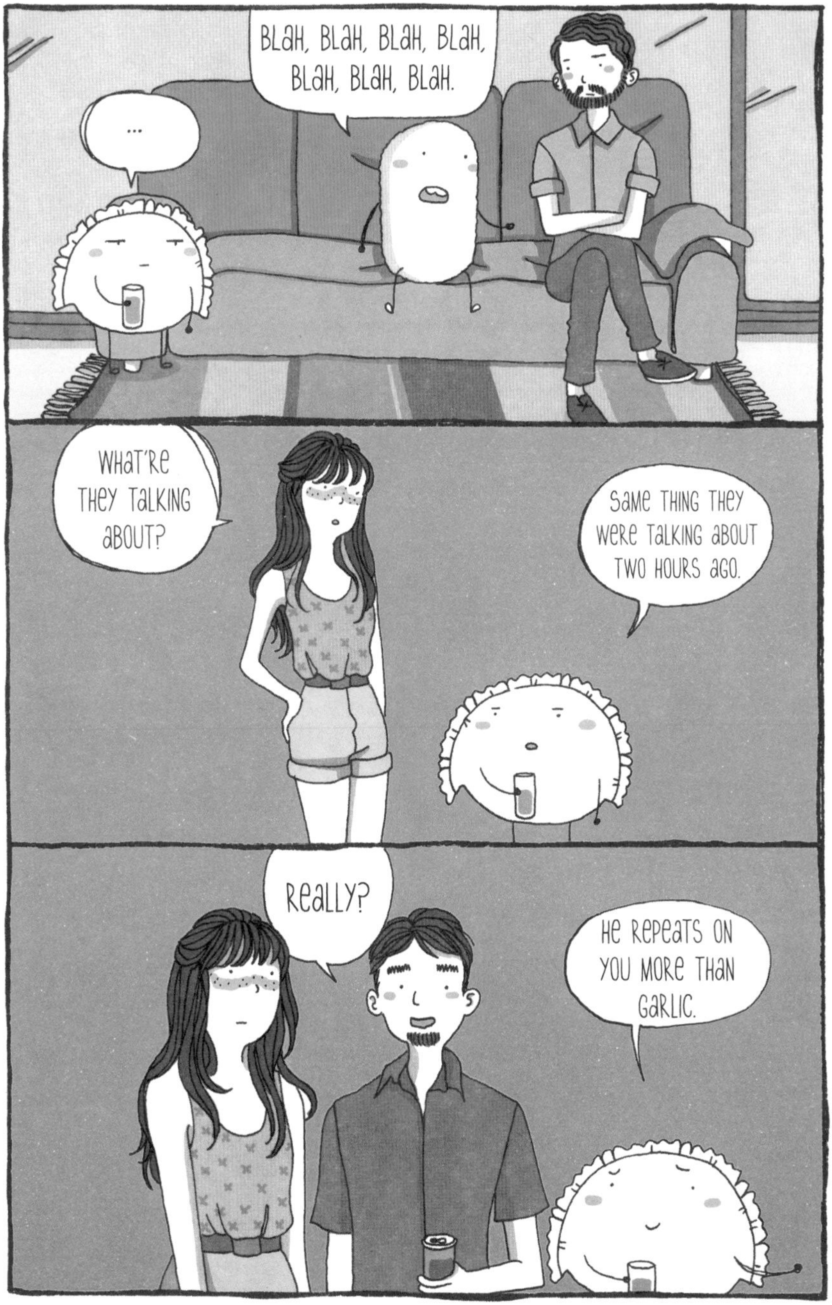
BLAH, BLAH, BLAH, BLAH,
BLAH, BLAH, BLAH.
...
WHAT'RE THEY TALKING ABOUT?
SAME THING THEY WERE TALKING ABOUT TWO HOURS AGO.
REALLY?
HE REPEATS ON YOU MORE THAN GARLIC.

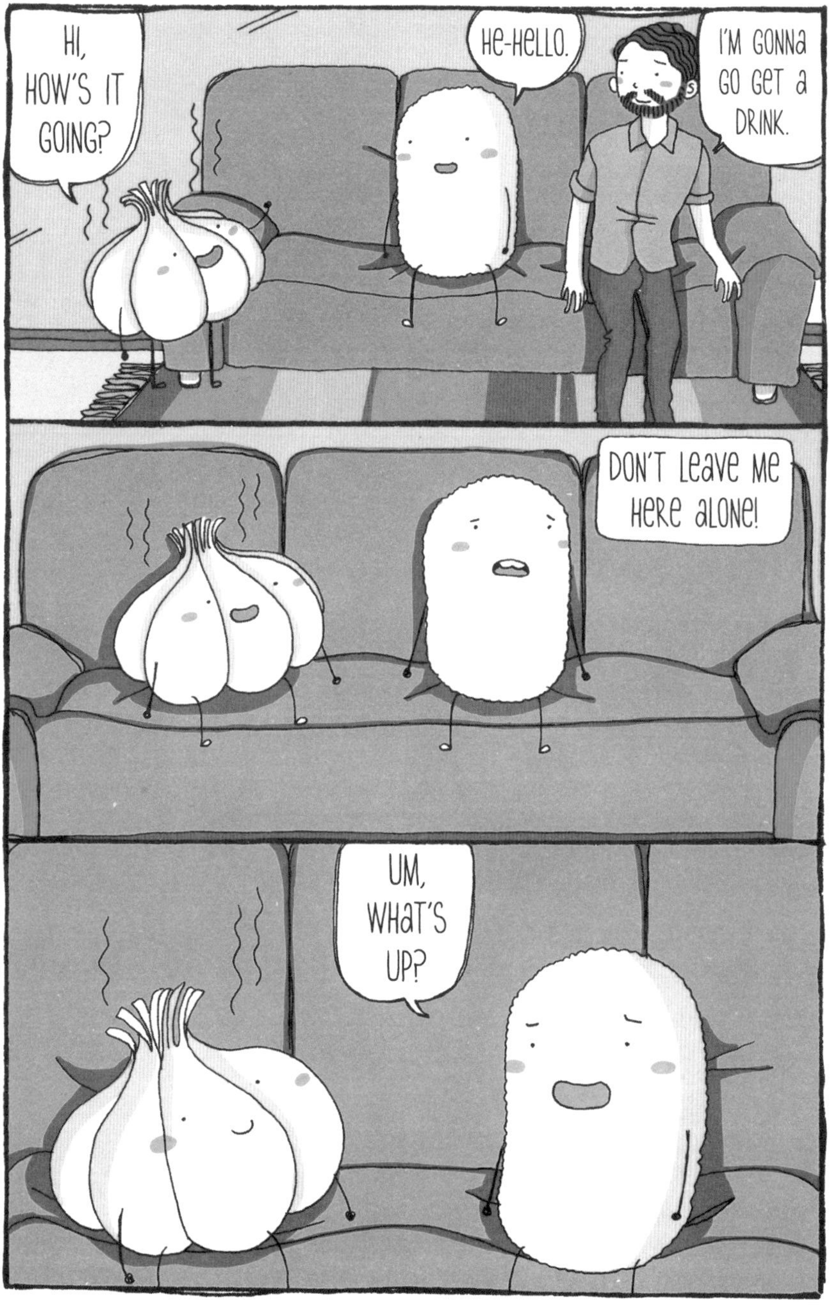
HI, HOW'S IT GOING?
HE-HELLO.
I'M GONNA GO GET A DRINK.
DON'T LEAVE ME HERE ALONE!
UM, WHAT'S UP?

- HOME SWEET HOME (SOMETIMES) -

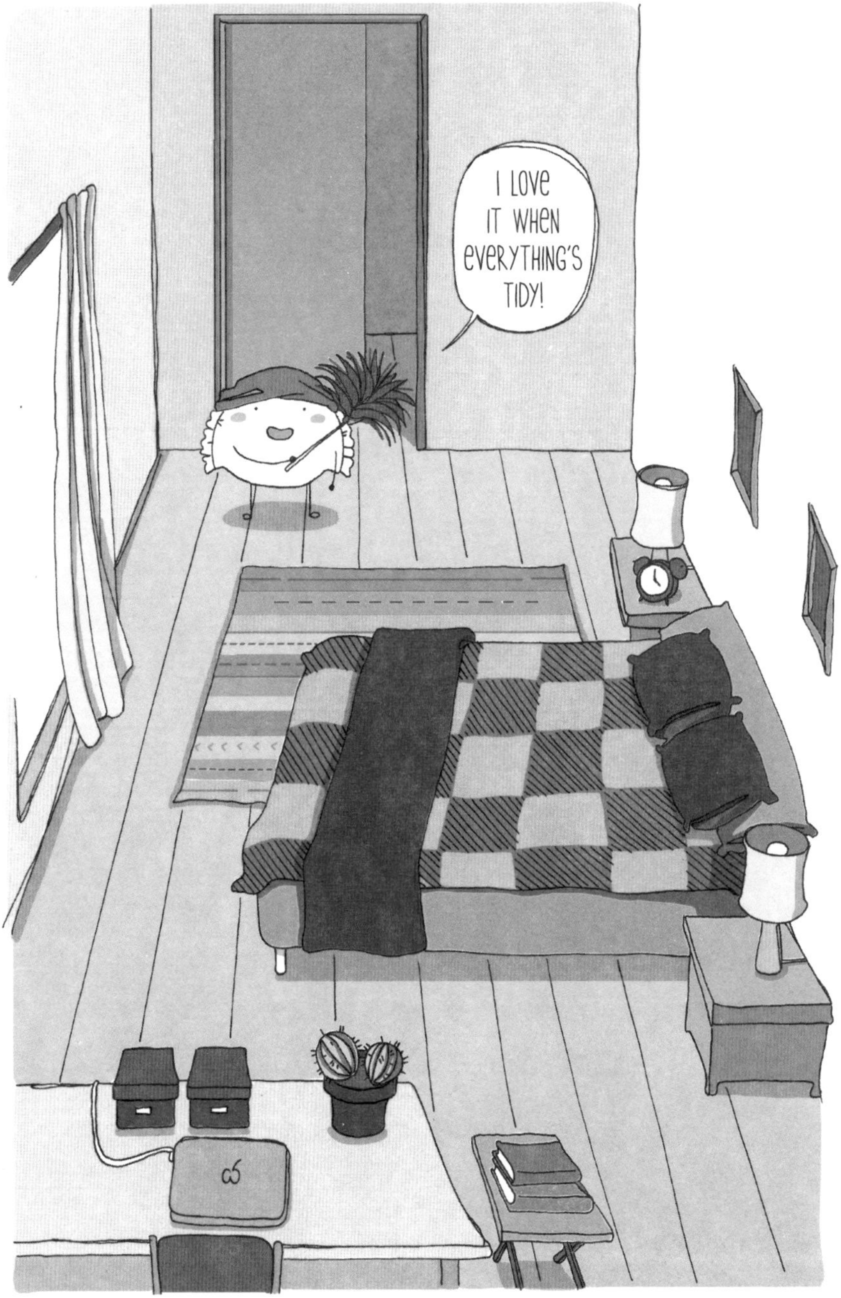
I LOVE IT WHEN EVERYTHING'S TIDY!

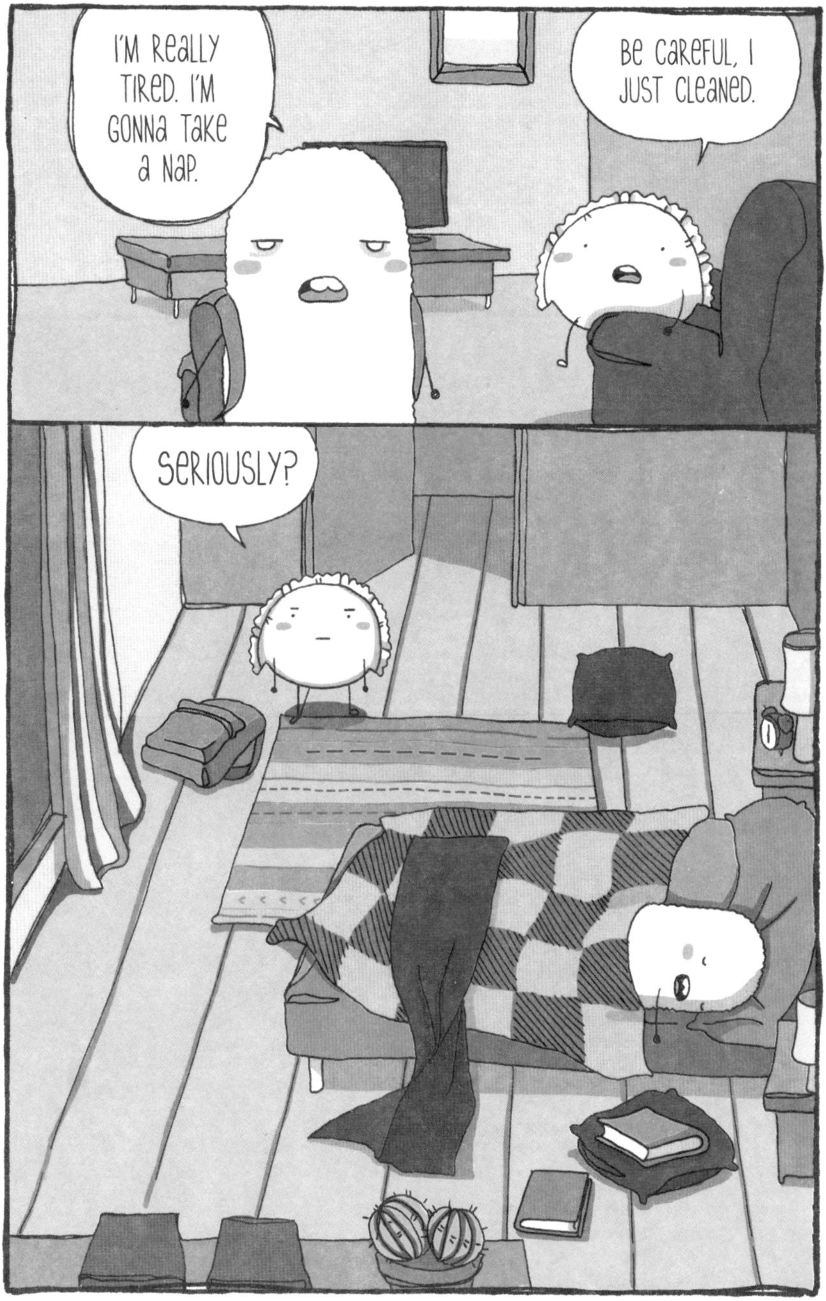
I'M REALLY TIRED. I'M GONNA TAKE A NAP.
BE CAREFUL, I JUST CLEANED.
SERIOUSLY?

- WHO'S THE BOSS? -

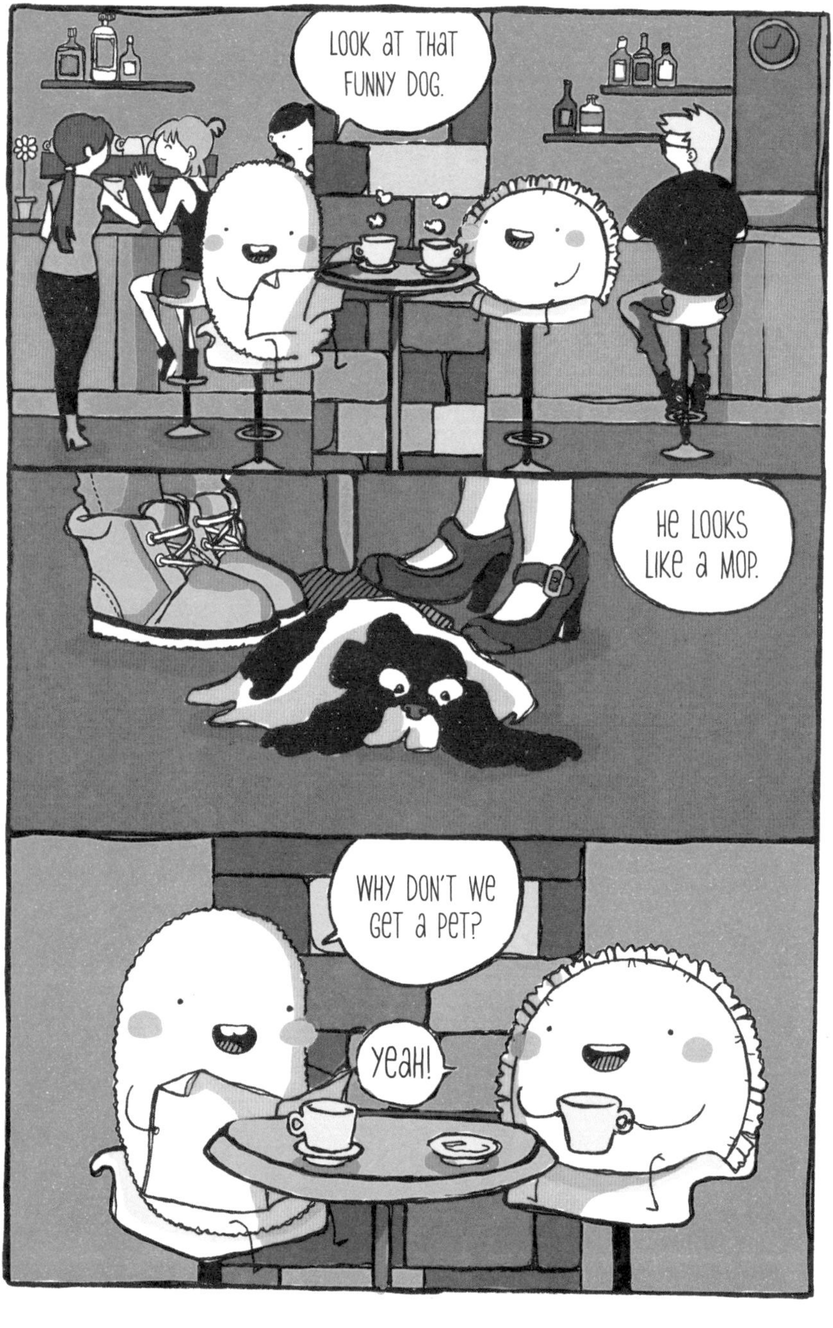
LOOK AT THAT FUNNY DOG.
HE LOOKS LIKE A MOP.
WHY DON'T WE GET A PET?
YEAH!

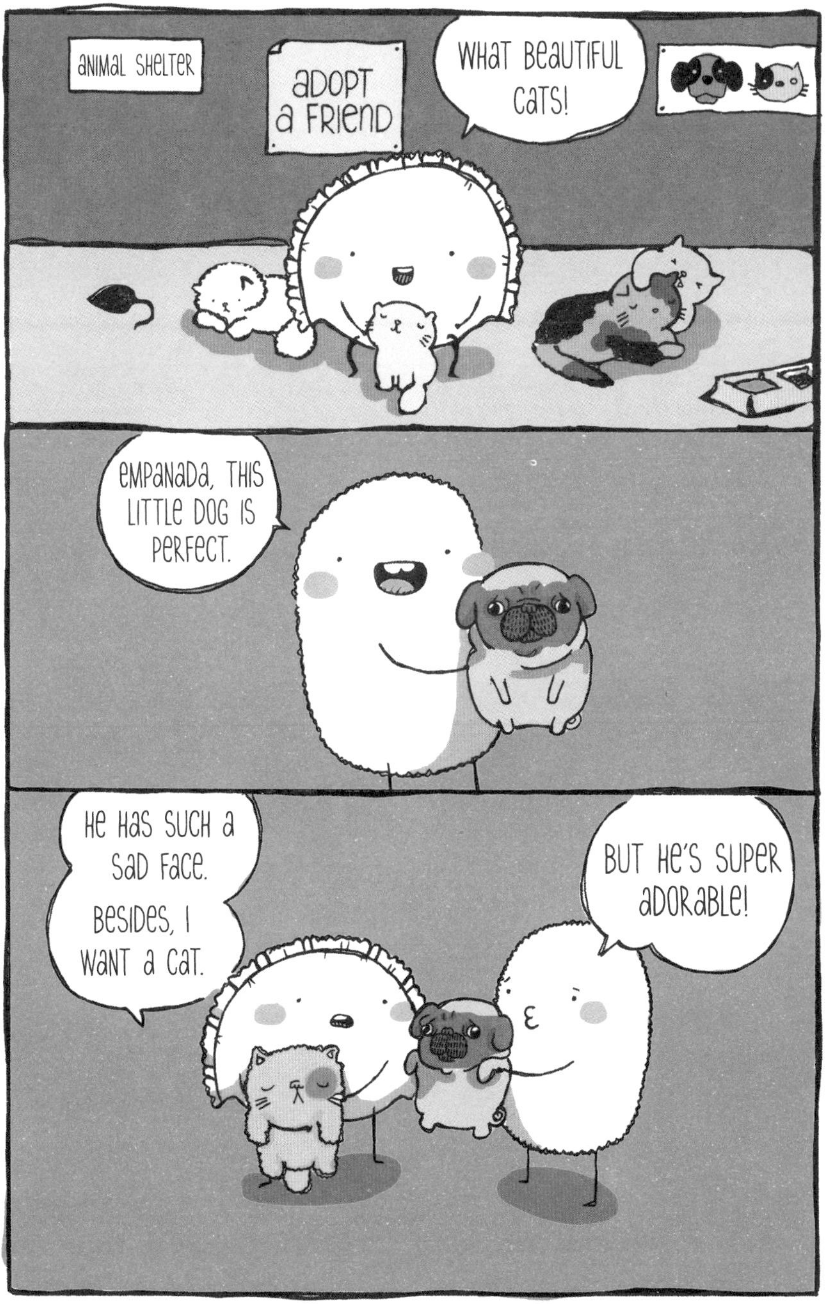
ANIMAL SHELTER
ADOPT A FRIEND
WHAT BEAUTIFUL CATS!
EMPANADA, THIS LITTLE DOG IS PERFECT.
HE HAS SUCH A SAD FACE.
BESIDES, I WANT A CAT.
BUT HE'S SUPER ADORABLE!

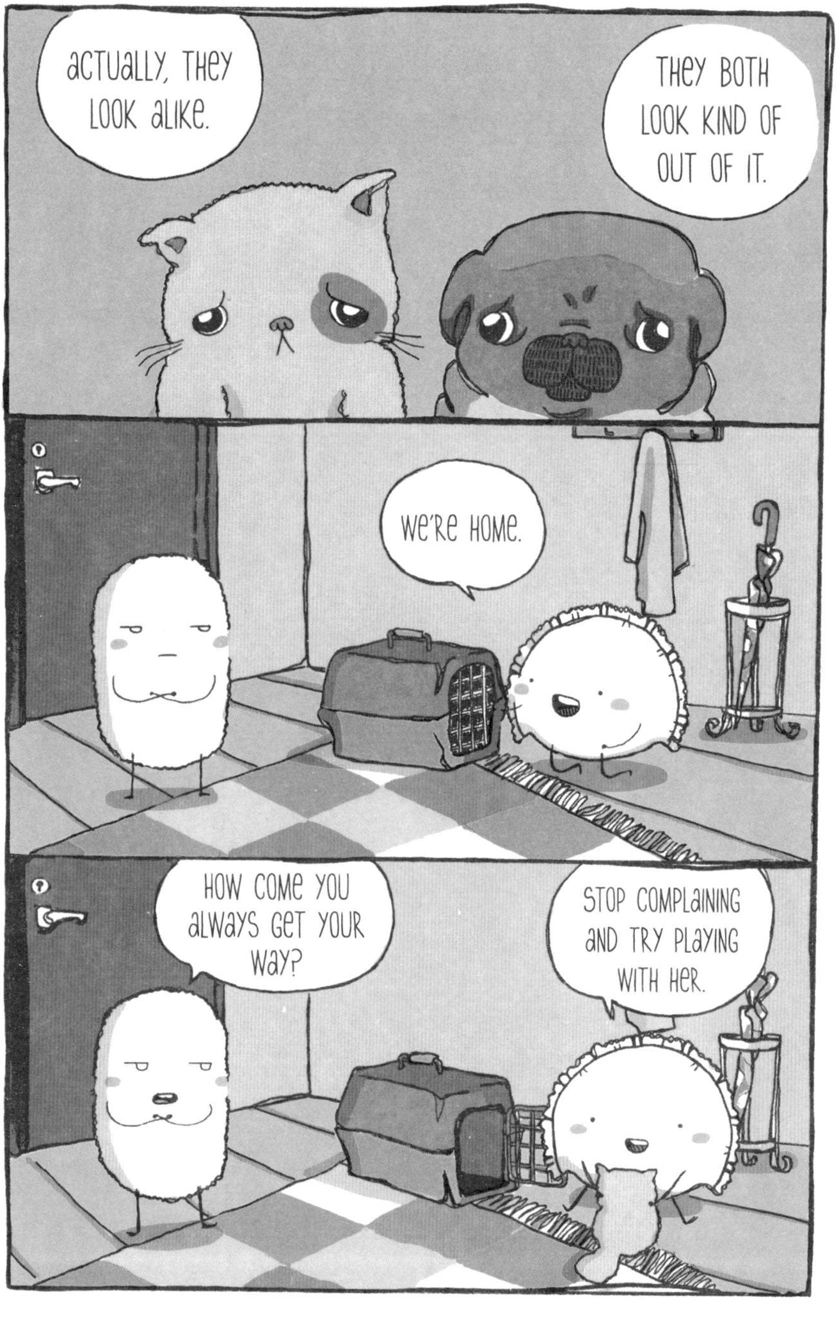
actually, they look alike.
They both look kind of out of it.
We're home.
How come you always get your way?
Stop complaining and try playing with her.

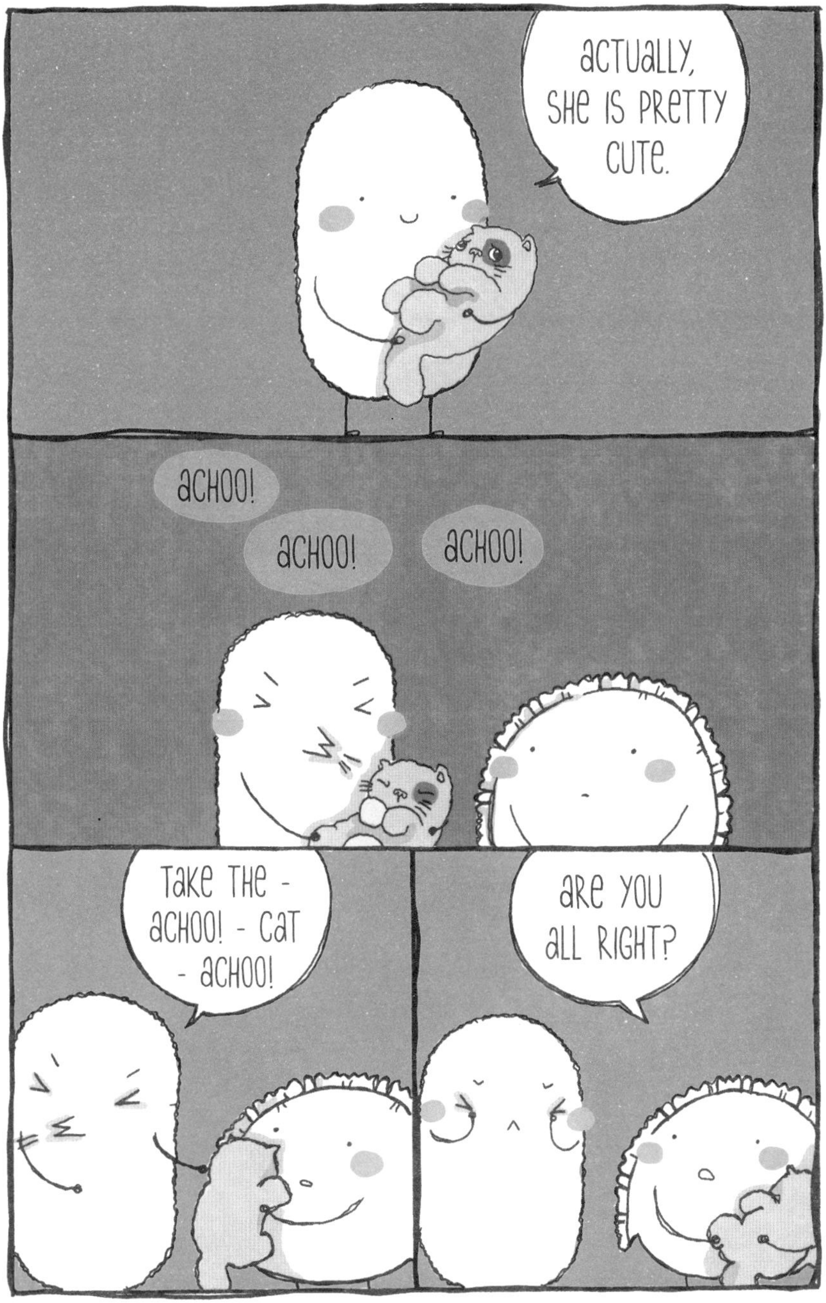
Actually, she is pretty cute.
Achoo!
Achoo!
Achoo!
Take the - achoo! - cat - achoo!
Are you all right?

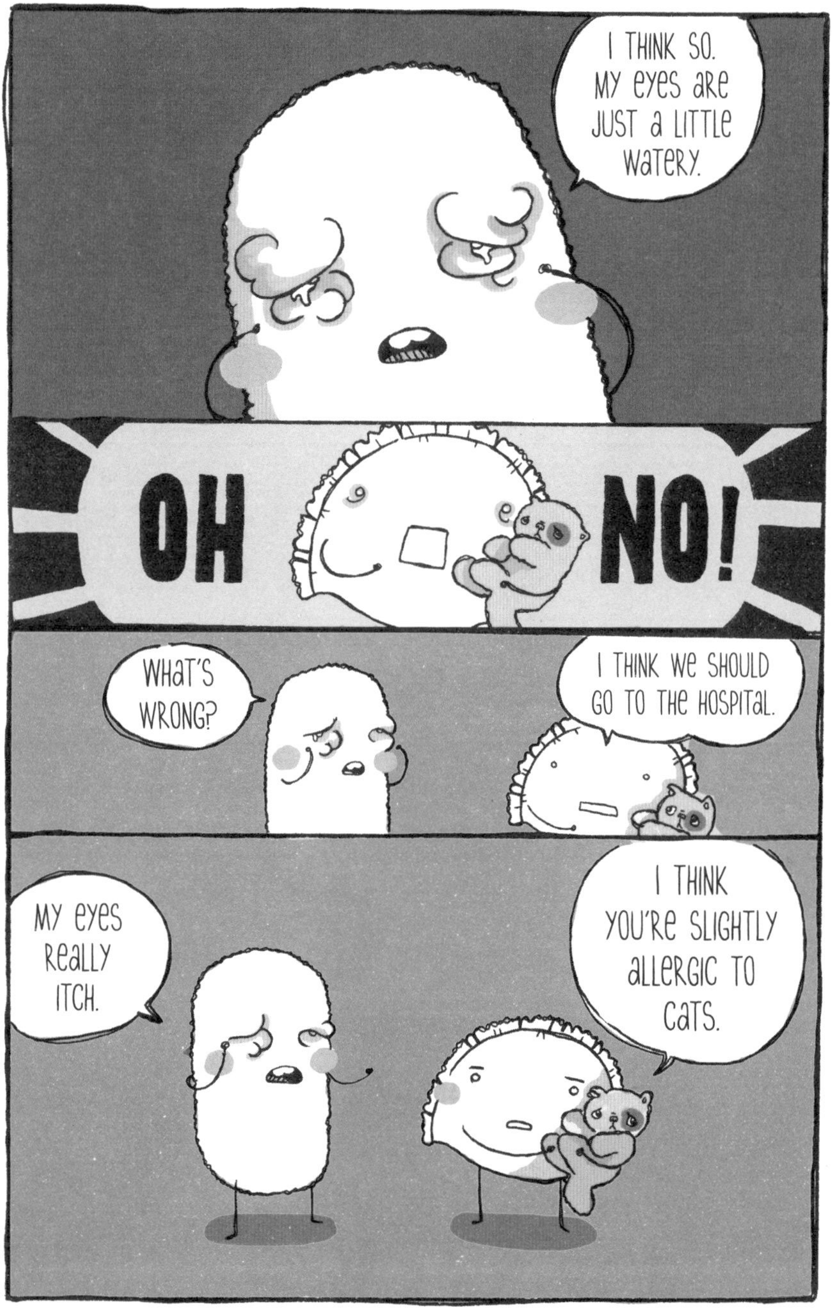
I THINK SO. MY EYES ARE JUST A LITTLE WATERY.
OH NO!
WHAT'S WRONG?
I THINK WE SHOULD GO TO THE HOSPITAL.
MY EYES REALLY ITCH.
I THINK YOU'RE SLIGHTLY ALLERGIC TO CATS.

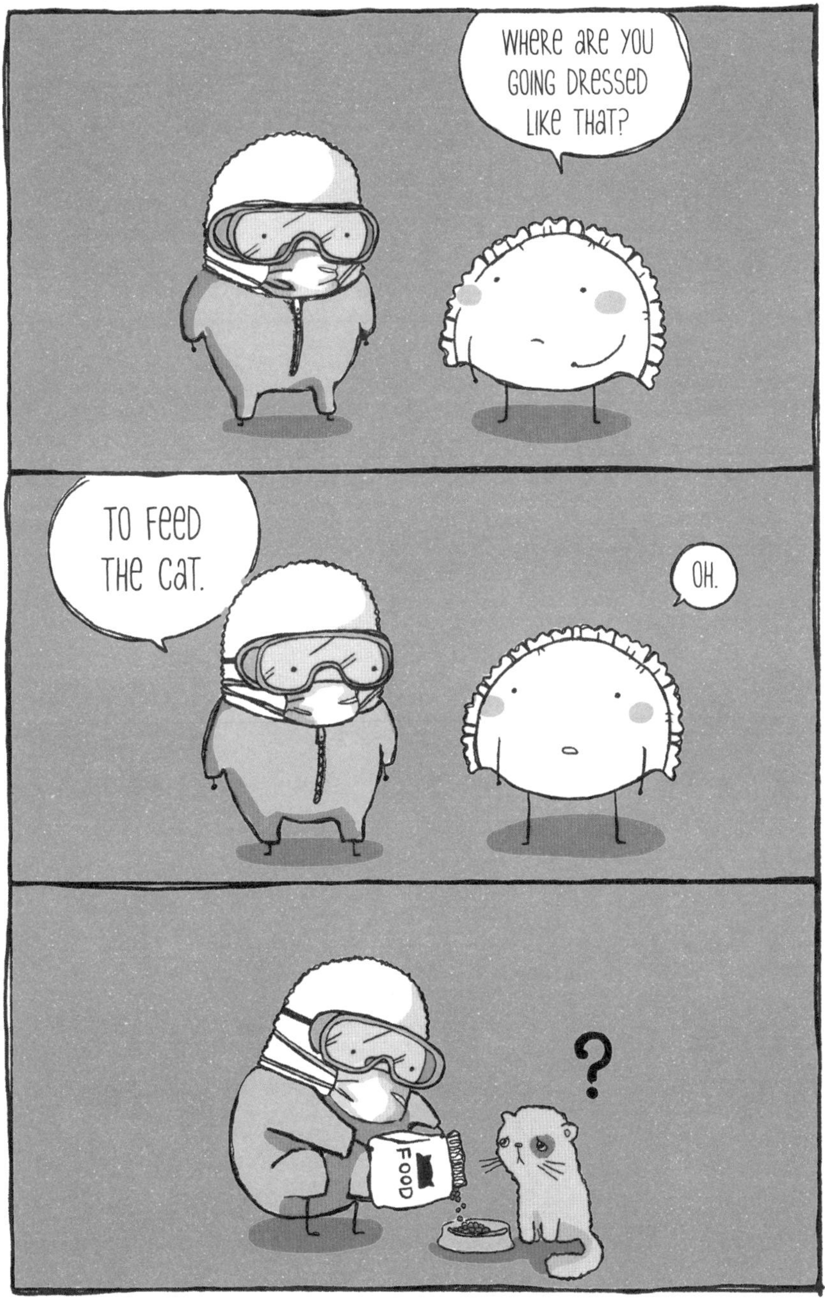
WHERE ARE YOU GOING DRESSED LIKE THAT?
TO FEED THE CAT.
OH.
?
FOOD

- SIGNS OF FALL -

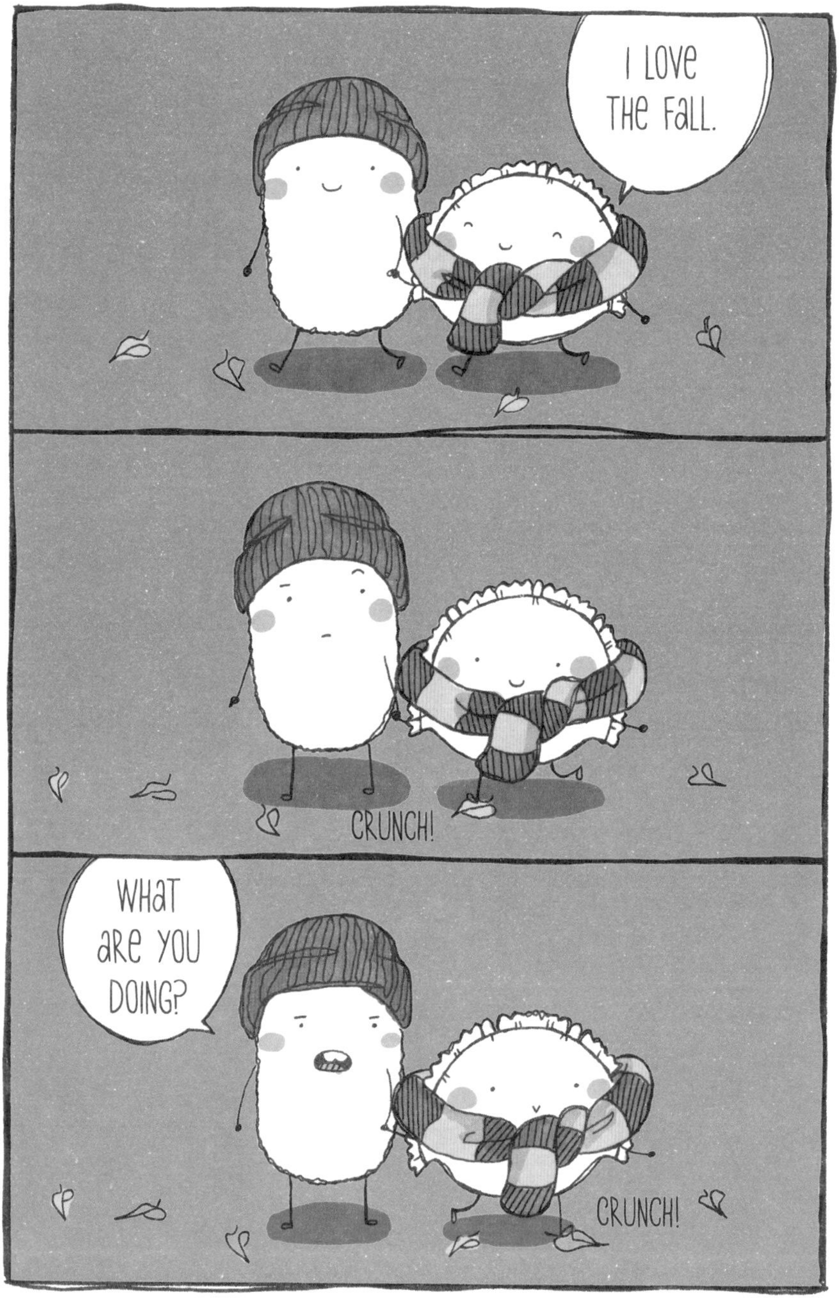
I LOVE THE FALL.
CRUNCH!
WHAT ARE YOU DOING?
CRUNCH!

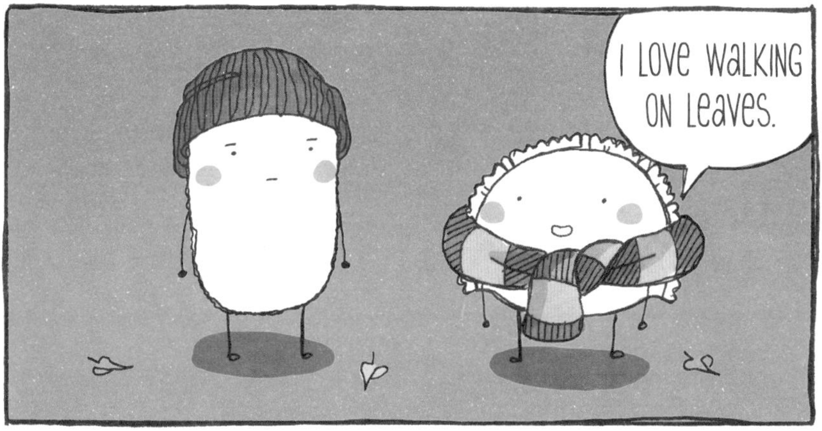
I LOVE WALKING ON LEAVES.

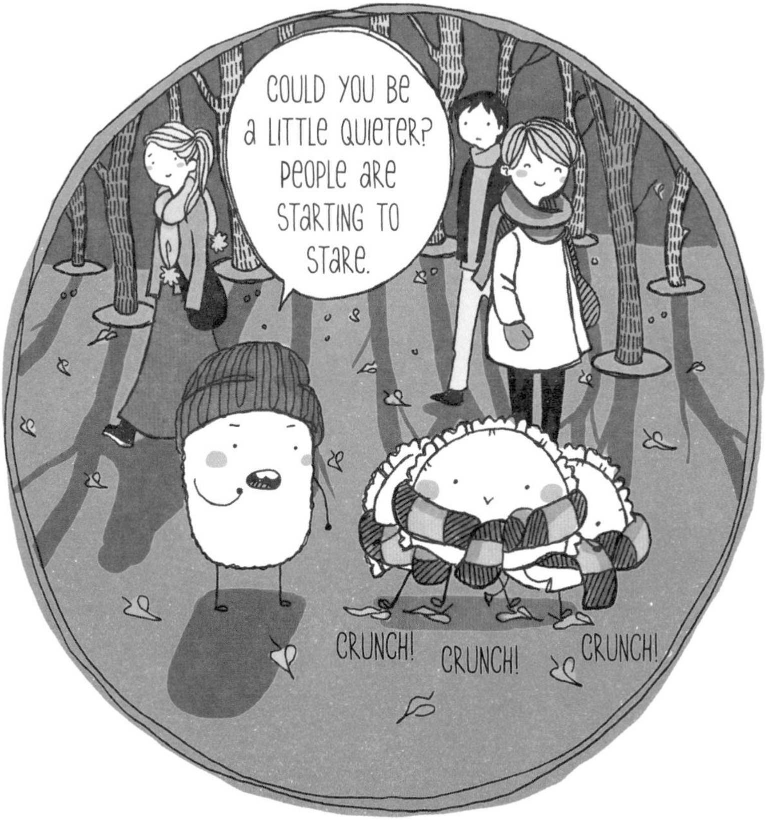
COULD YOU BE A LITTLE QUIETER? PEOPLE ARE STARTING TO STARE.
CRUNCH!
CRUNCH!
CRUNCH!

- SCARY BEDTIME STORIES -

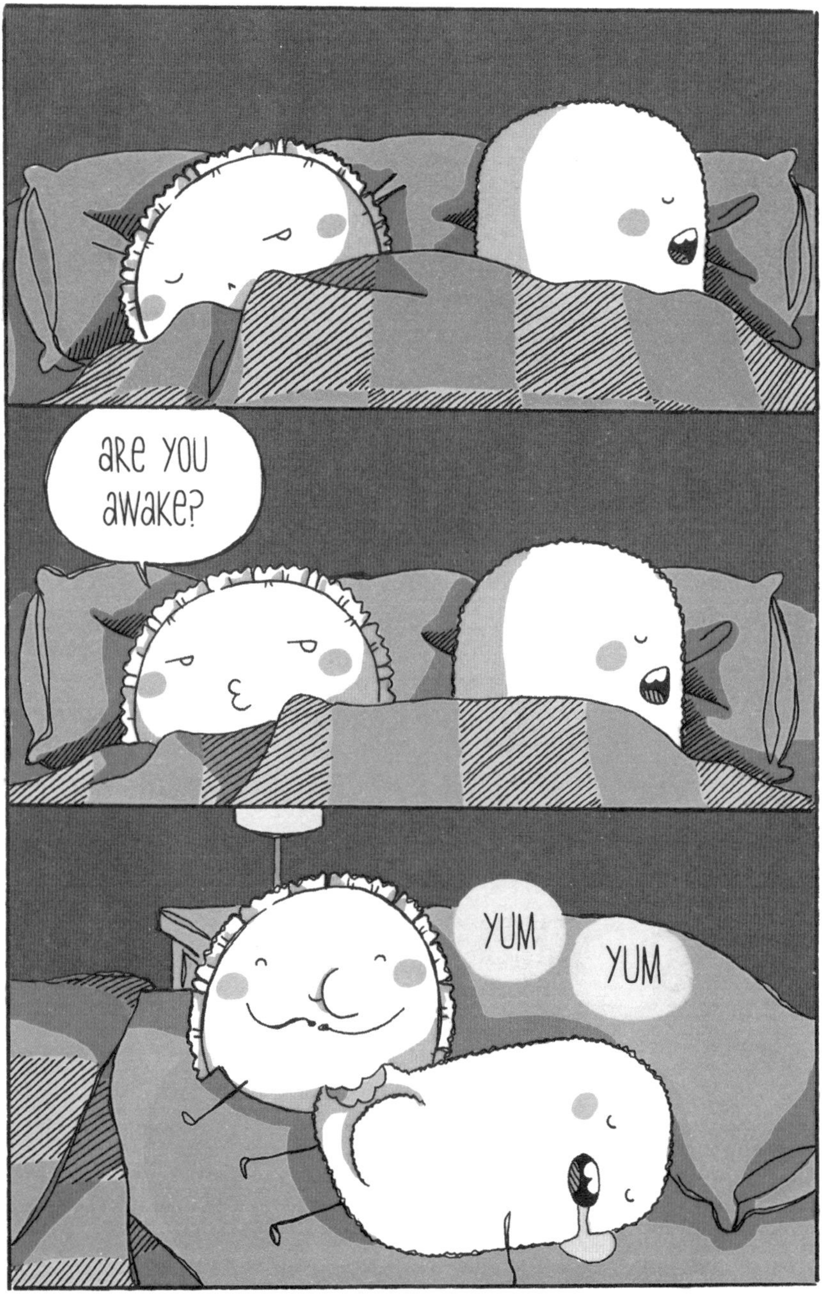
ARE YOU AWAKE?
YUM
YUM

- DIFFERENT PERSPECTIVES -

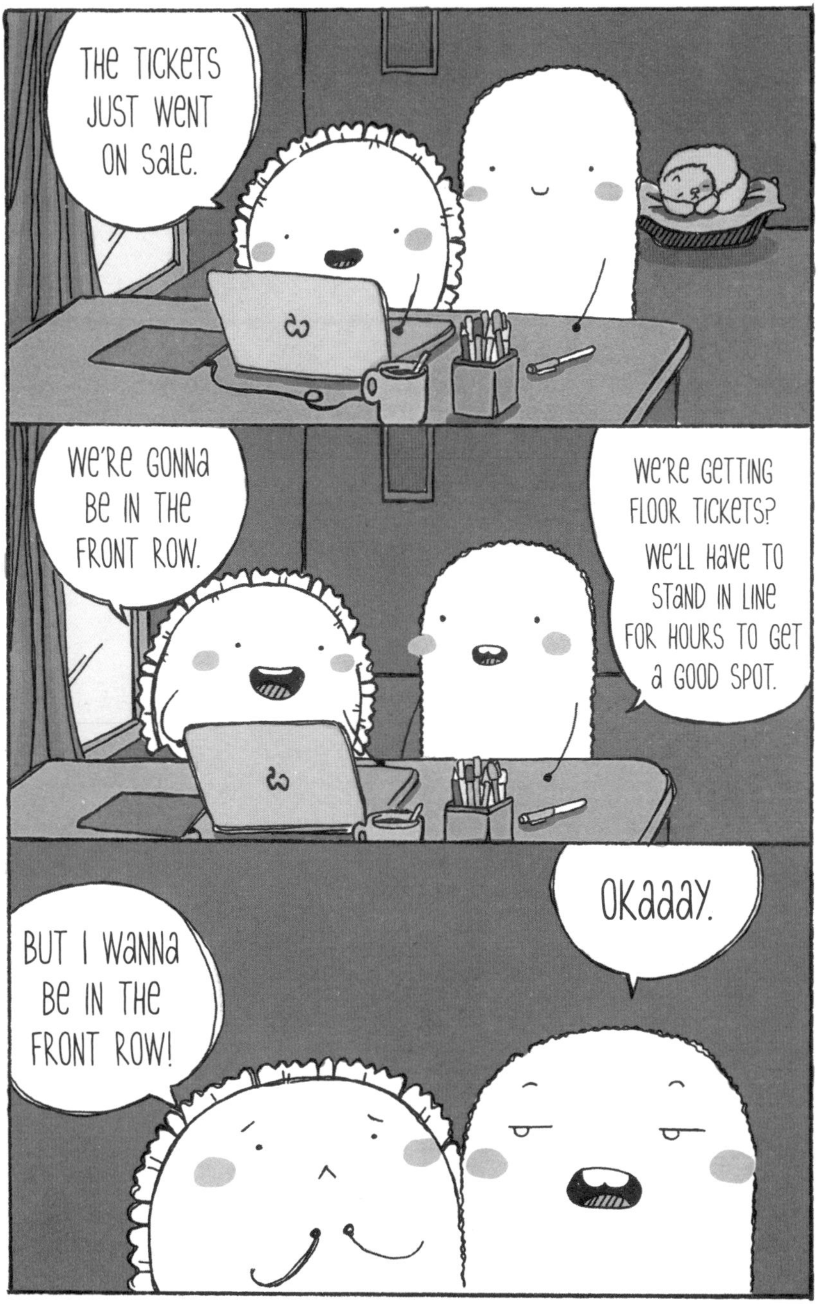
THE TICKETS JUST WENT ON SALE.
WE'RE GONNA BE IN THE FRONT ROW.
WE'RE GETTING FLOOR TICKETS? WE'LL HAVE TO STAND IN LINE FOR HOURS TO GET A GOOD SPOT.
BUT I WANNA BE IN THE FRONT ROW!
OKAAAY.

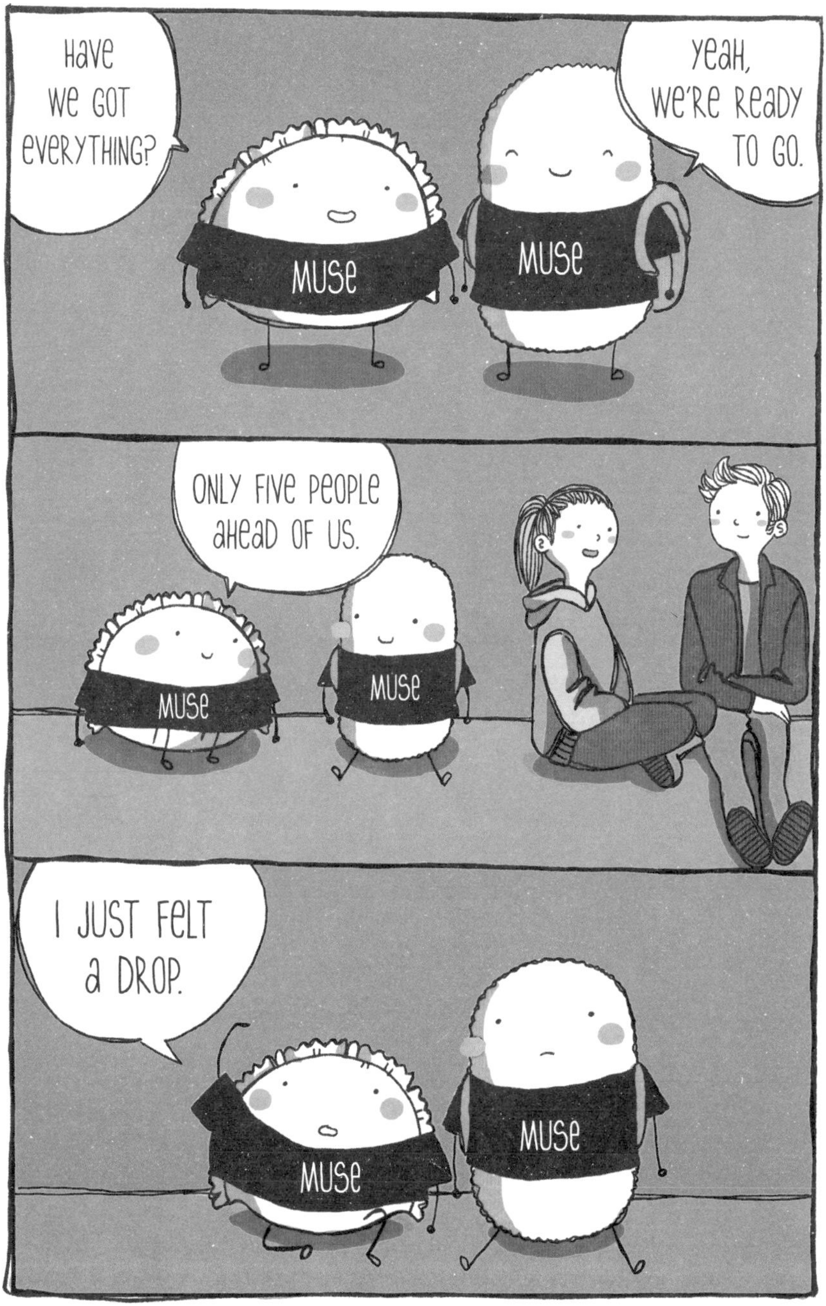
Have we got everything?
Yeah, we're ready to go.
MUSE
MUSE
Only five people ahead of us.
MUSE
MUSE
I just felt a drop.
MUSE
MUSE

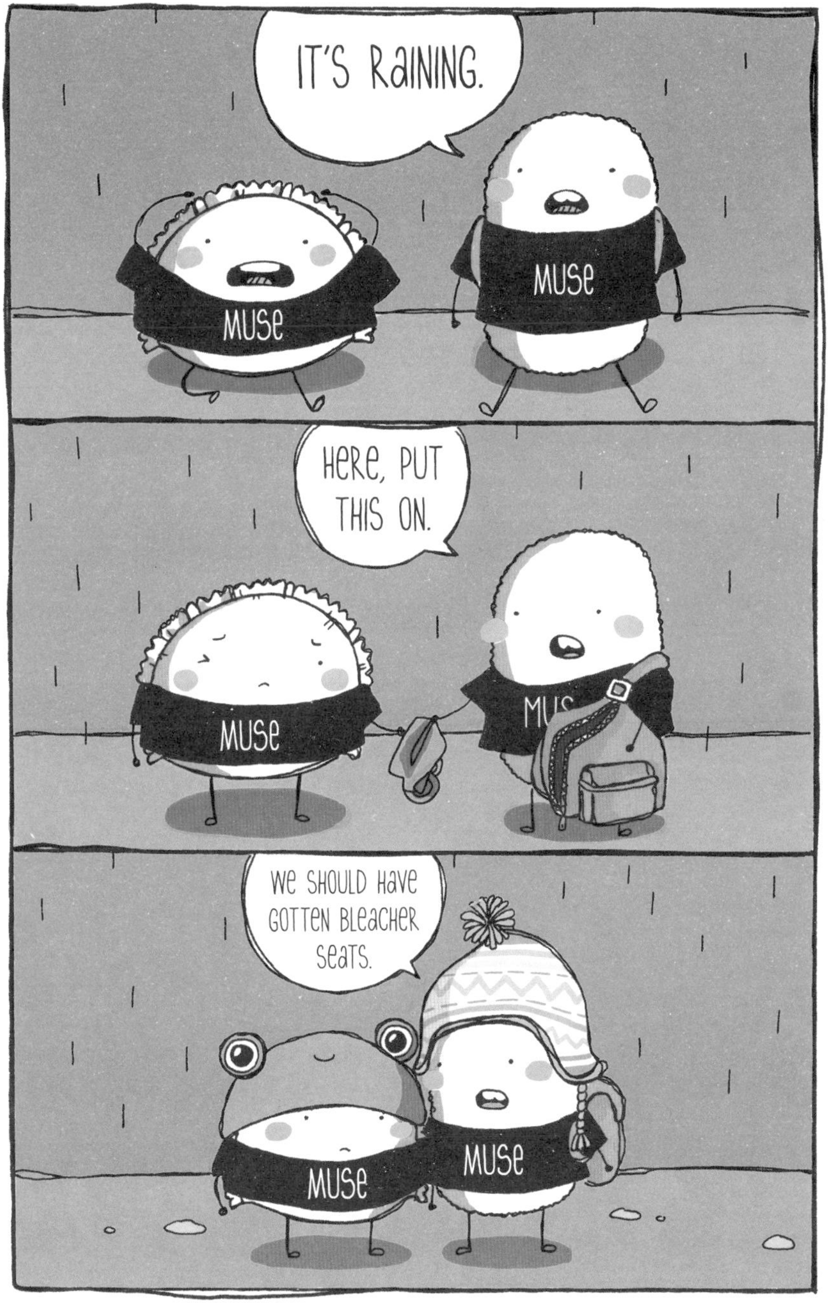
IT'S RAINING.
MUSE
MUSE
HERE, PUT THIS ON.
MUSE
WE SHOULD HAVE GOTTEN BLEACHER SEATS.
MUSE
MUSE

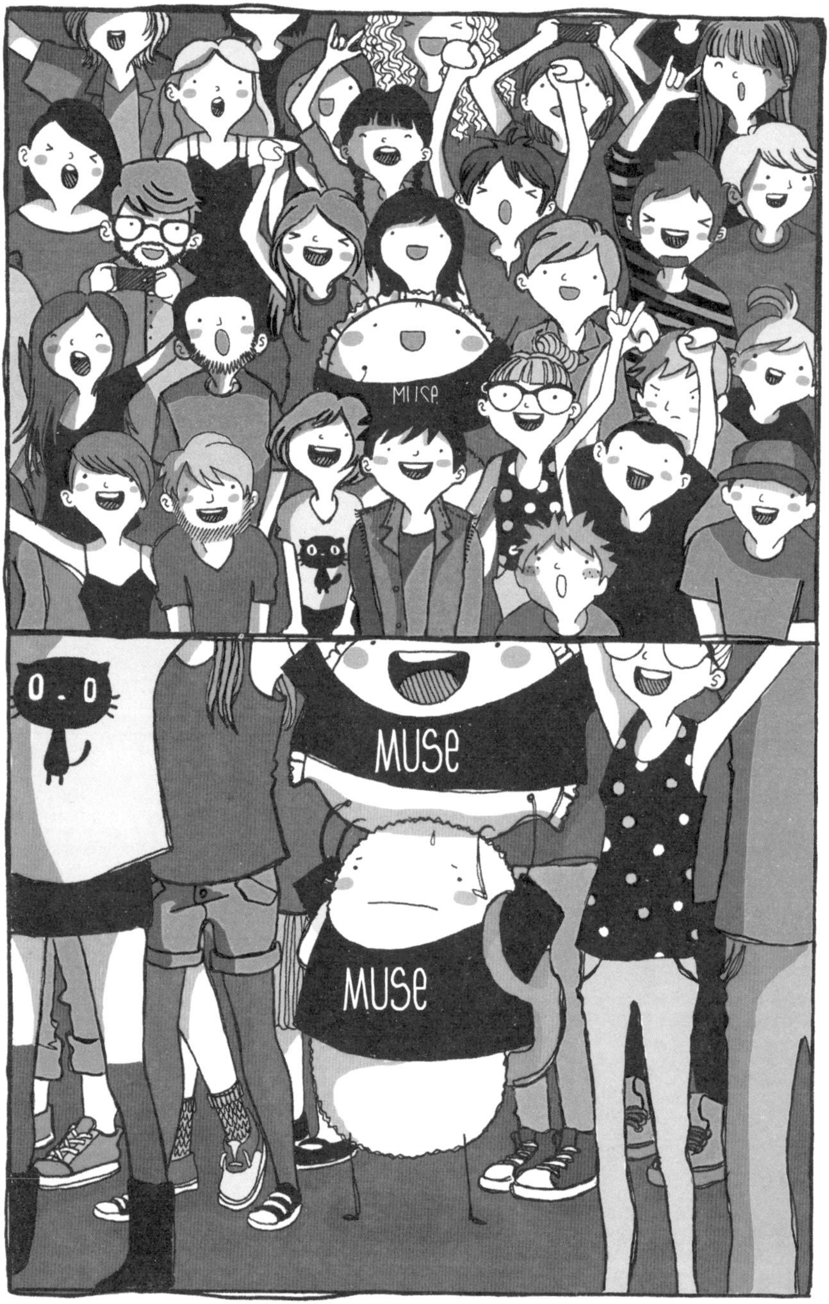
MUSE
MUSE
MUSE

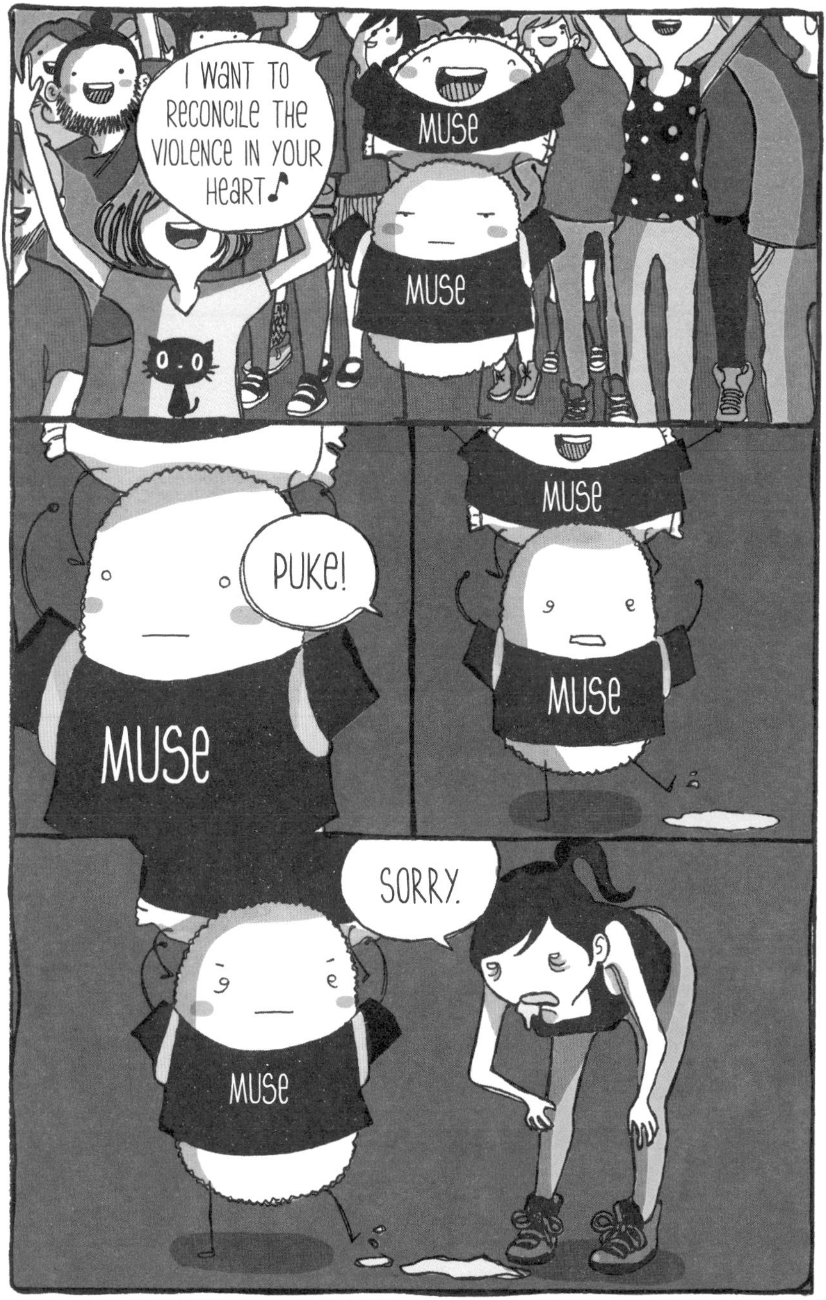
I WANT TO RECONCILE THE VIOLENCE IN YOUR HEART♪
MUSE
MUSE
PUKE!
MUSE
MUSE
MUSE
SORRY.
MUSE

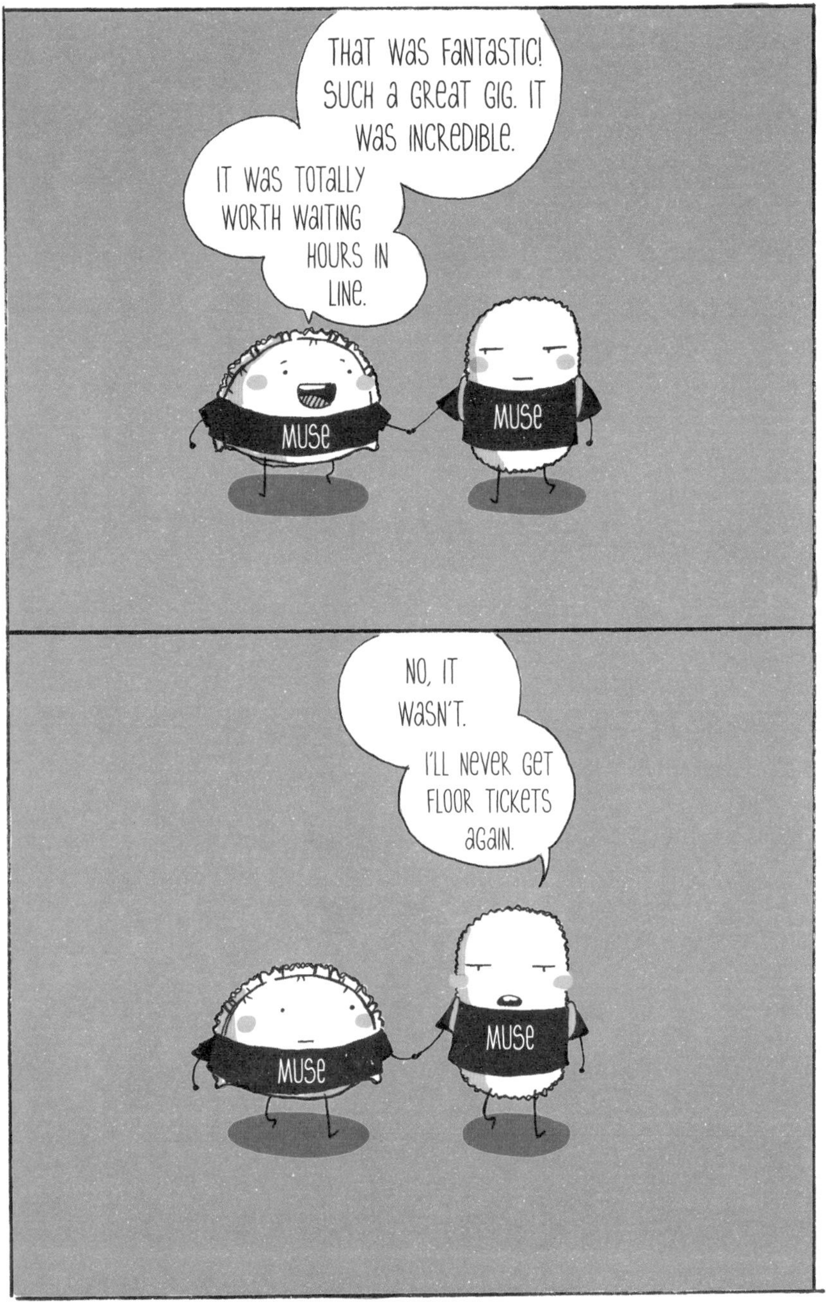
THAT WAS FANTASTIC! SUCH A GREAT GIG. IT WAS INCREDIBLE.
IT WAS TOTALLY WORTH WAITING HOURS IN LINE.
MUSE
MUSE
NO, IT WASN'T.
I'LL NEVER GET FLOOR TICKETS AGAIN.
MUSE
MUSE

- SCARY BEDTIME STORIES -

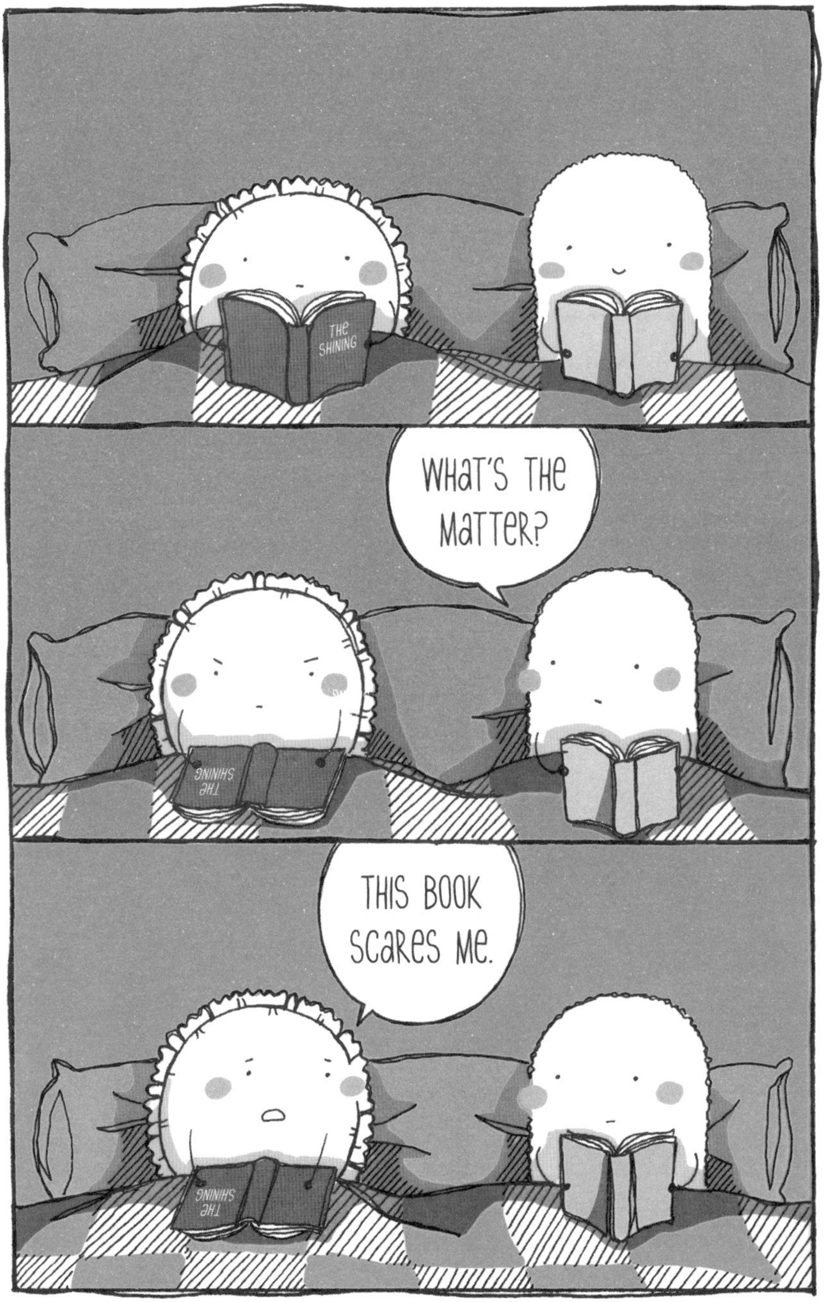
THE SHINING
WHAT'S THE MATTER?
THIS BOOK SCARES ME.

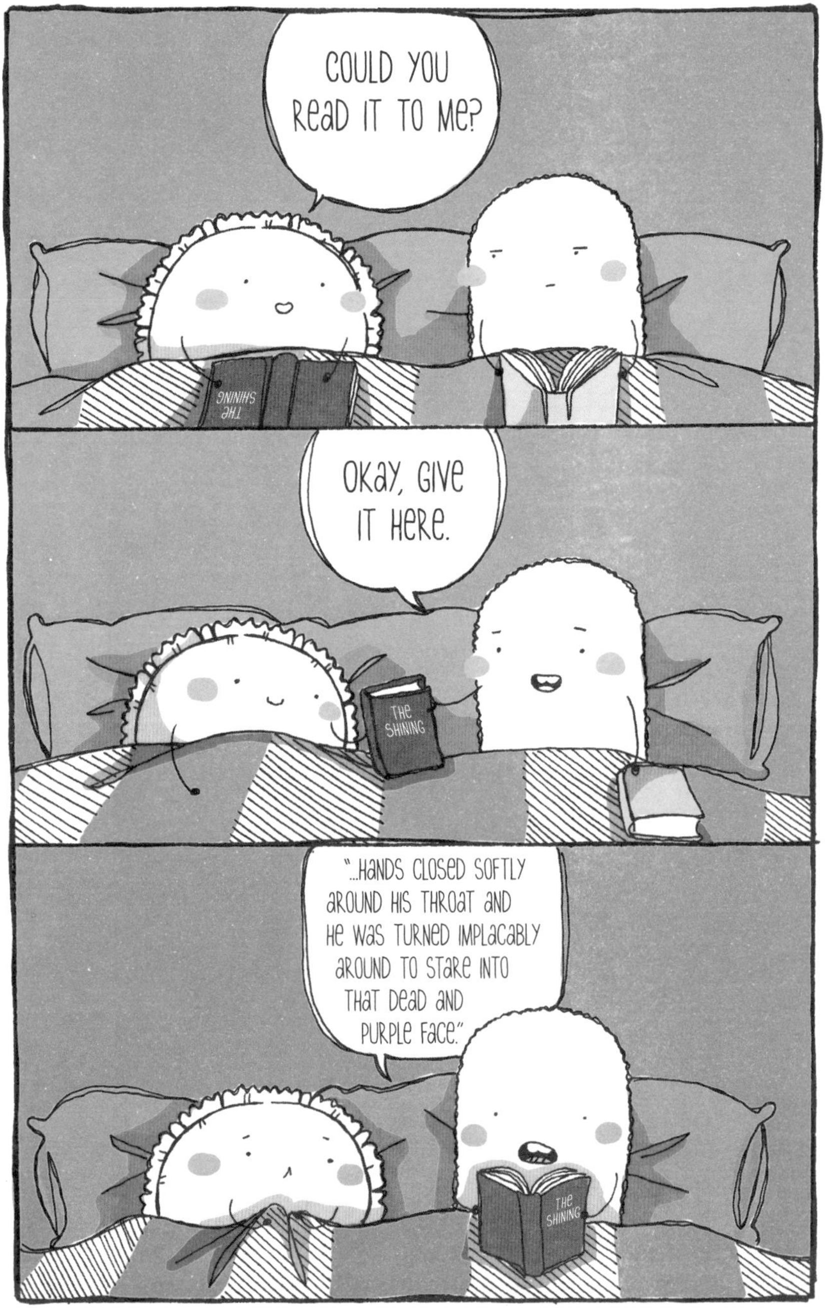
COULD YOU READ IT TO ME?
THE SHINING
OKAY, GIVE IT HERE.
THE SHINING
"...HANDS CLOSED SOFTLY AROUND HIS THROAT AND HE WAS TURNED IMPLACABLY AROUND TO STARE INTO THAT DEAD AND PURPLE FACE."
THE SHINING

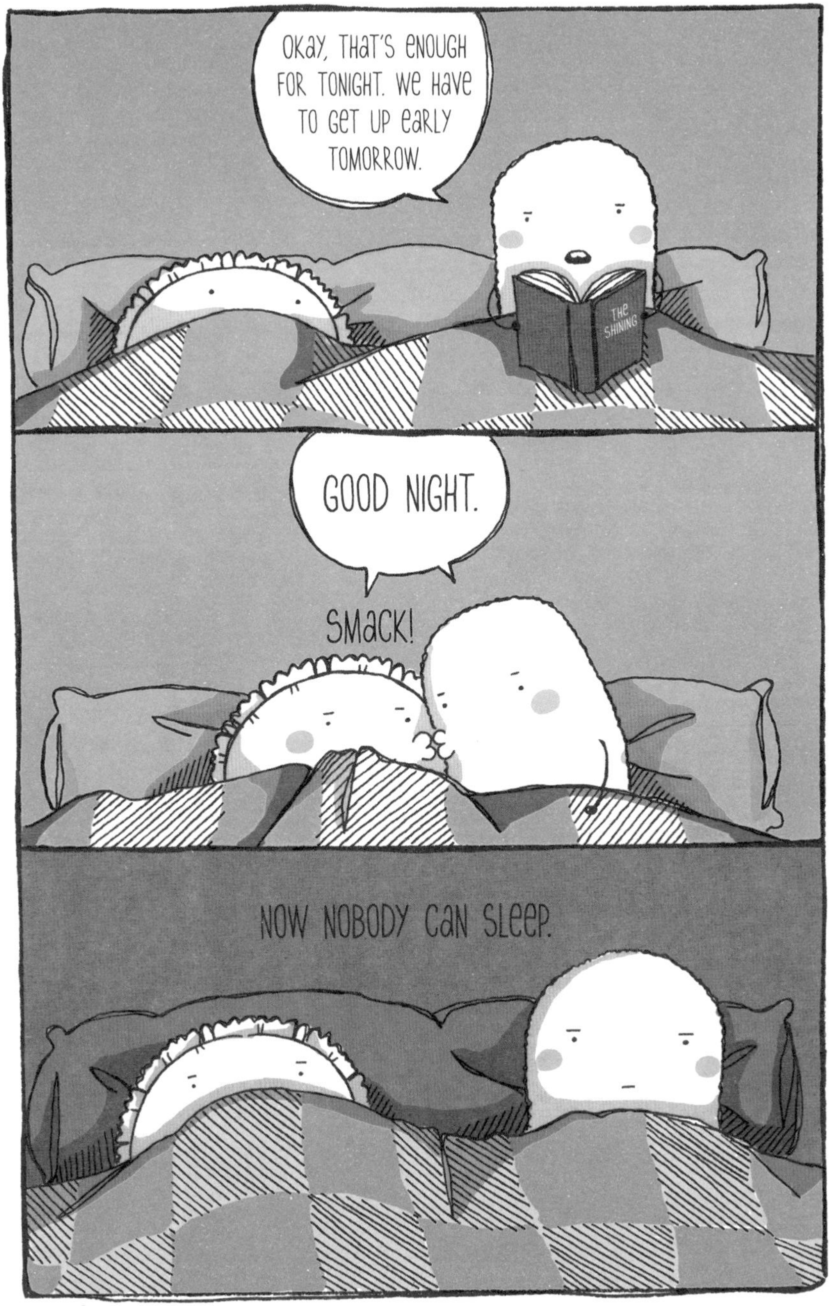
OKAY, THAT'S ENOUGH FOR TONIGHT. WE HAVE TO GET UP EARLY TOMORROW.
THE SHINING
GOOD NIGHT.
SMACK!
NOW NOBODY CAN SLEEP.

- LOVE PANDA TOUR -

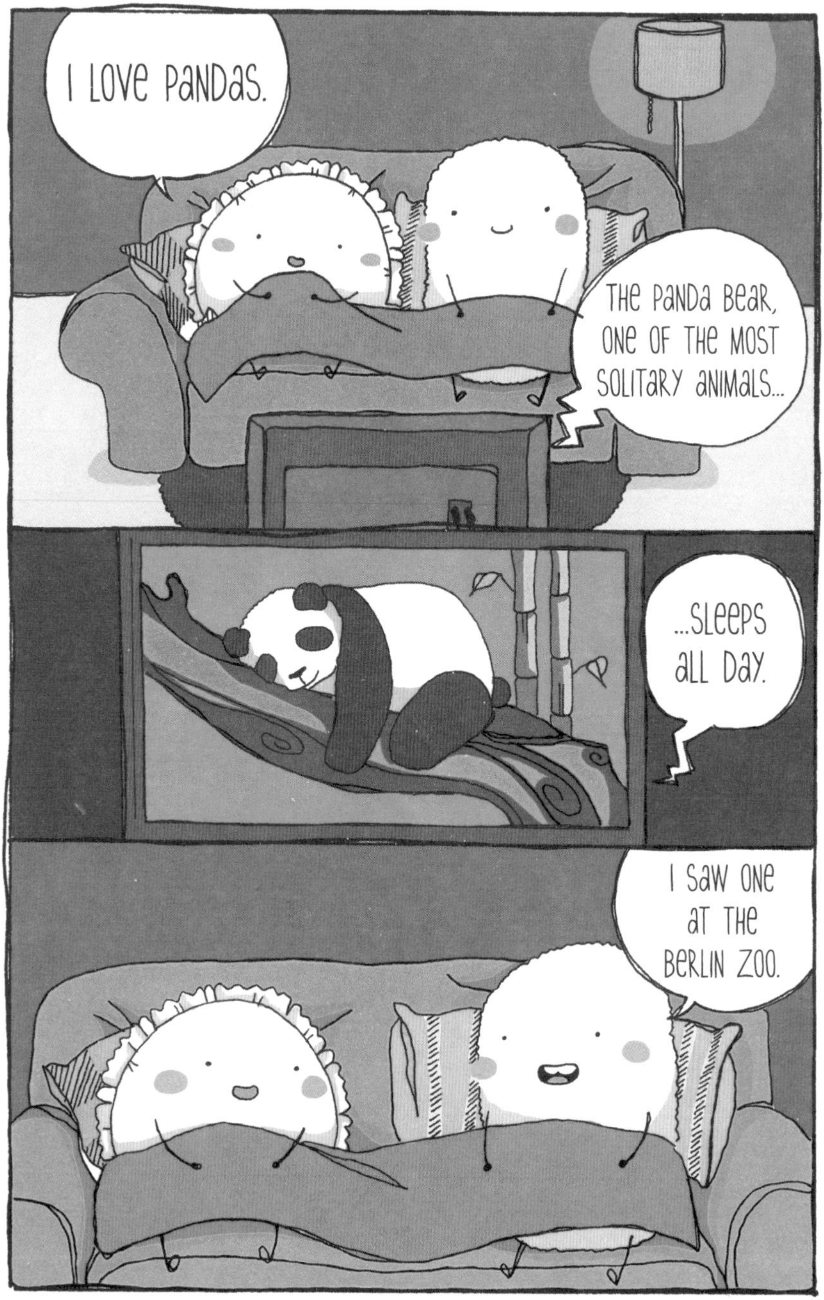
I LOVE PANDAS.
THE PANDA BEAR, ONE OF THE MOST SOLITARY ANIMALS...
...SLEEPS ALL DAY.
I SAW ONE AT THE BERLIN ZOO.

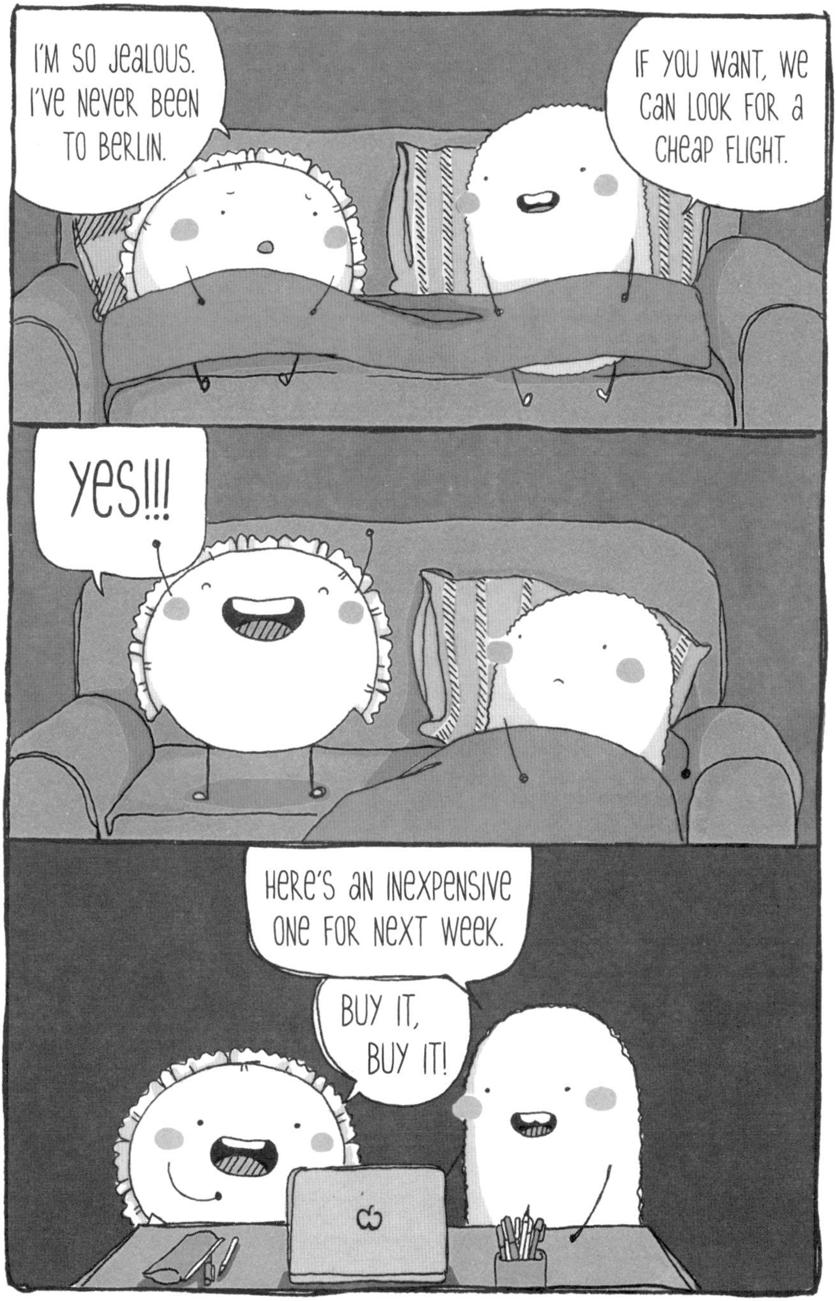
I'M SO JEALOUS. I'VE NEVER BEEN TO BERLIN.
IF YOU WANT, WE CAN LOOK FOR A CHEAP FLIGHT.
YES!!!
HERE'S AN INEXPENSIVE ONE FOR NEXT WEEK.
BUY IT, BUY IT!

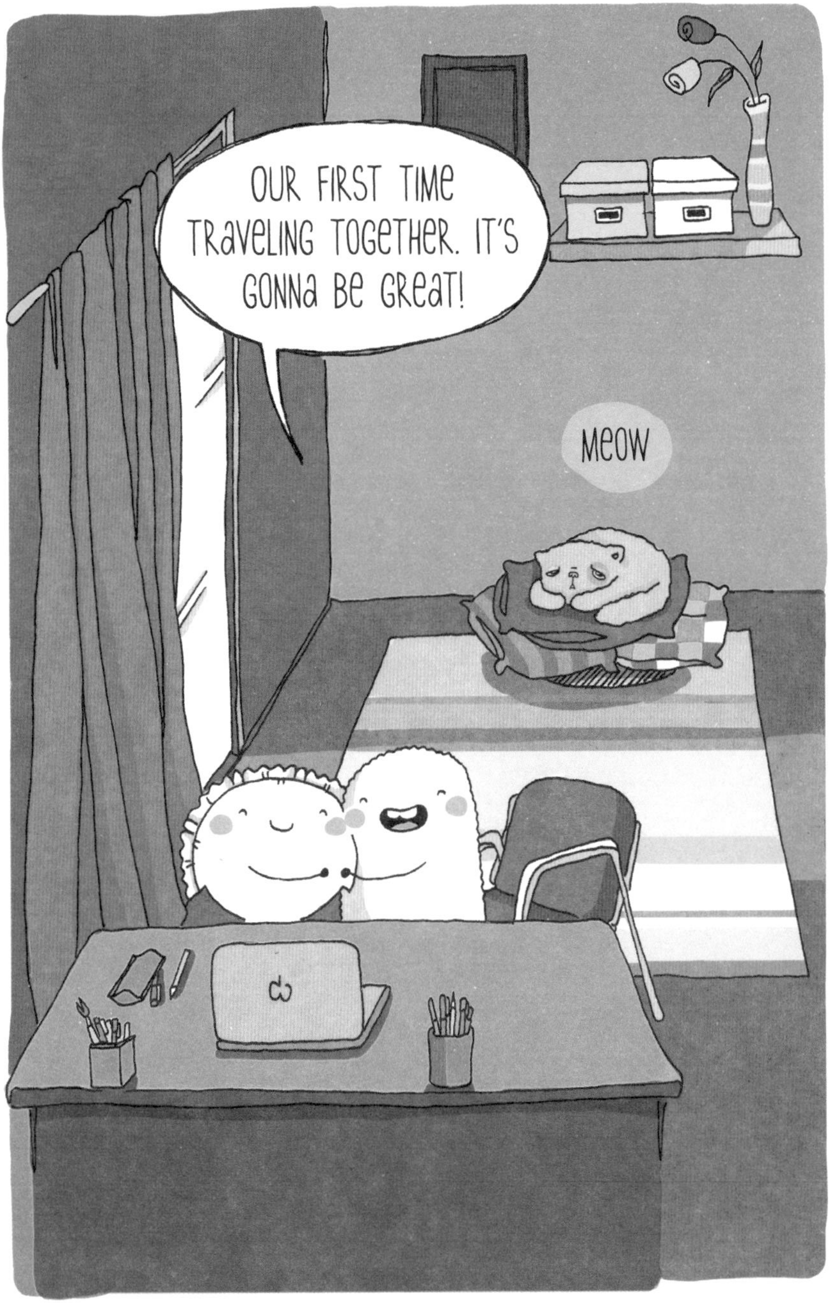
OUR FIRST TIME TRAVELING TOGETHER. IT'S GONNA BE GREAT!
MEOW

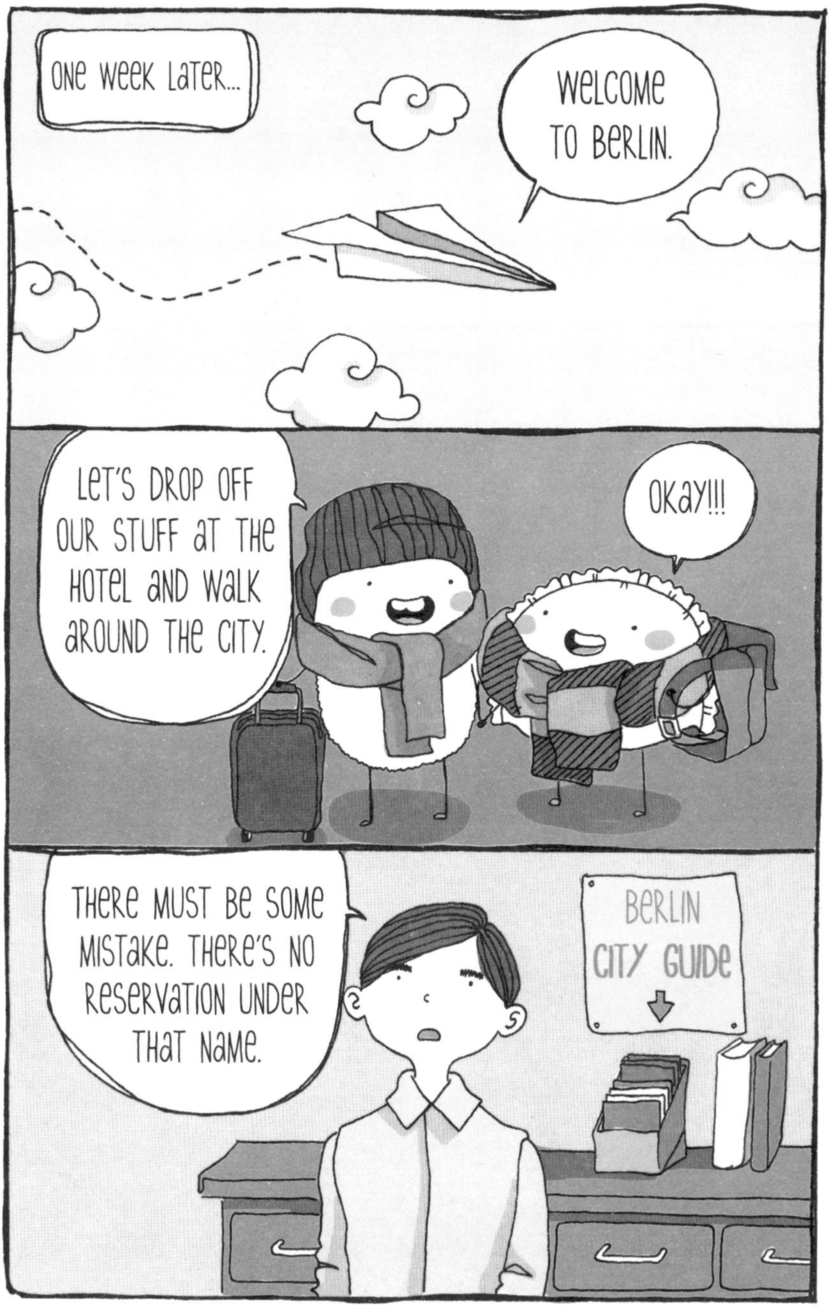
ONE WEEK LATER...
WELCOME TO BERLIN.
LET'S DROP OFF OUR STUFF AT THE HOTEL AND WALK AROUND THE CITY.
OKAY!!!
THERE MUST BE SOME MISTAKE. THERE'S NO RESERVATION UNDER THAT NAME.
BERLIN CITY GUIDE

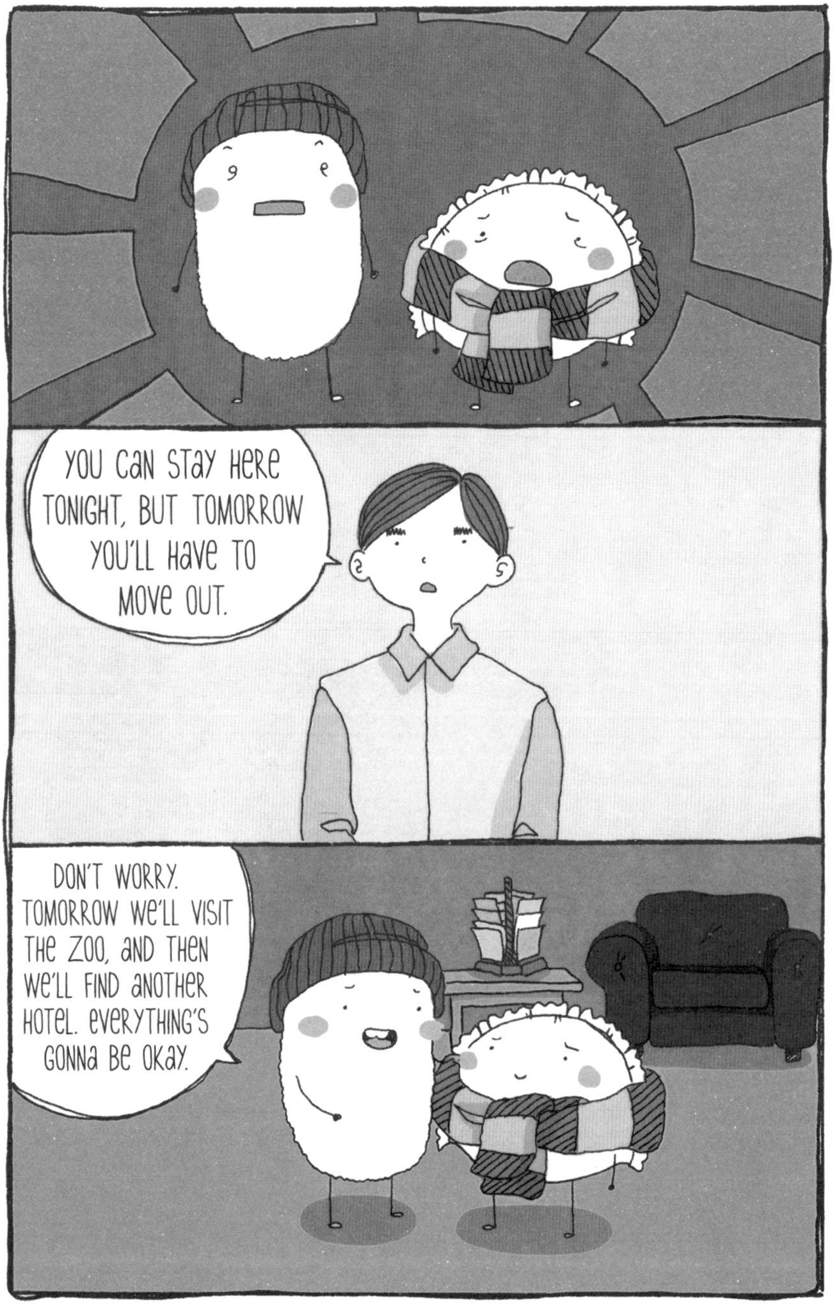
YOU CAN STAY HERE TONIGHT, BUT TOMORROW YOU'LL HAVE TO MOVE OUT.
DON'T WORRY. TOMORROW WE'LL VISIT THE ZOO, AND THEN WE'LL FIND ANOTHER HOTEL. EVERYTHING'S GONNA BE OKAY.

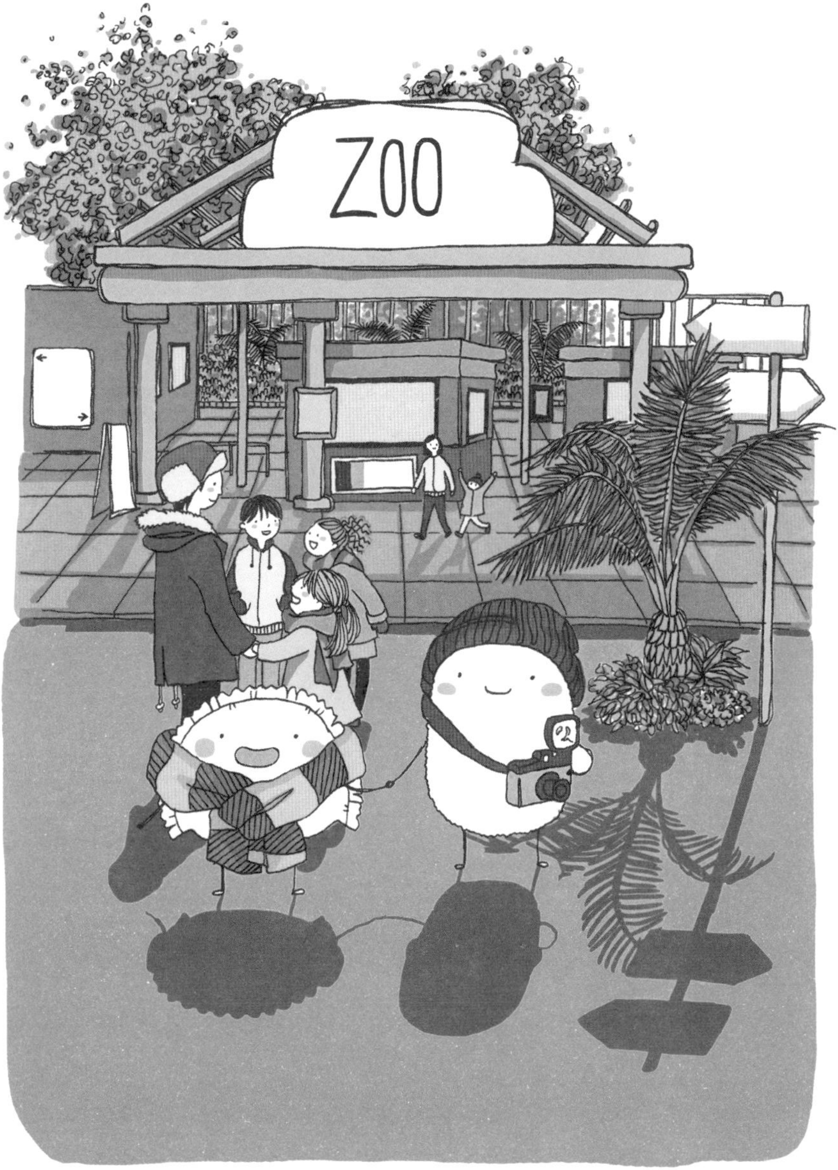
ZOO

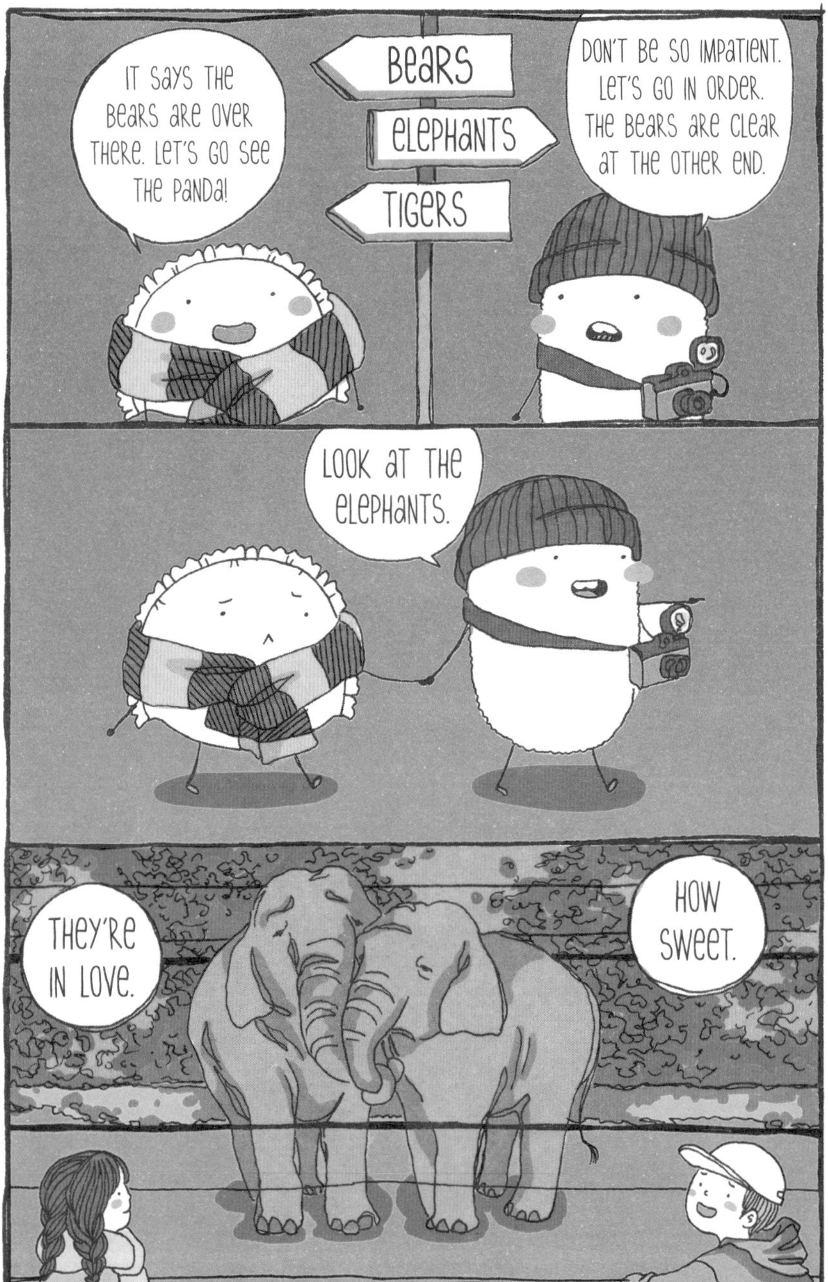
IT SAYS THE BEARS ARE OVER THERE. LET'S GO SEE THE PANDA!
BEARS
ELEPHANTS
TIGERS
DON'T BE SO IMPATIENT. LET'S GO IN ORDER. THE BEARS ARE CLEAR AT THE OTHER END.
LOOK AT THE ELEPHANTS.
THEY'RE IN LOVE.
HOW SWEET.

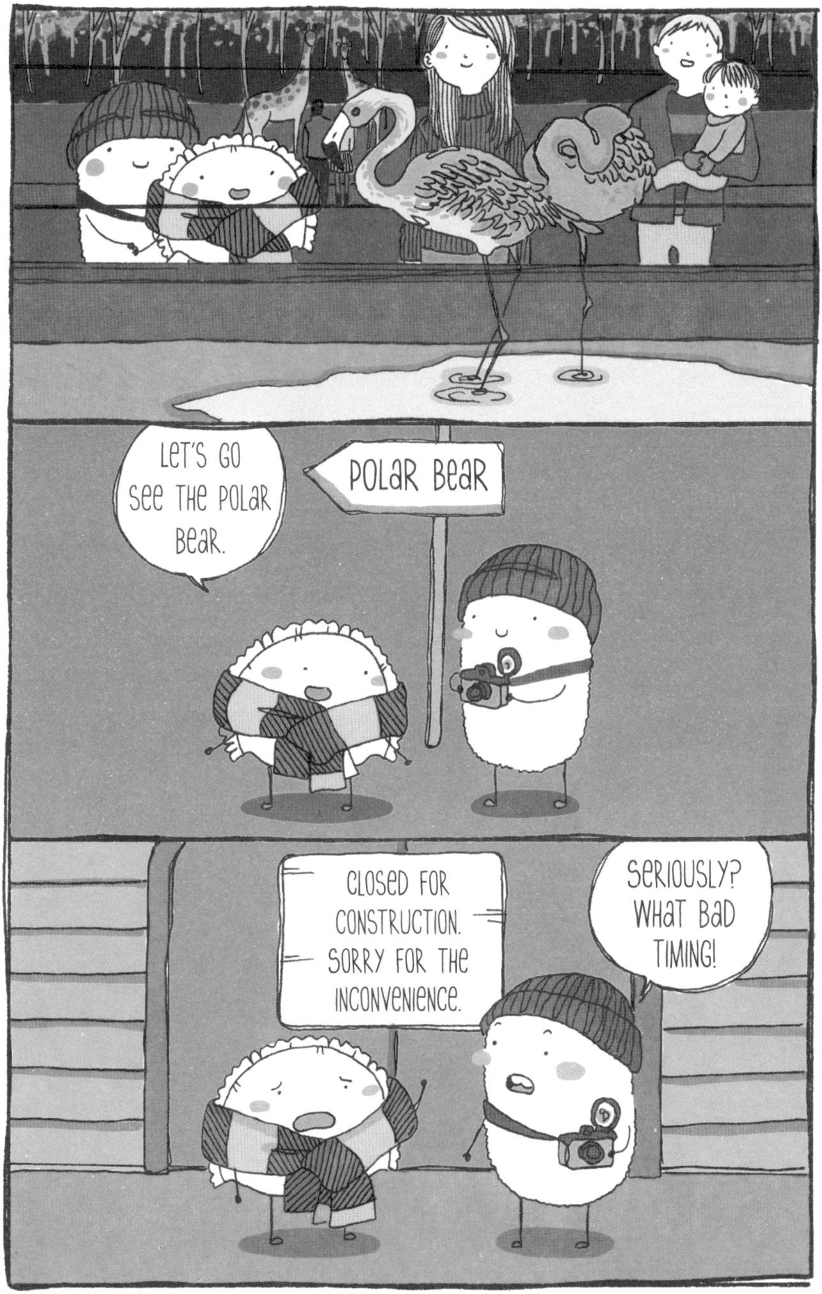
LET'S GO SEE THE POLAR BEAR.
POLAR BEAR
CLOSED FOR CONSTRUCTION. SORRY FOR THE INCONVENIENCE.
SERIOUSLY? WHAT BAD TIMING!

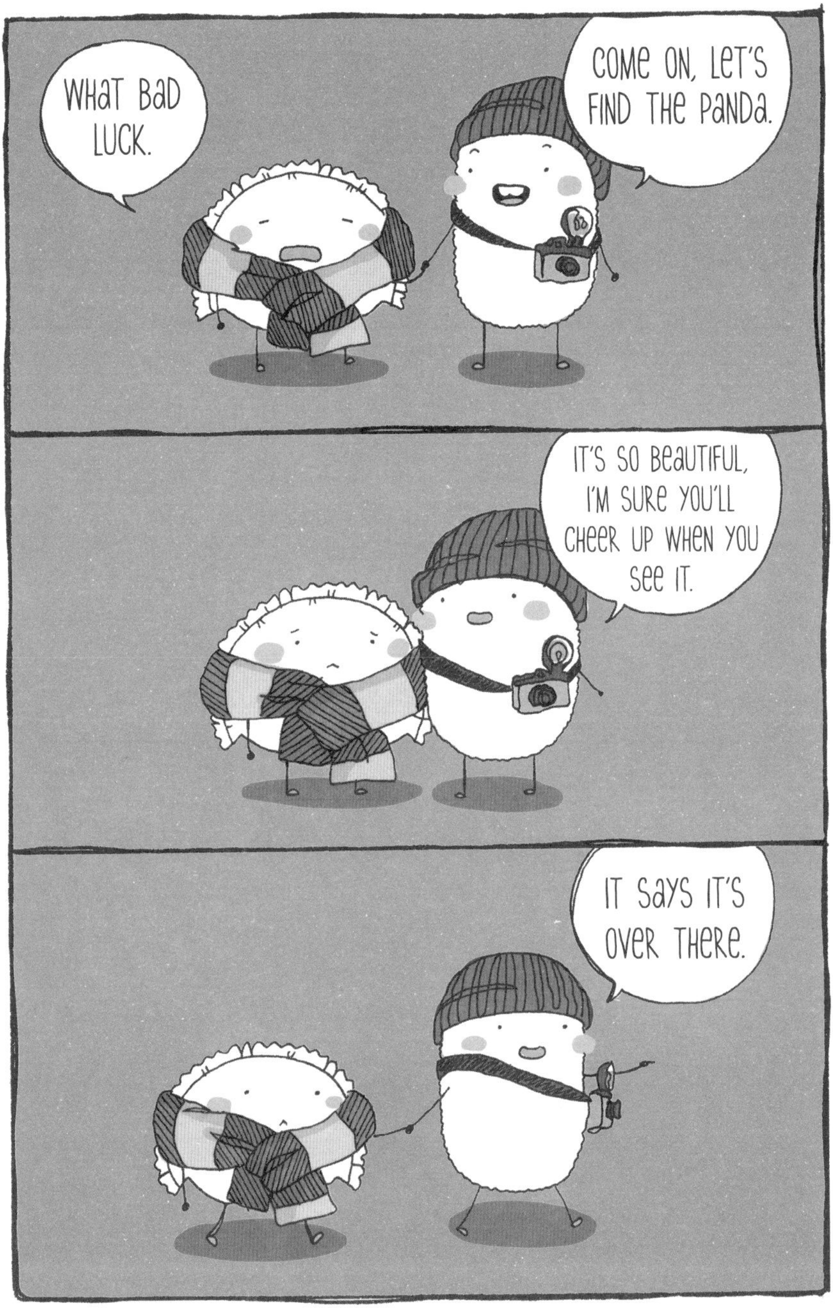
WHAT BAD LUCK.
COME ON, LET'S FIND THE PANDA.
IT'S SO BEAUTIFUL, I'M SURE YOU'LL CHEER UP WHEN YOU SEE IT.
IT SAYS IT'S OVER THERE.

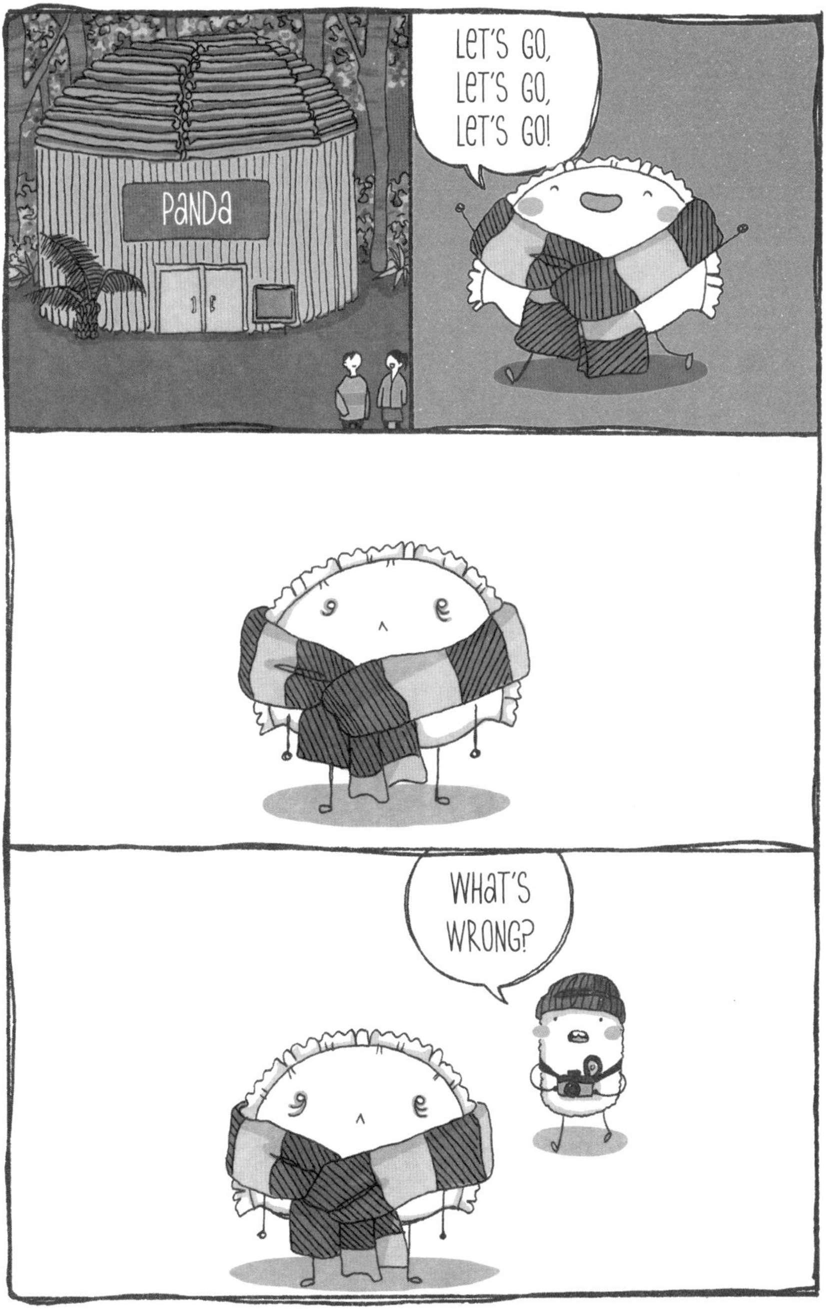
PANDA
LET'S GO, LET'S GO, LET'S GO!
WHAT'S WRONG?

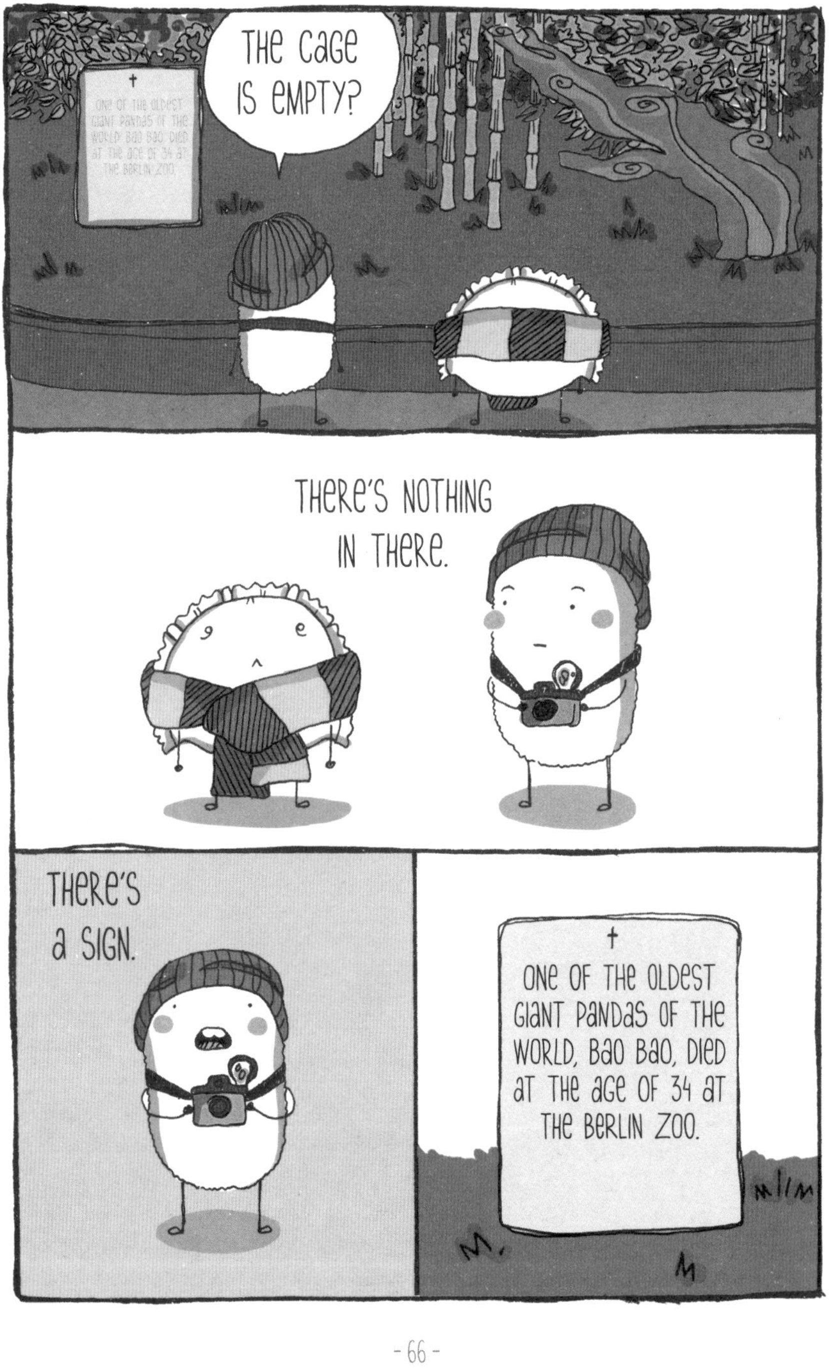
THE CAGE IS EMPTY?
THERE'S NOTHING IN THERE.
THERE'S A SIGN.
†
ONE OF THE OLDEST GIANT PANDAS OF THE WORLD, BAO BAO, DIED AT THE AGE OF 34 AT THE BERLIN ZOO.

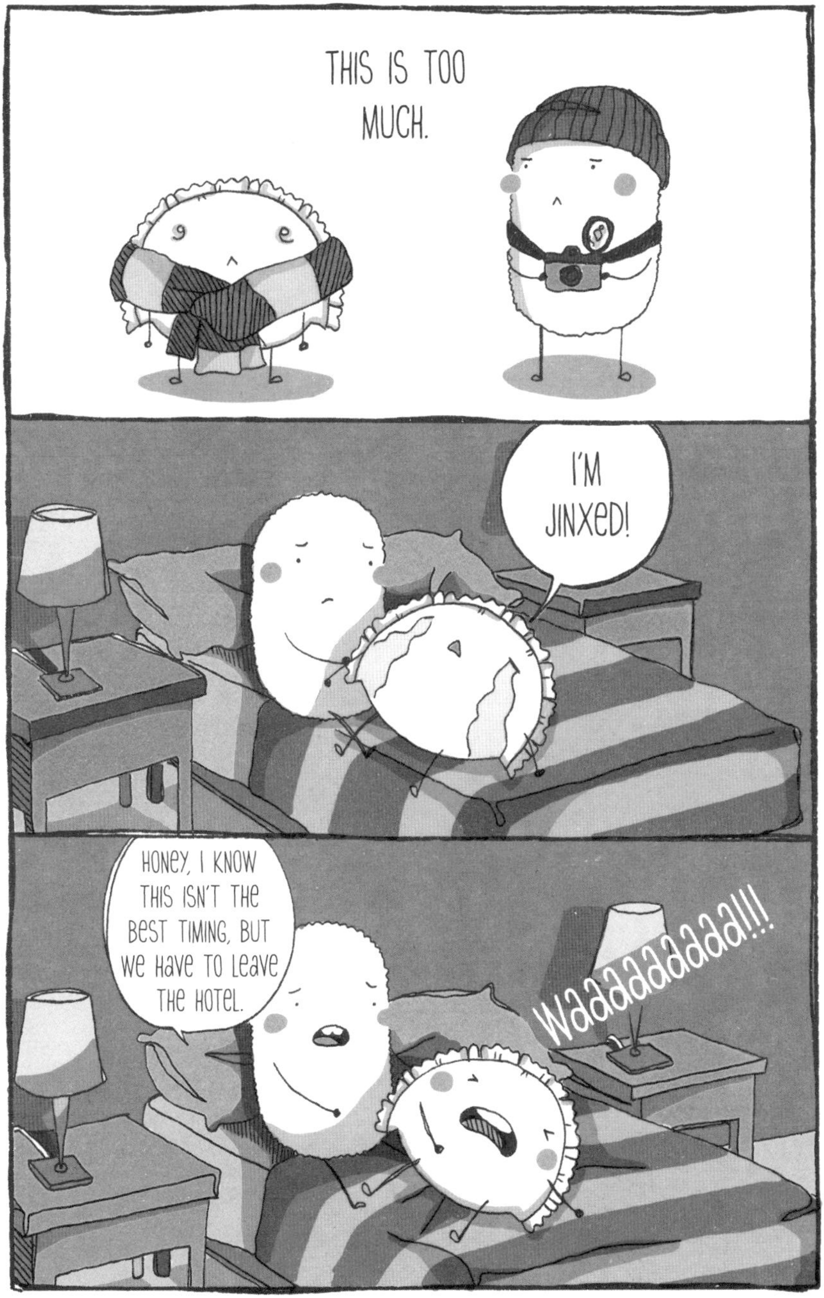
THIS IS TOO MUCH.
I'M JINXED!
HONEY, I KNOW THIS ISN'T THE BEST TIMING, BUT WE HAVE TO LEAVE THE HOTEL.
Waaaaaaaaaa!!!

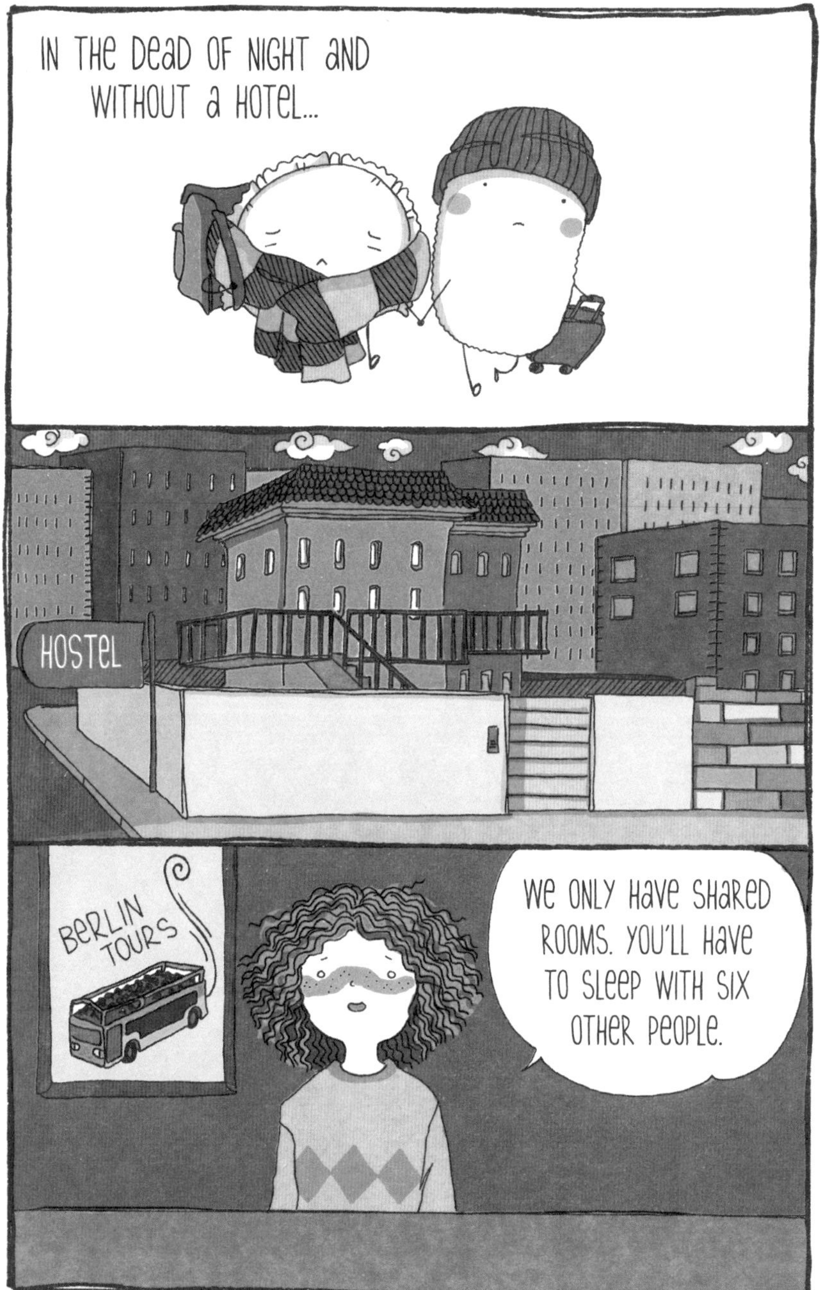
IN THE DEAD OF NIGHT AND WITHOUT A HOTEL...
HOSTEL
BERLIN TOURS
WE ONLY HAVE SHARED ROOMS. YOU'LL HAVE TO SLEEP WITH SIX OTHER PEOPLE.

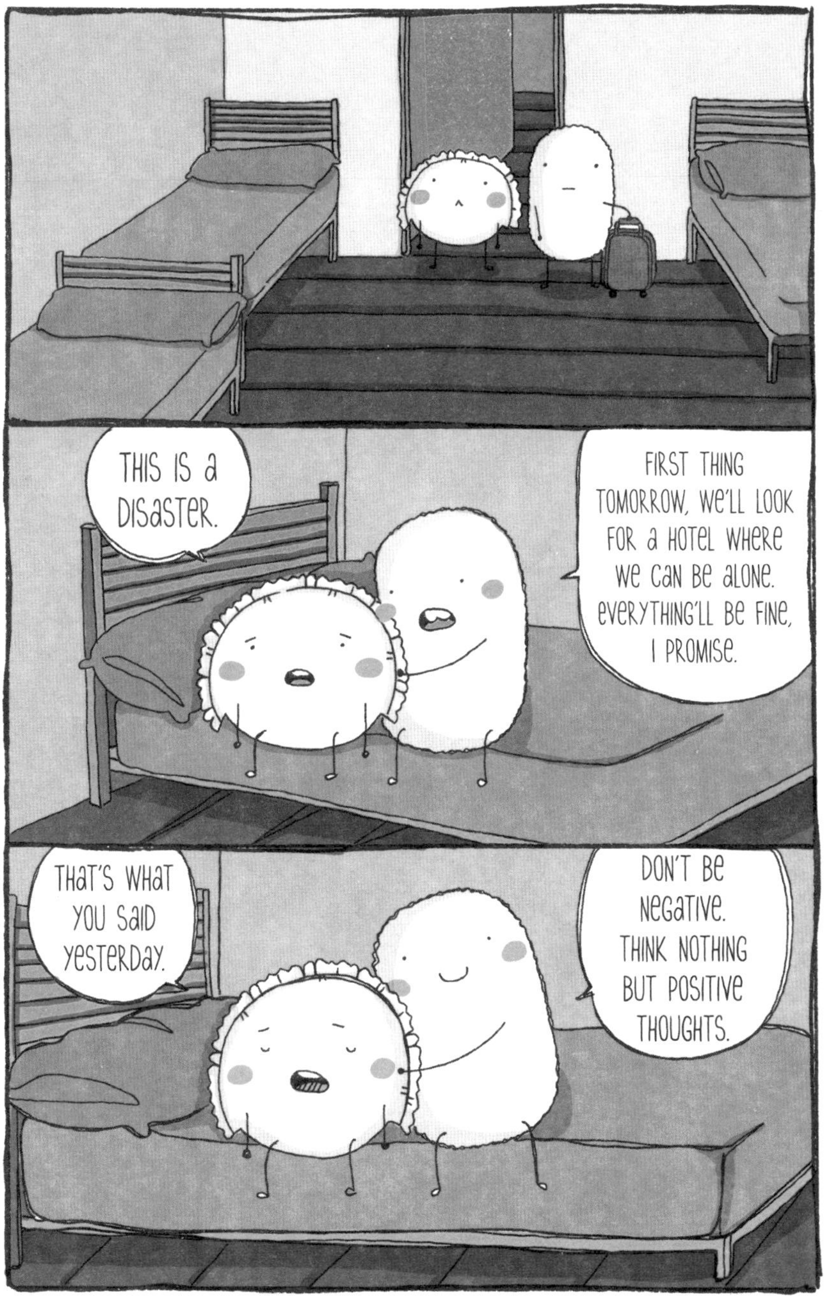
THIS IS a DISASTER.
FIRST THING TOMORROW, WE'LL LOOK FOR a HOTEL WHERE WE CAN BE ALONE. EVERYTHING'LL BE FINE, I PROMISE.
THAT'S WHAT YOU SaID YESTERDAY.
DON'T BE NEGaTIVE. THINK NOTHING BUT POSITIVE THOUGHTS.

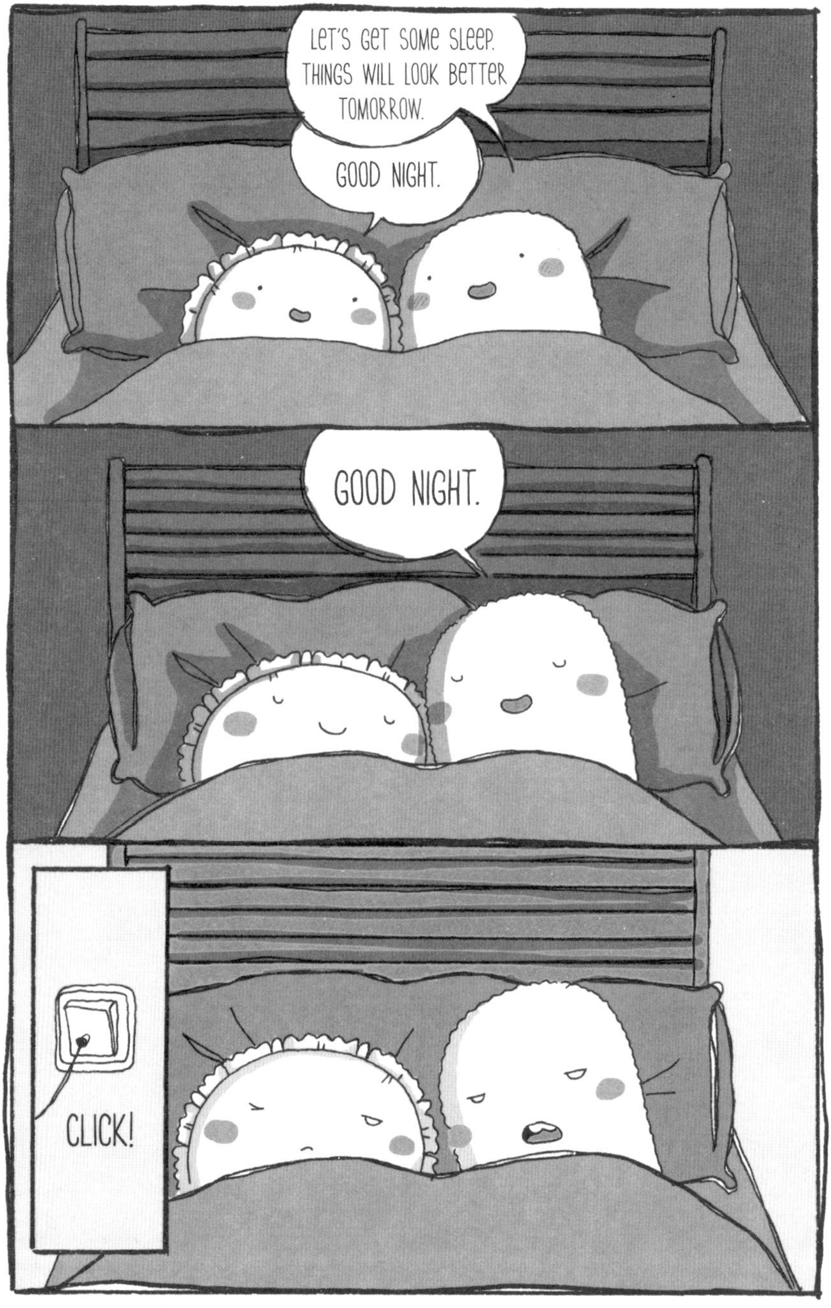
LET'S GET SOME SLEEP. THINGS WILL LOOK BETTER TOMORROW.
GOOD NIGHT.
GOOD NIGHT.
CLICK!

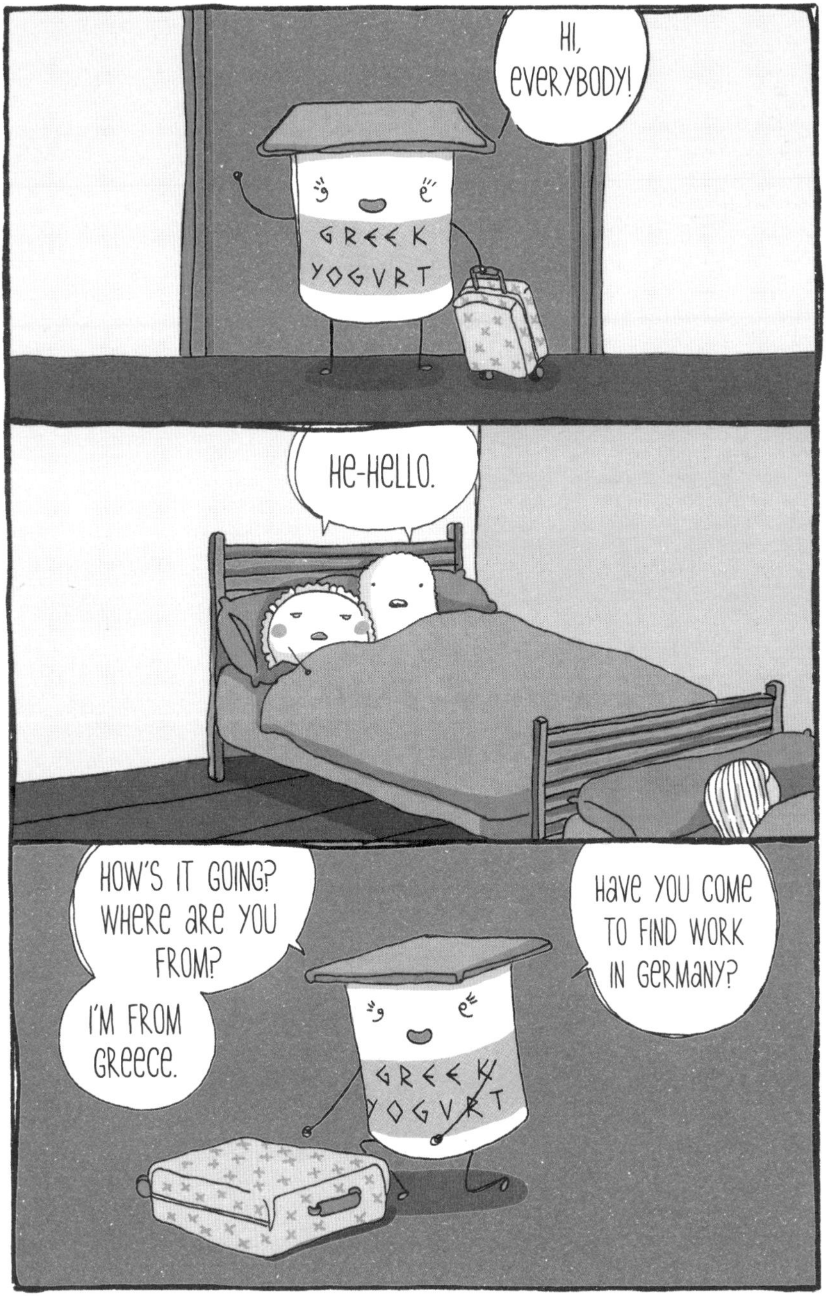
HI, EVERYBODY!
GREEK YOGURT
HE-HELLO.
HOW'S IT GOING? WHERE ARE YOU FROM?
I'M FROM GREECE.
HAVE YOU COME TO FIND WORK IN GERMANY?
GREEK YOGURT

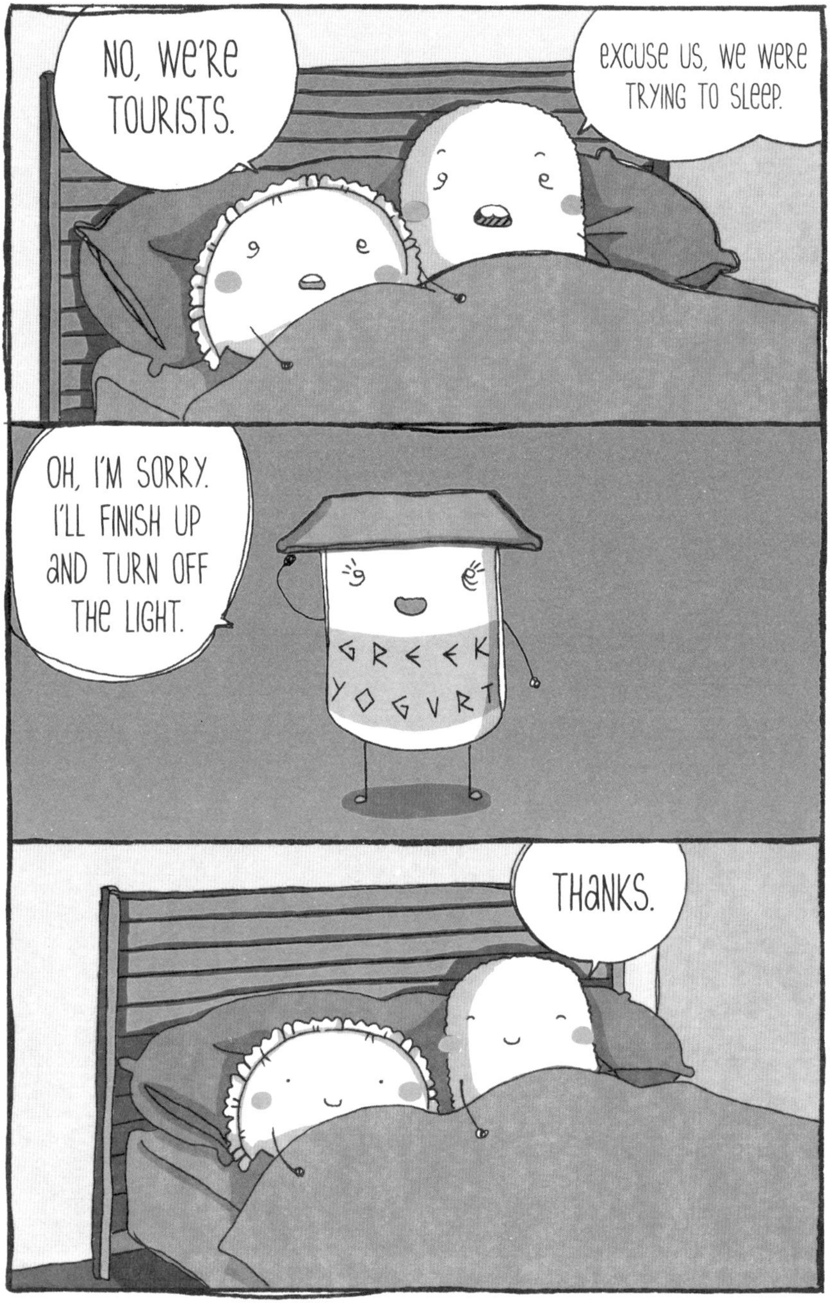
NO, WE'RE TOURISTS.
EXCUSE US, WE WERE TRYING TO SLEEP.
OH, I'M SORRY. I'LL FINISH UP AND TURN OFF THE LIGHT.
GREEK YOGURT
THANKS.

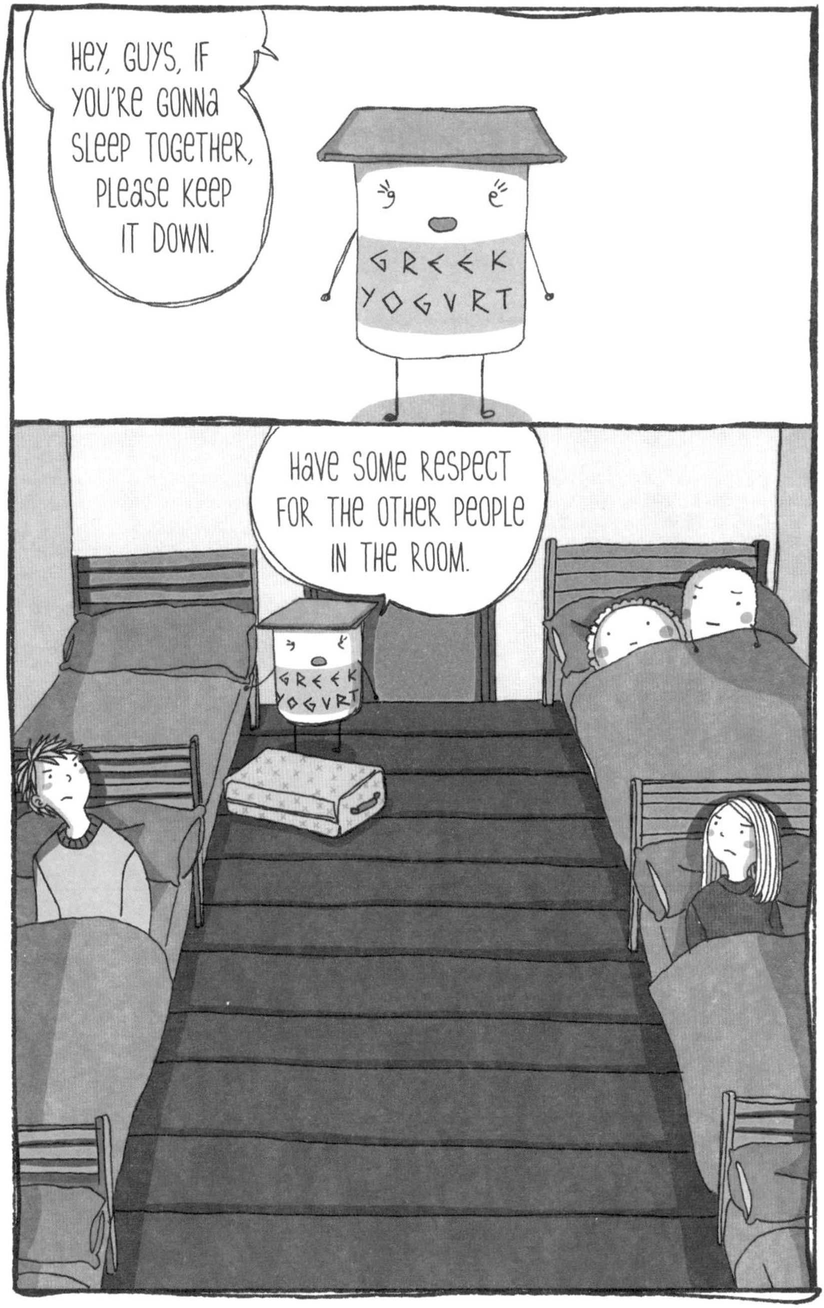
HEY, GUYS, IF YOU'RE GONNA SLEEP TOGETHER, PLEASE KEEP IT DOWN.
GREEK YOGURT
HAVE SOME RESPECT FOR THE OTHER PEOPLE IN THE ROOM.
GREEK YOGURT

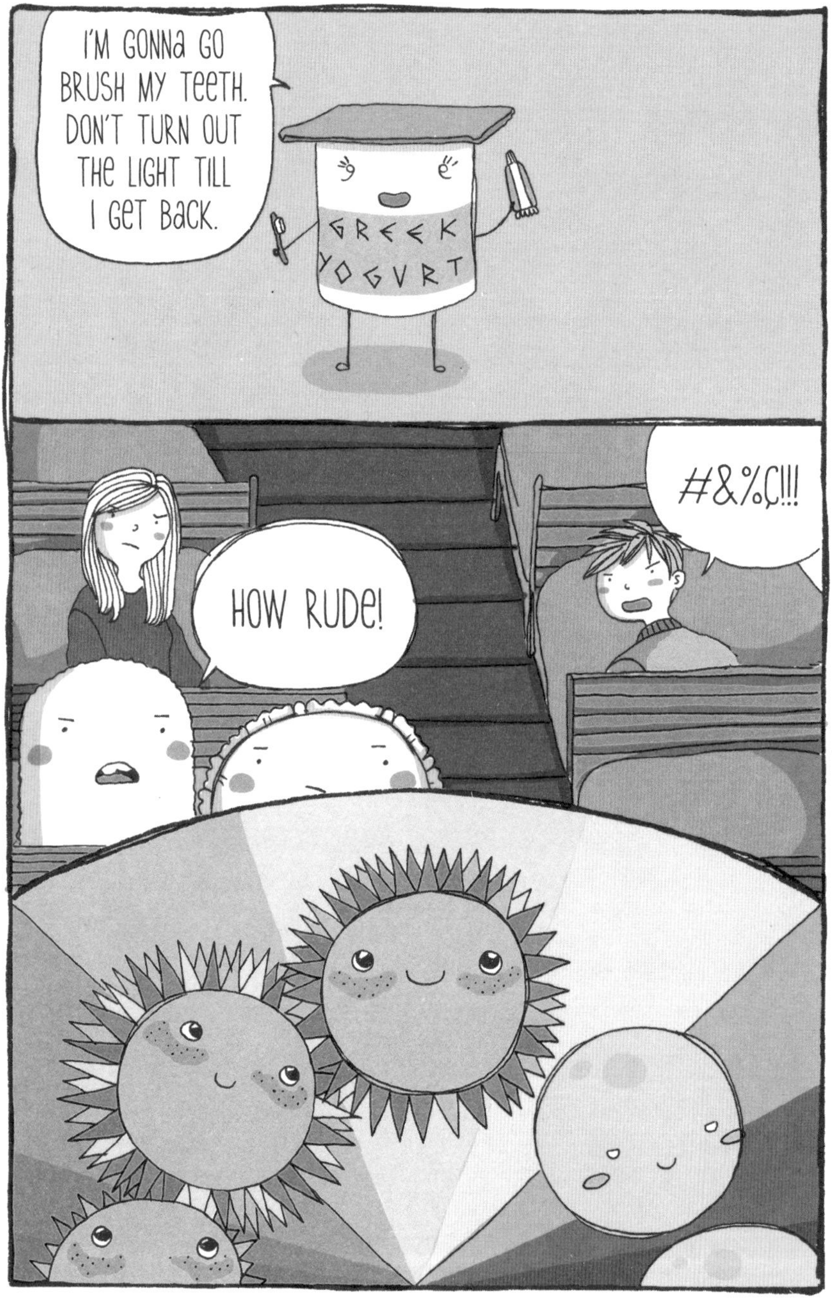
I'M GONNA GO BRUSH MY TEETH. DON'T TURN OUT THE LIGHT TILL I GET BACK.
GREEK YOGURT
HOW RUDE!
#&%Ç!!!

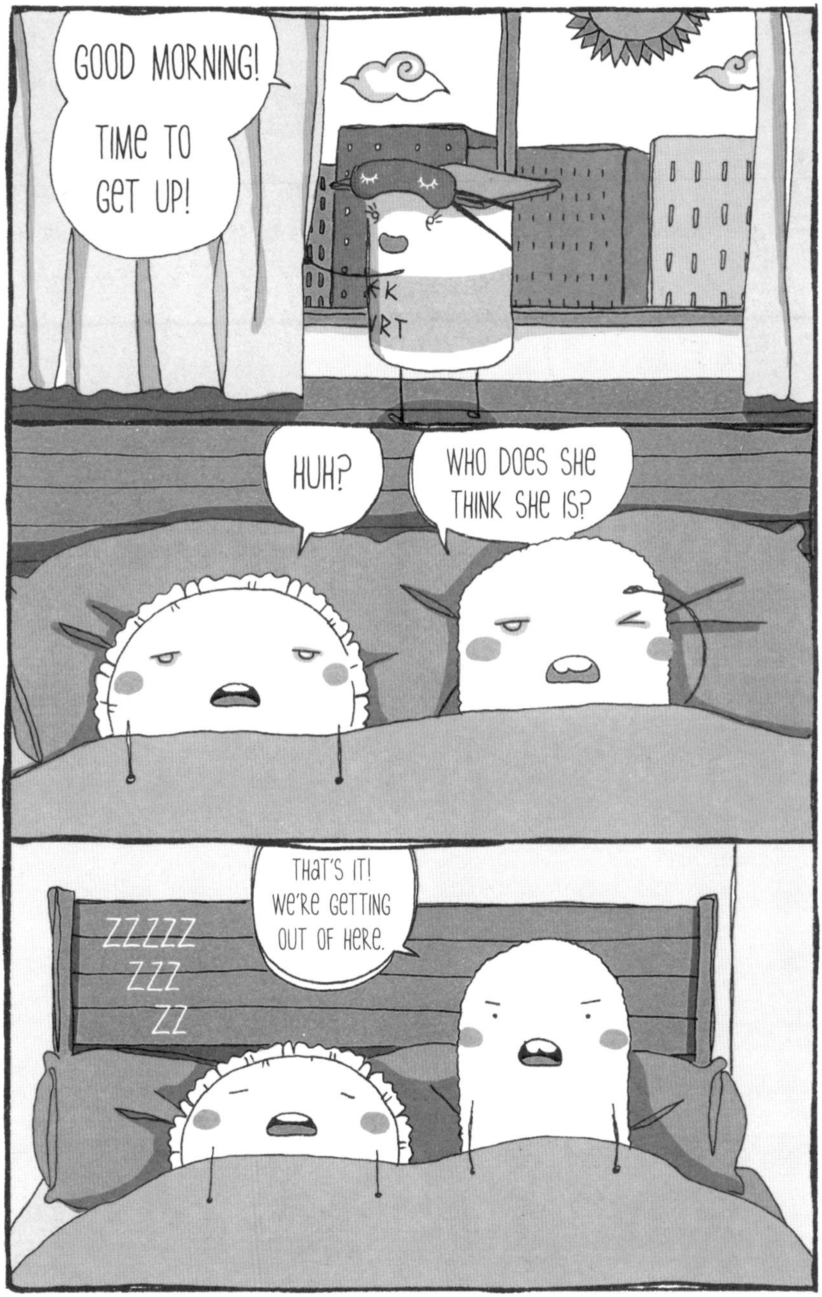
GOOD MORNING!
TIME TO GET UP!
HUH?
WHO DOES SHE THINK SHE IS?
ZZZZZ ZZZ ZZ
THAT'S IT! WE'RE GETTING OUT OF HERE.

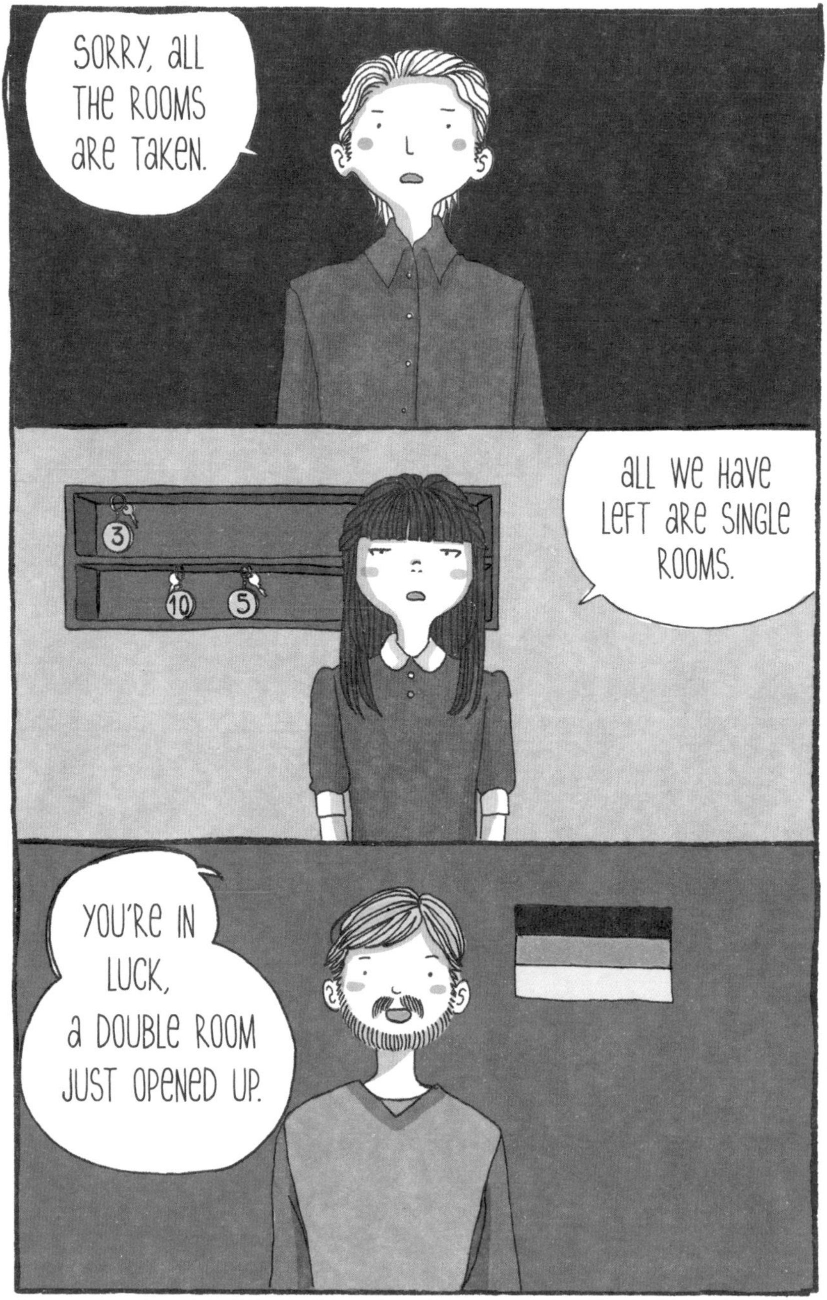
SORRY, ALL THE ROOMS ARE TAKEN.
ALL WE HAVE LEFT ARE SINGLE ROOMS.
3
10
5
YOU'RE IN LUCK, A DOUBLE ROOM JUST OPENED UP.

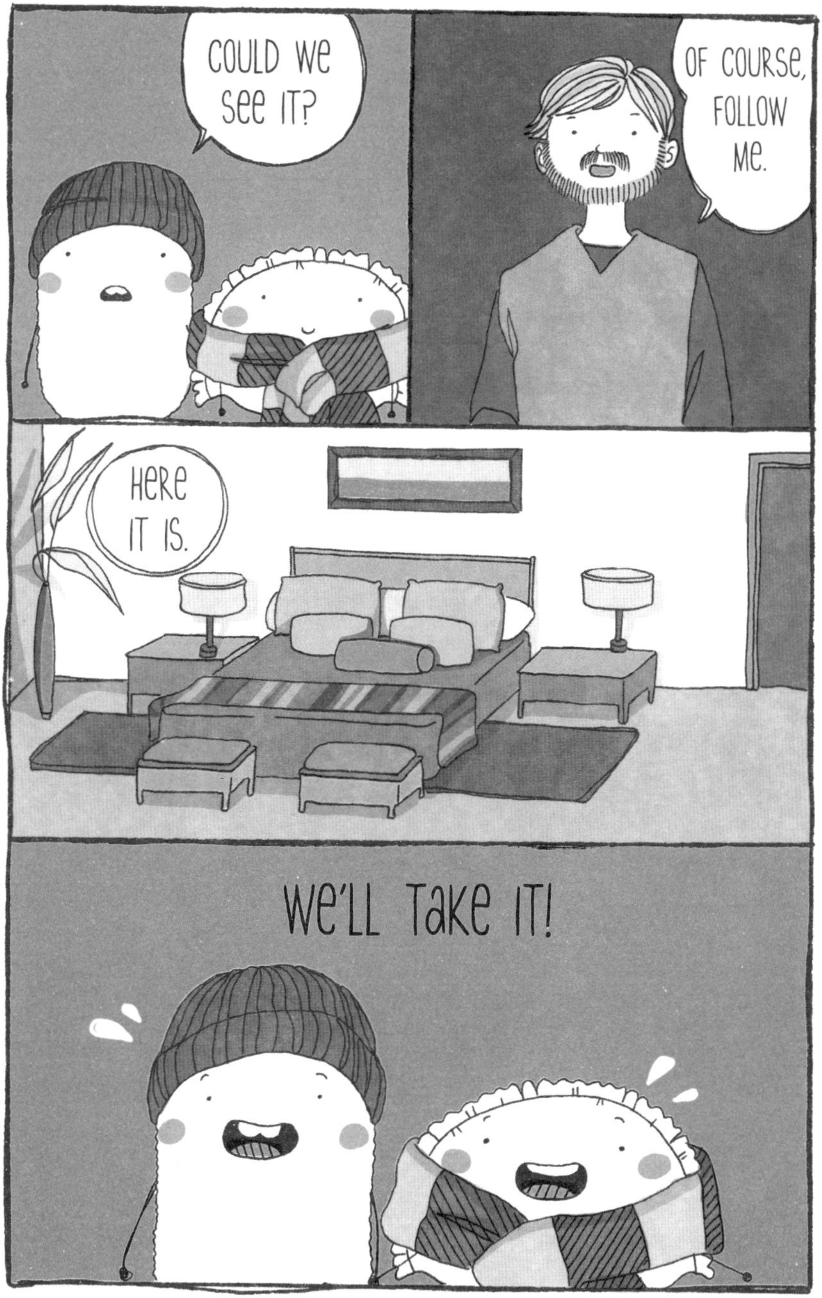
COULD WE SEE IT?
OF COURSE, FOLLOW ME.
HERE IT IS.
WE'LL TAKE IT!

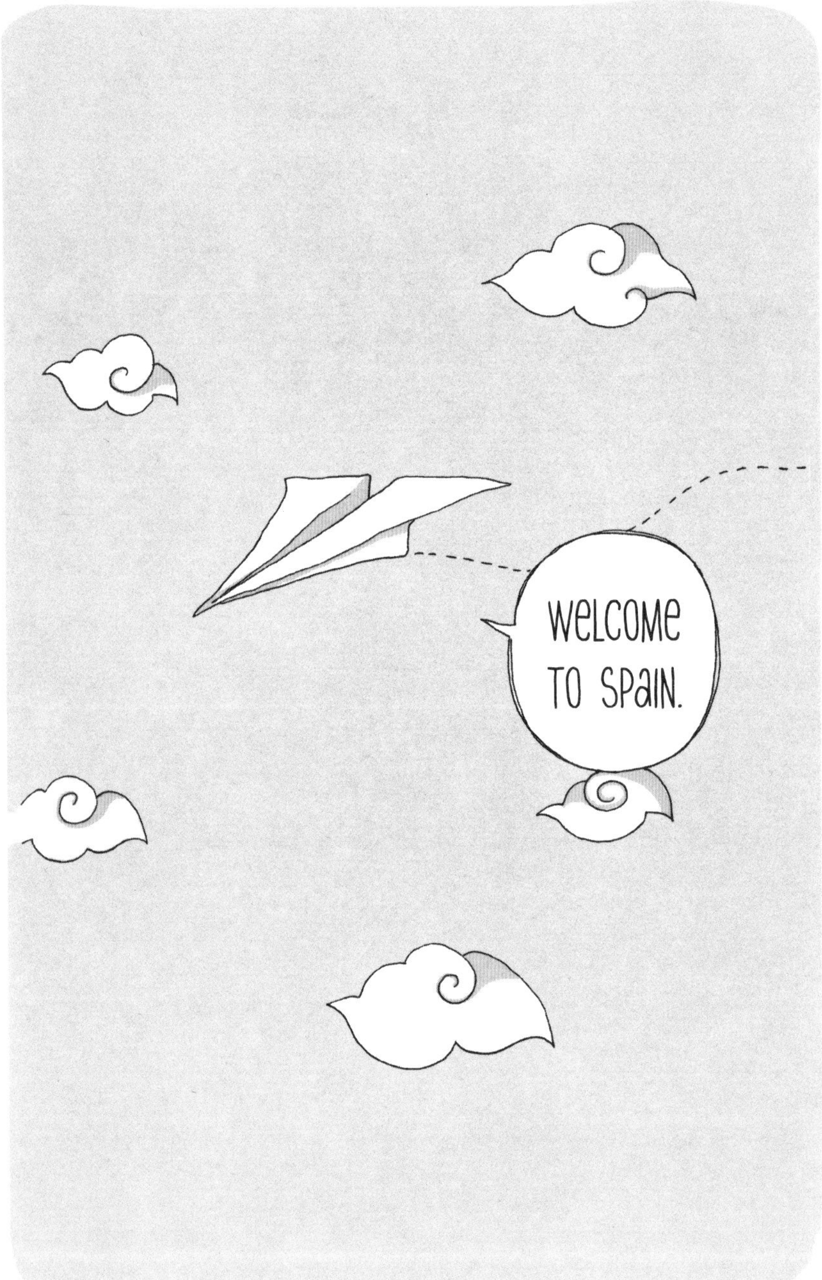
WELCOME TO SPAIN.

- Scary Bedtime Stories -

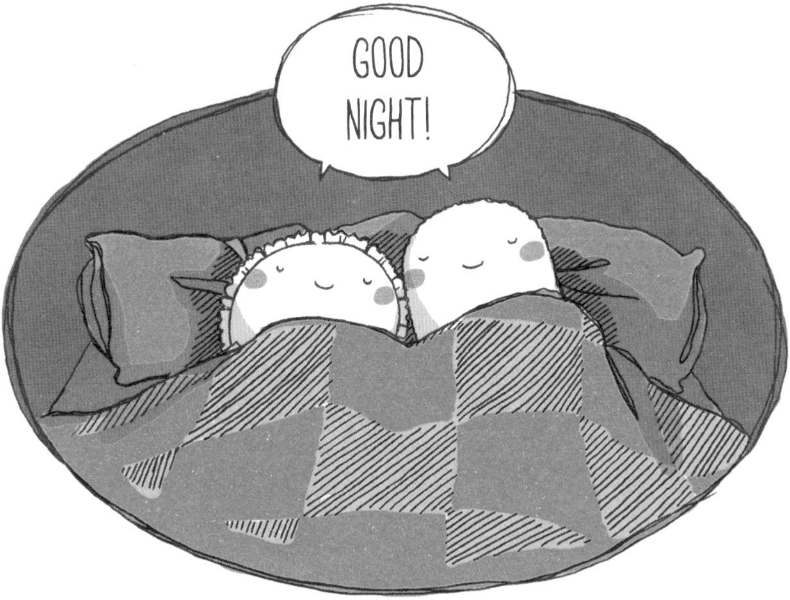
GOOD NIGHT!

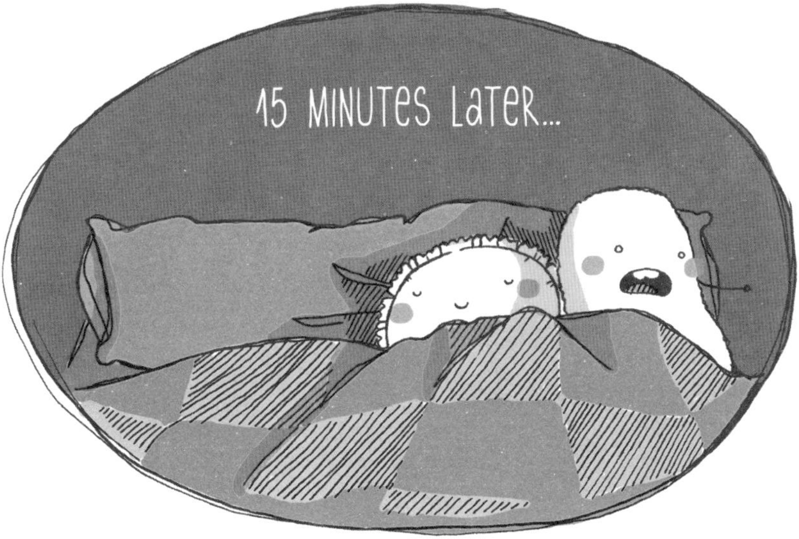
15 MINUTES LATER...

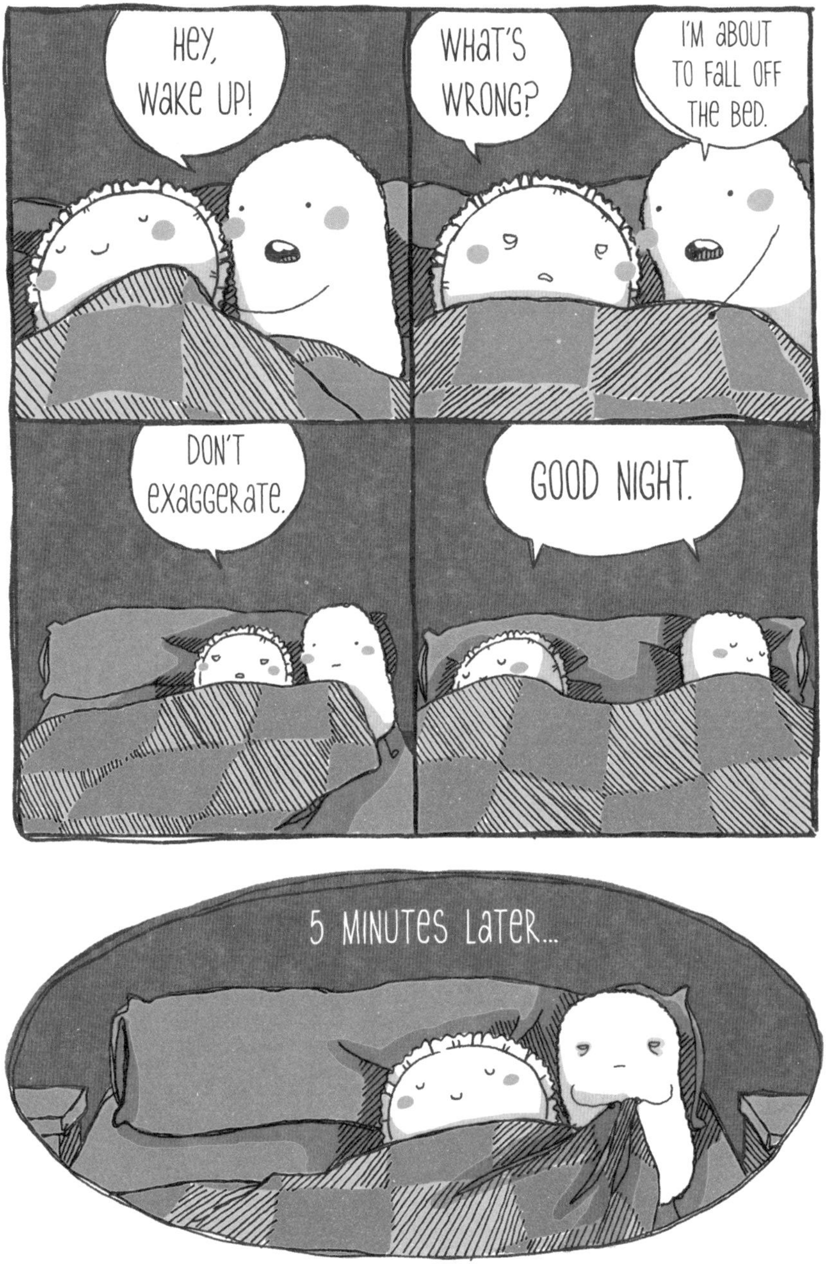
Hey, Wake up!
What's wrong?
I'm about to fall off the bed.
Don't exaggerate.
Good night.
5 minutes later...

- SLEEPING EMPANADA -

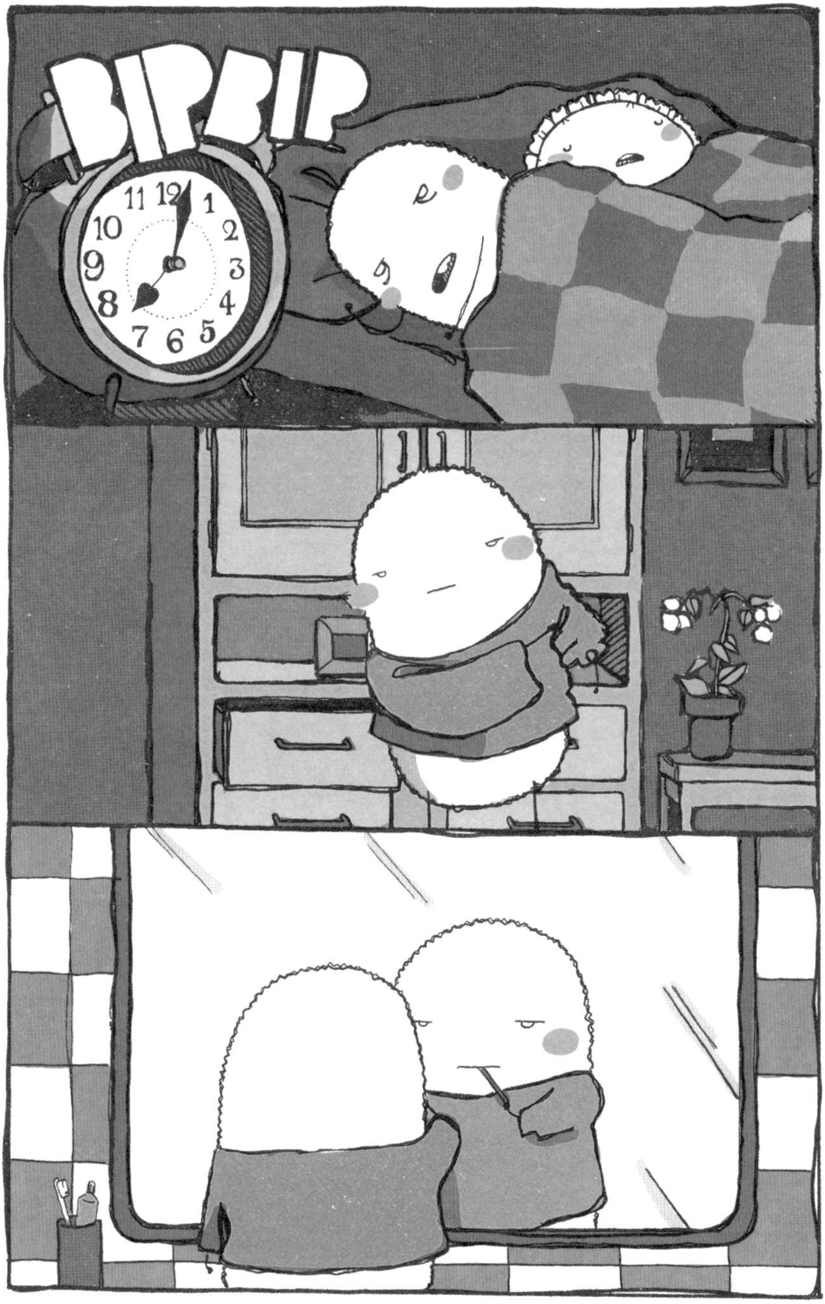
BIPBIP

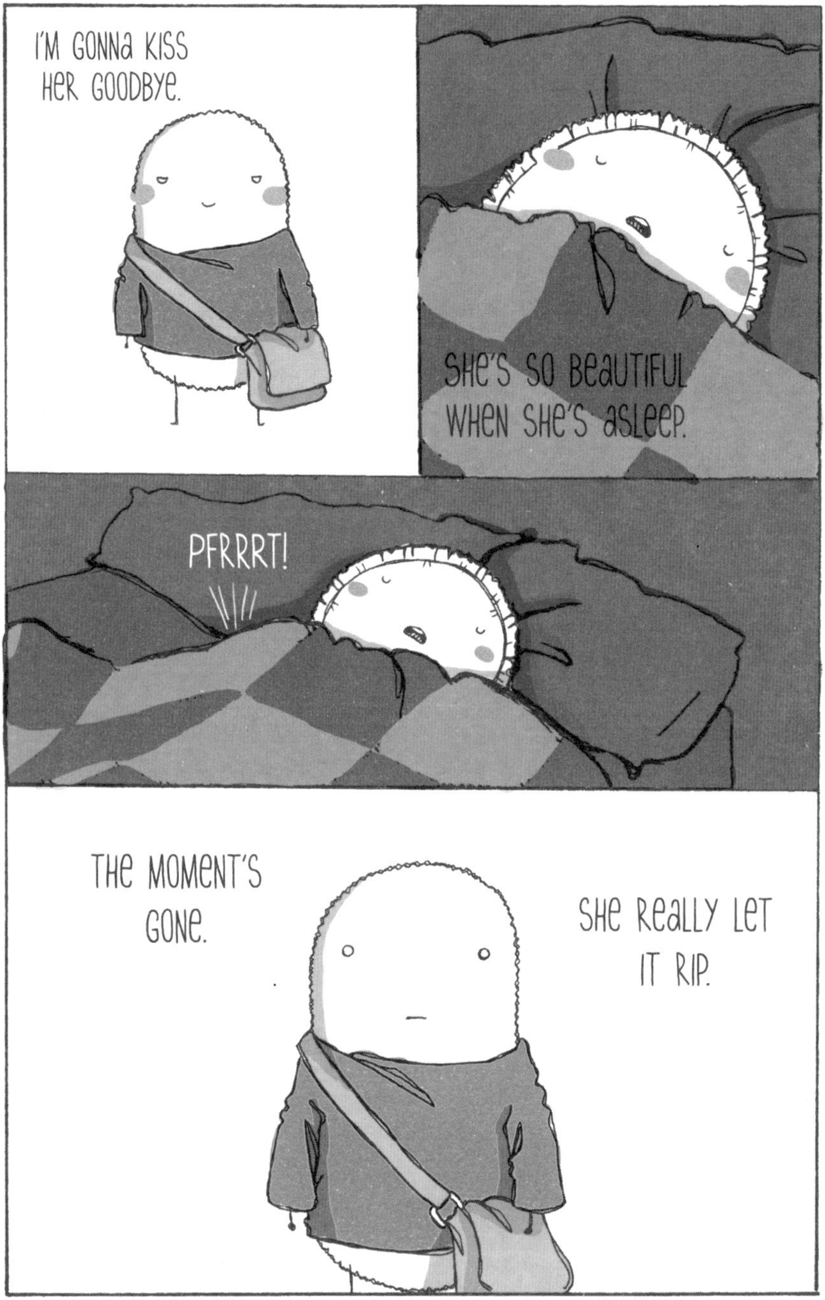
I'M GONNA KISS HER GOODBYE.
SHE'S SO BEAUTIFUL WHEN SHE'S ASLEEP.
PFRRRT!
THE MOMENT'S GONE.
SHE REALLY LET IT RIP.

- ALL I WANT FOR XMAS... -

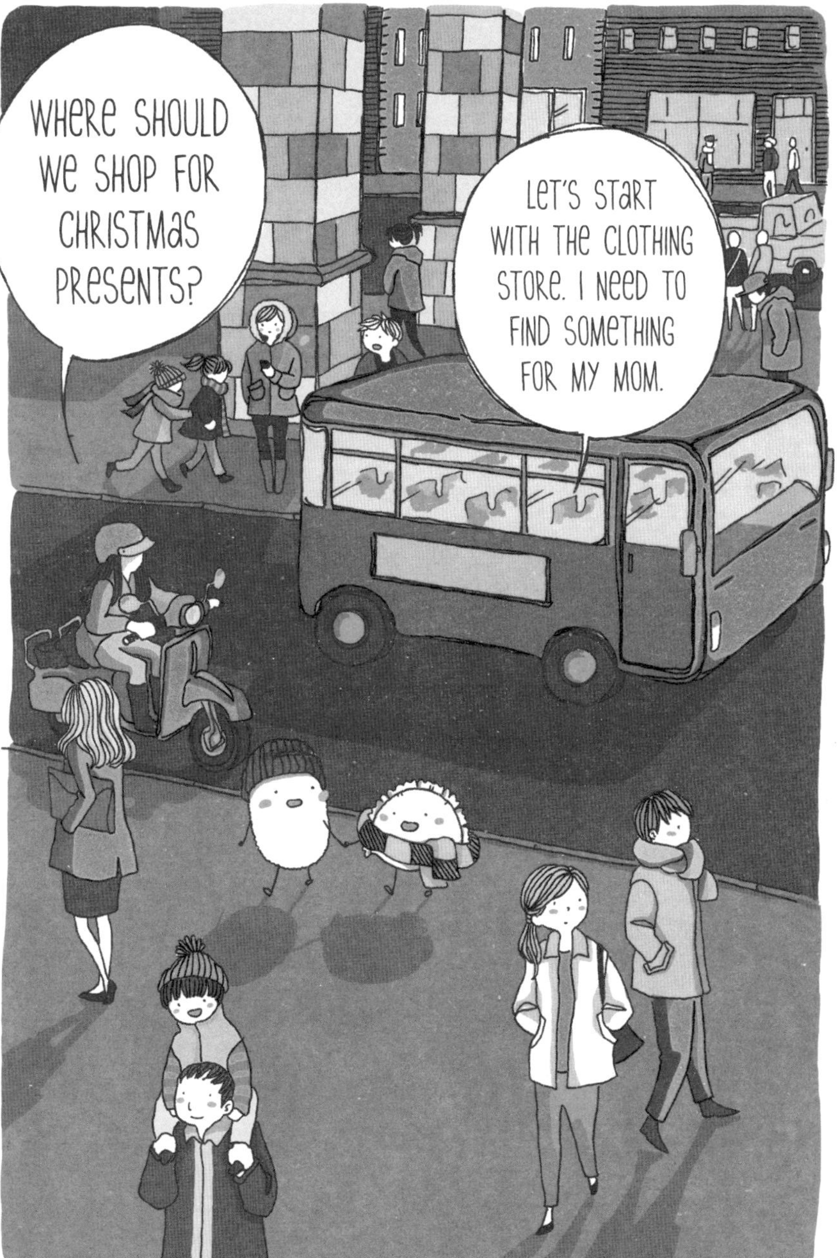
WHERE SHOULD WE SHOP FOR CHRISTMAS PRESENTS?
LET'S START WITH THE CLOTHING STORE. I NEED TO FIND SOMETHING FOR MY MOM.

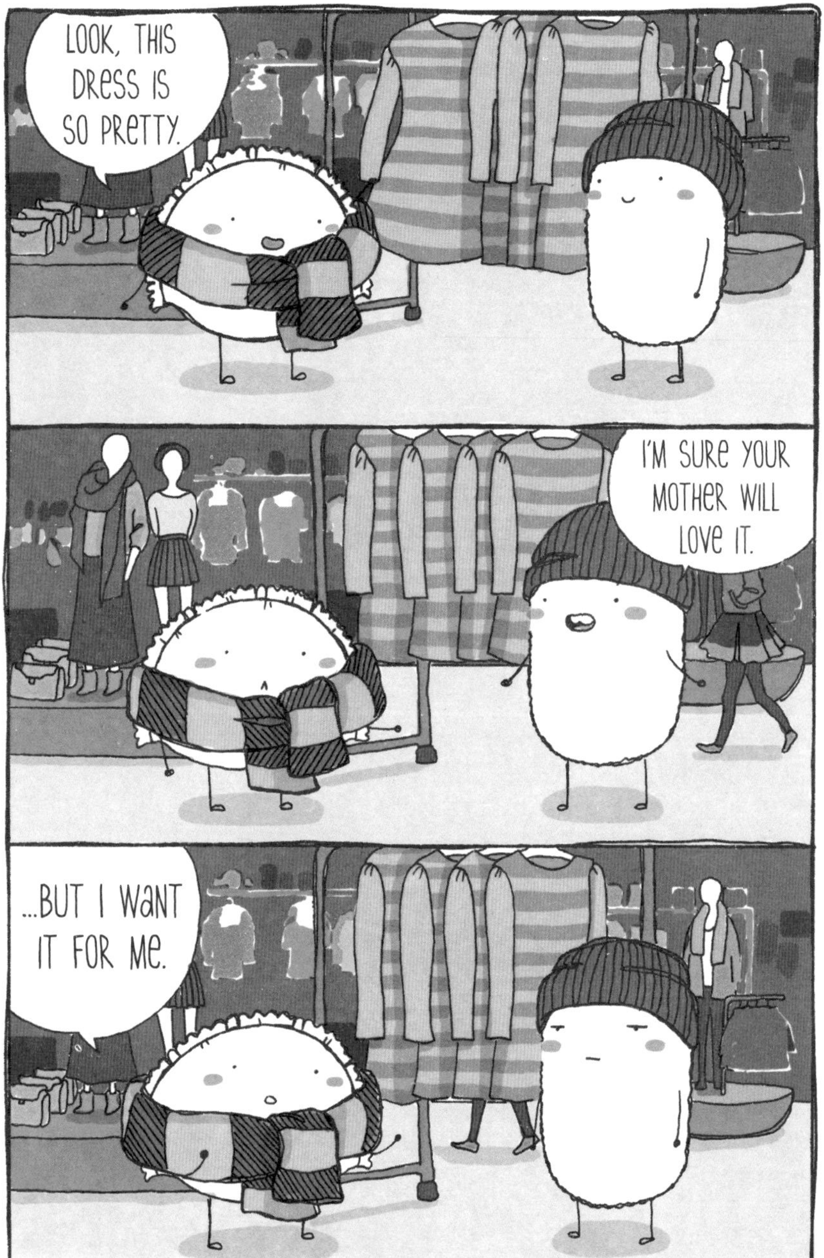
LOOK, THIS DRESS IS SO PRETTY.
I'M SURE YOUR MOTHER WILL LOVE IT.
...BUT I WANT IT FOR ME.

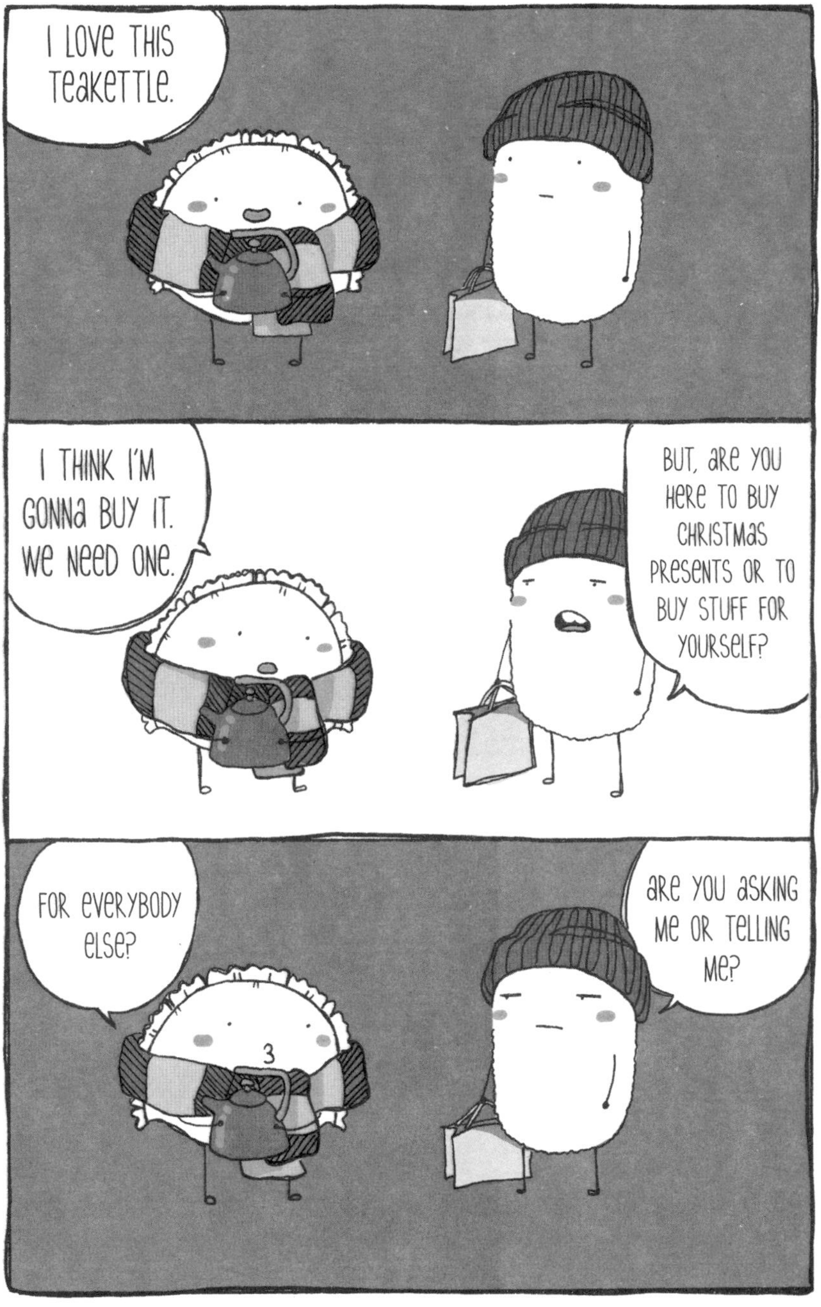
I LOVE THIS TEAKETTLE.
I THINK I'M GONNA BUY IT. WE NEED ONE.
BUT, ARE YOU HERE TO BUY CHRISTMAS PRESENTS OR TO BUY STUFF FOR YOURSELF?
FOR EVERYBODY ELSE?
ARE YOU ASKING ME OR TELLING ME?

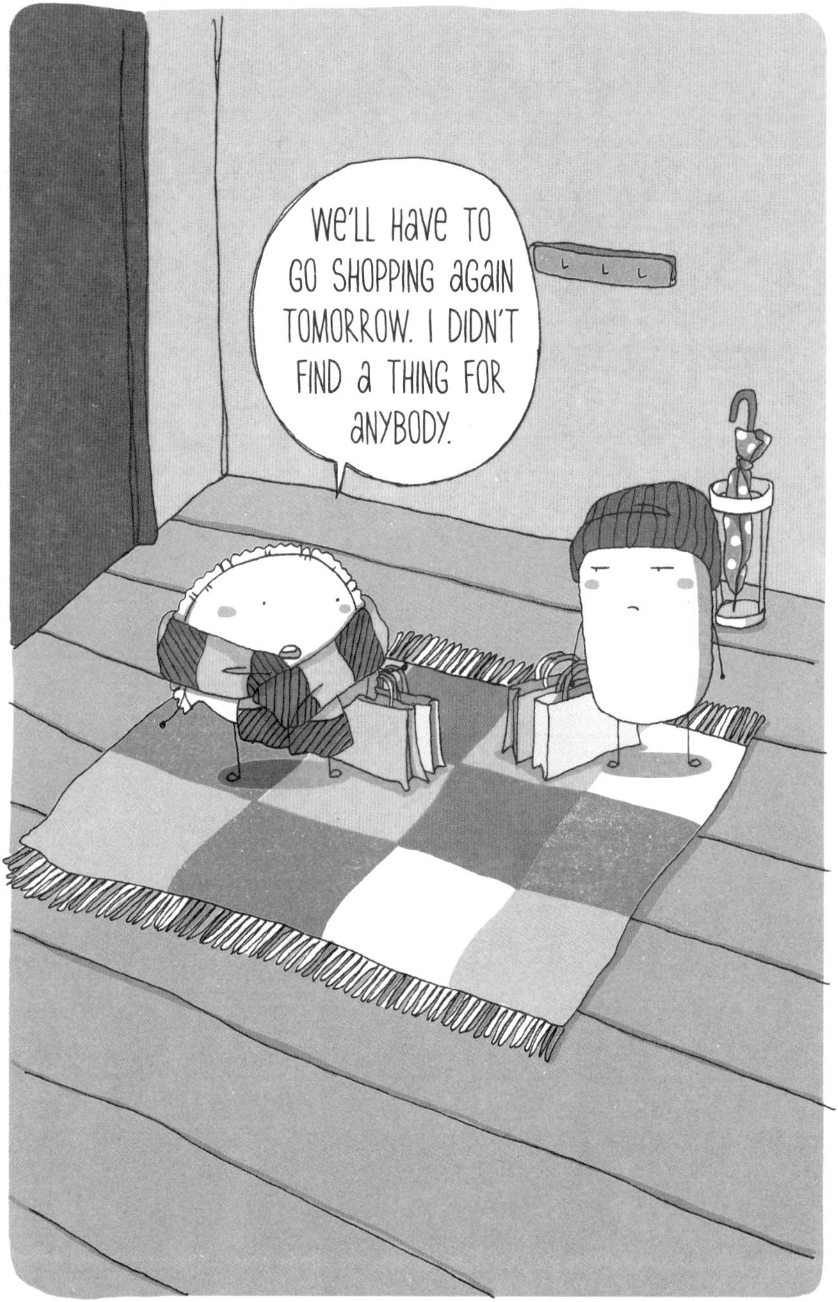
WE'LL HAVE TO GO SHOPPING AGAIN TOMORROW. I DIDN'T FIND A THING FOR ANYBODY.

- SCARY BEDTIME STORIES -

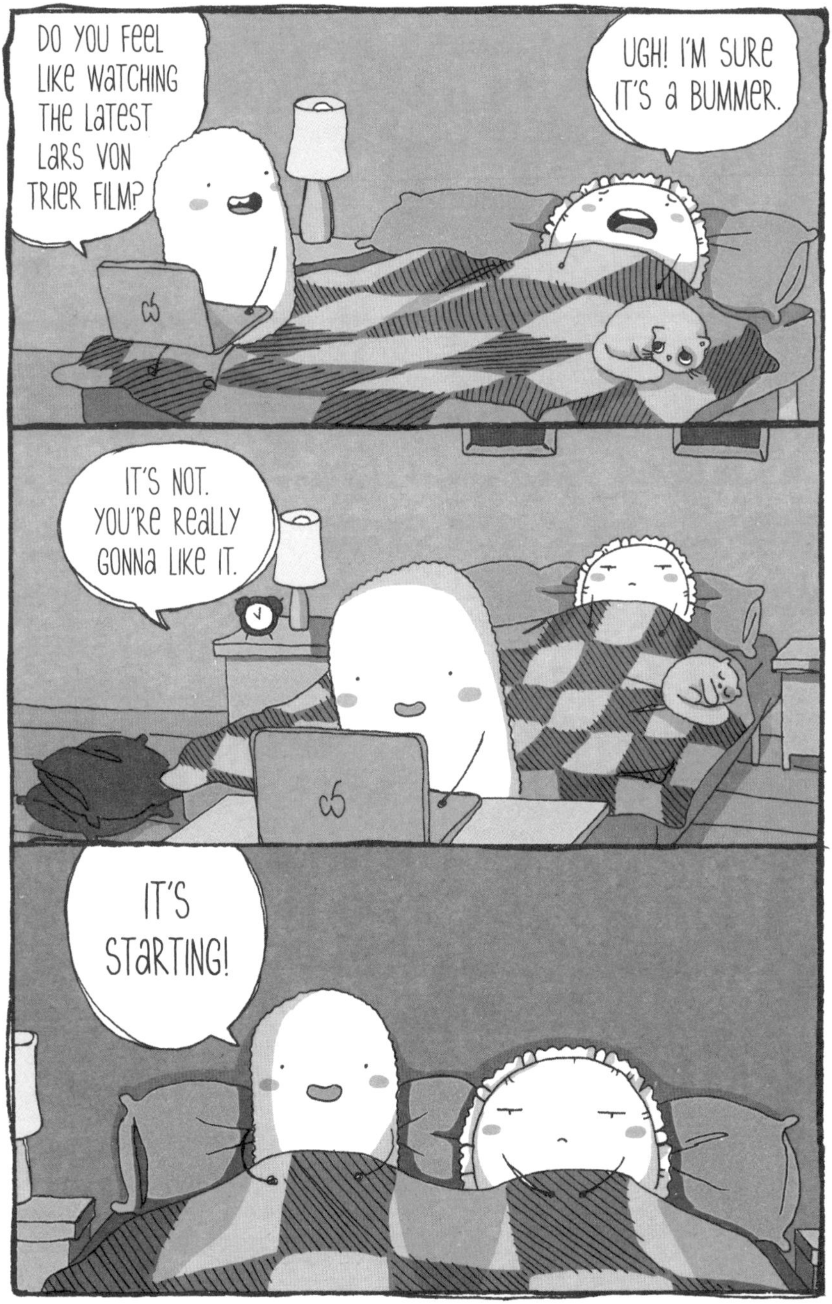
DO YOU FEEL LIKE WATCHING THE LATEST LARS VON TRIER FILM?
UGH! I'M SURE IT'S A BUMMER.
IT'S NOT. YOU'RE REALLY GONNA LIKE IT.
IT'S STARTING!

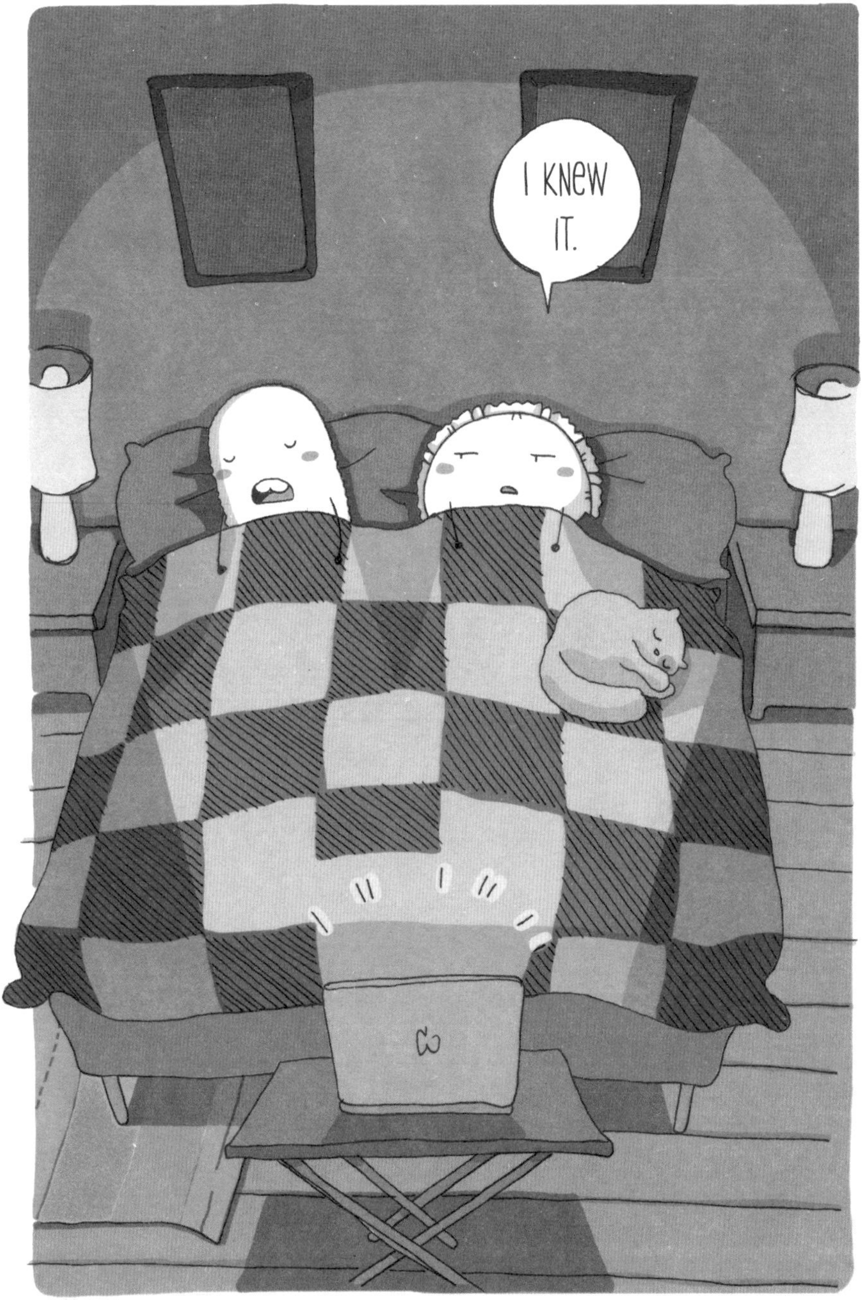
I KNEW IT.

- New Year's Eve -

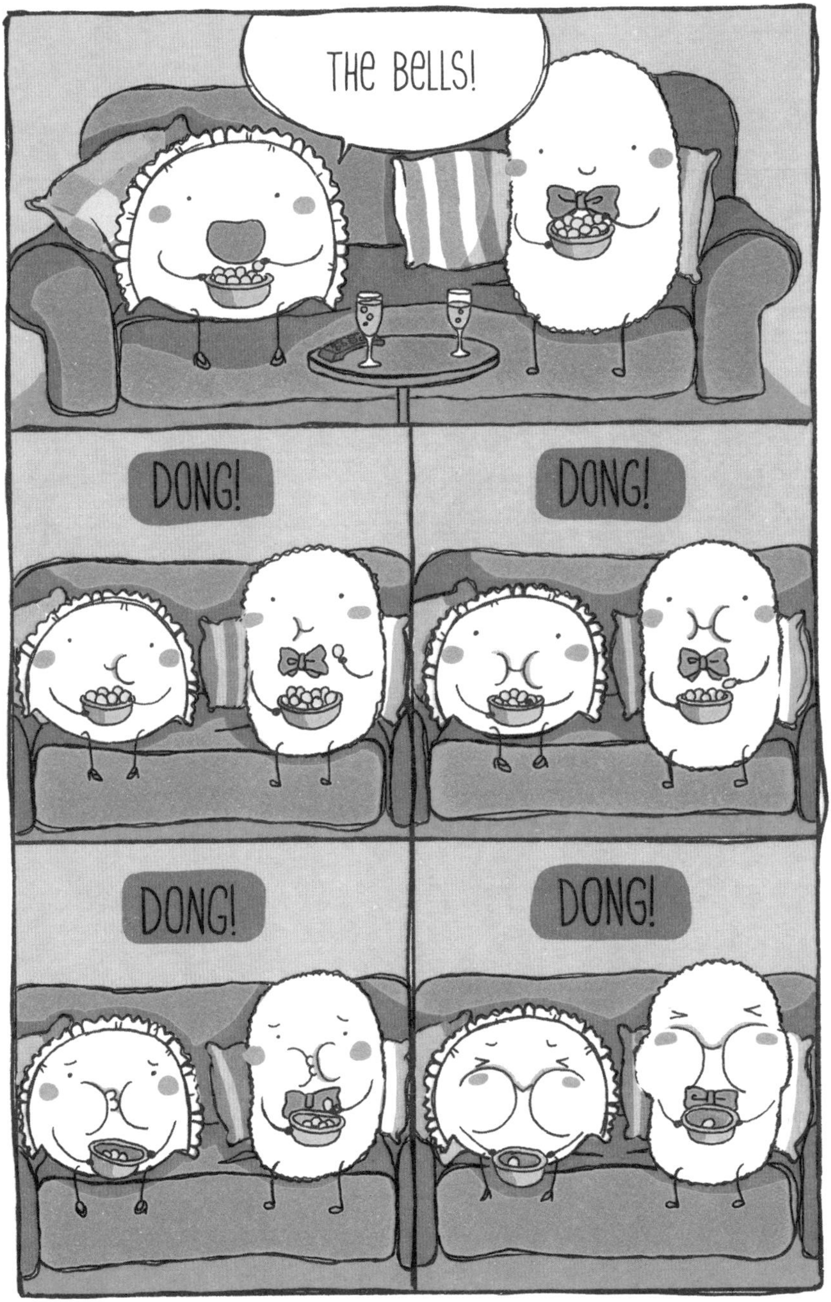

THE BELLS!
DONG!
DONG!
DONG!
DONG!

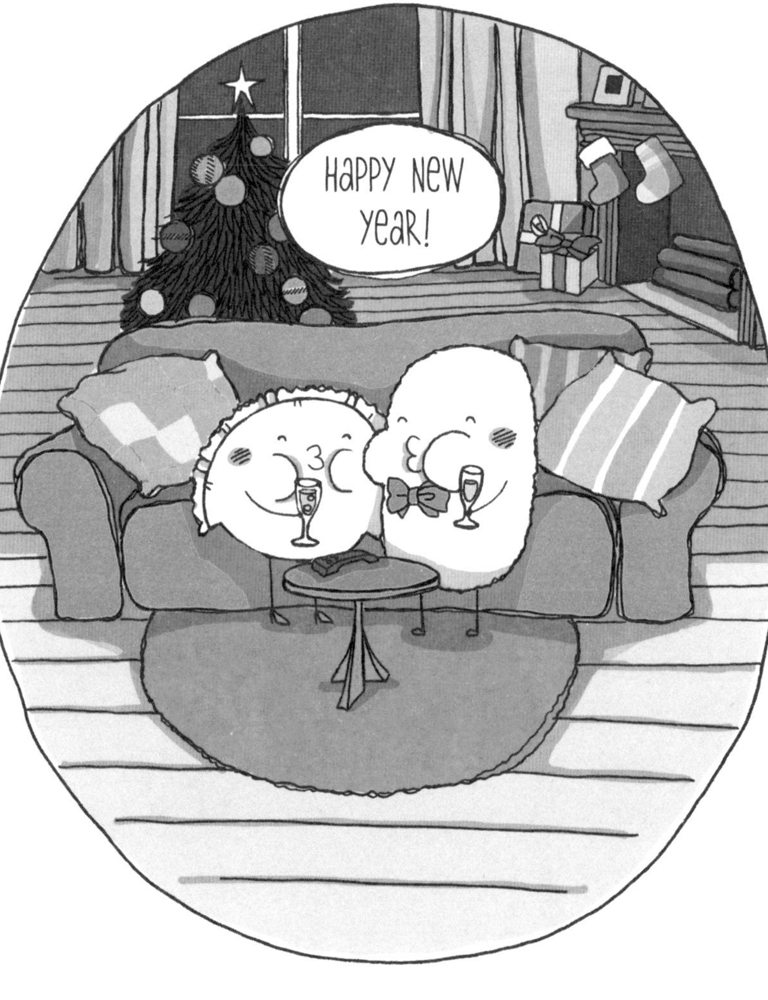
HAPPY NEW YEAR!

- SCARY BEDTIME STORIES -

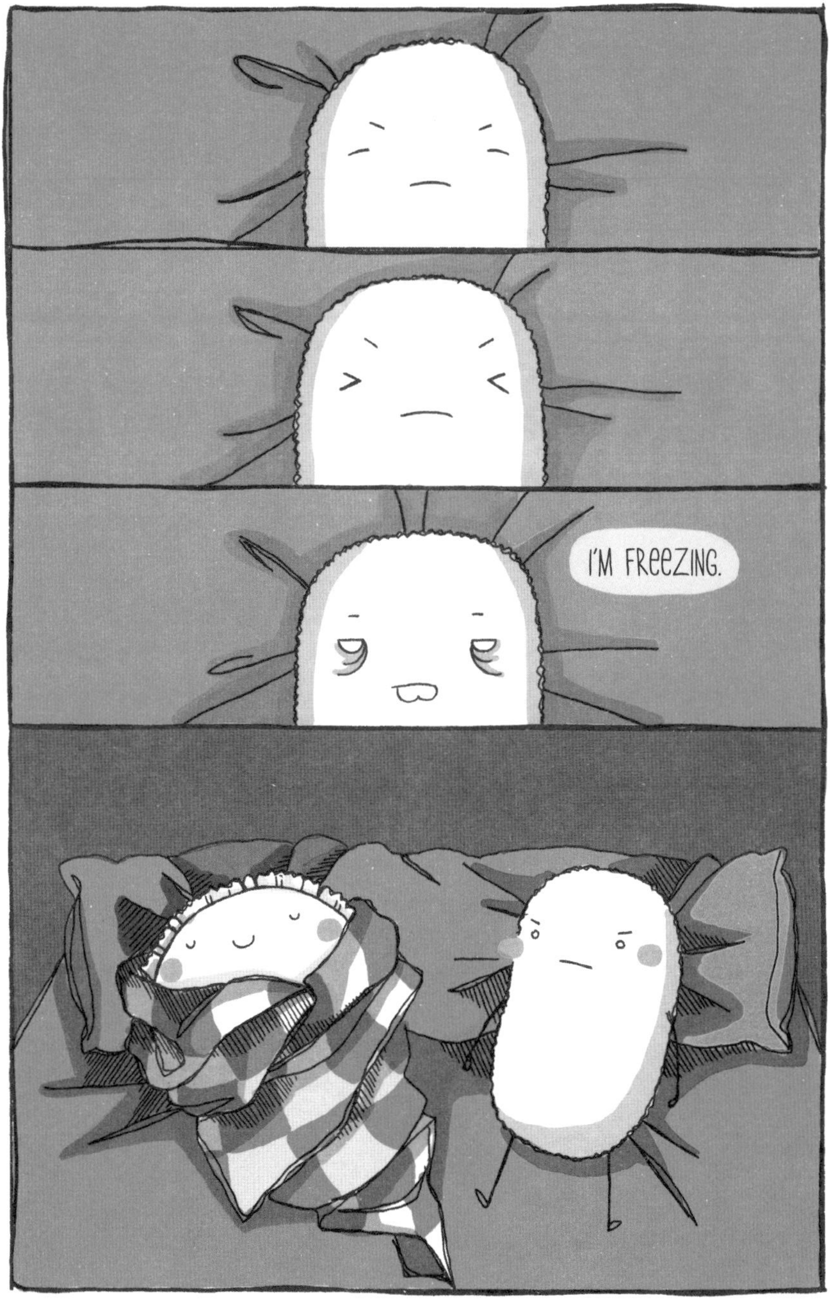
I'M FREEZING.

- ETERNAL TUPPERWARE -

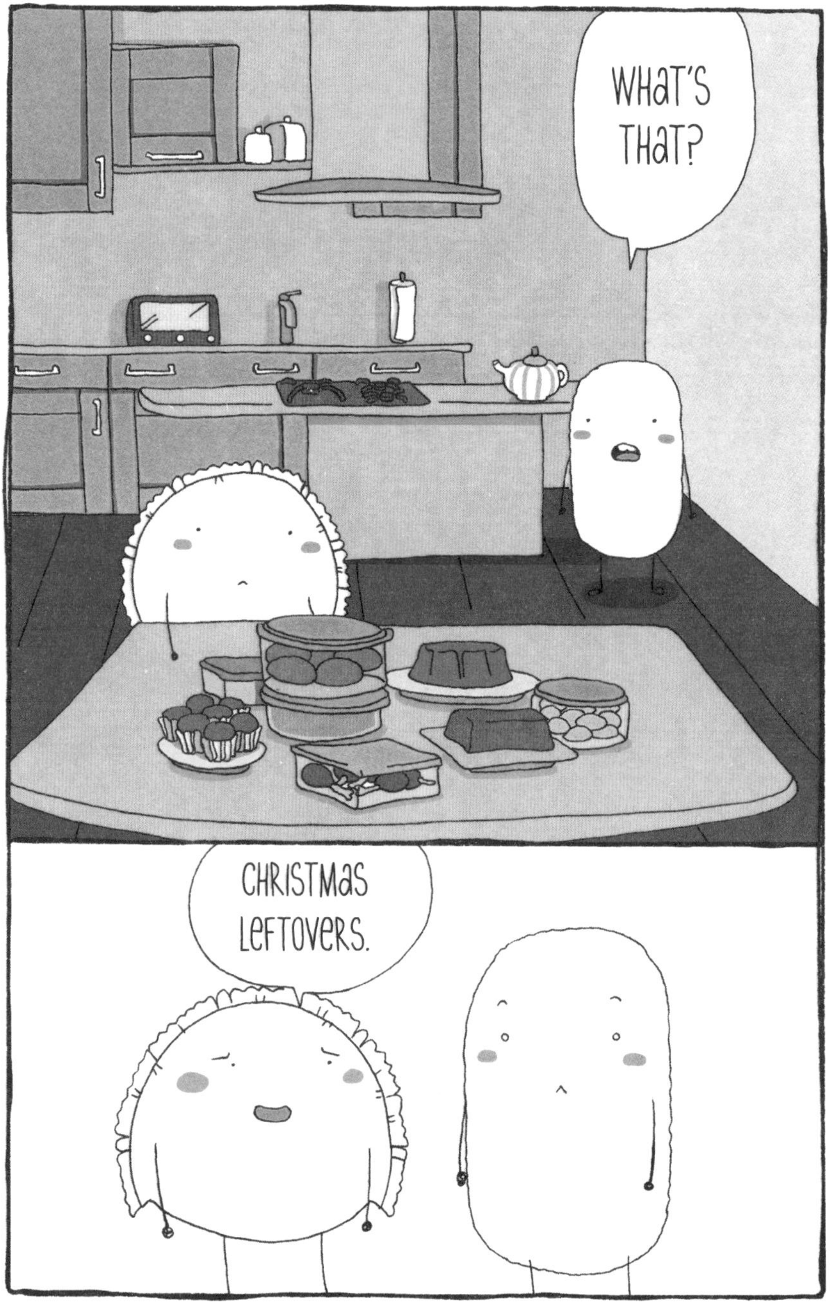

WHAT'S THAT?
CHRISTMAS LEFTOVERS.

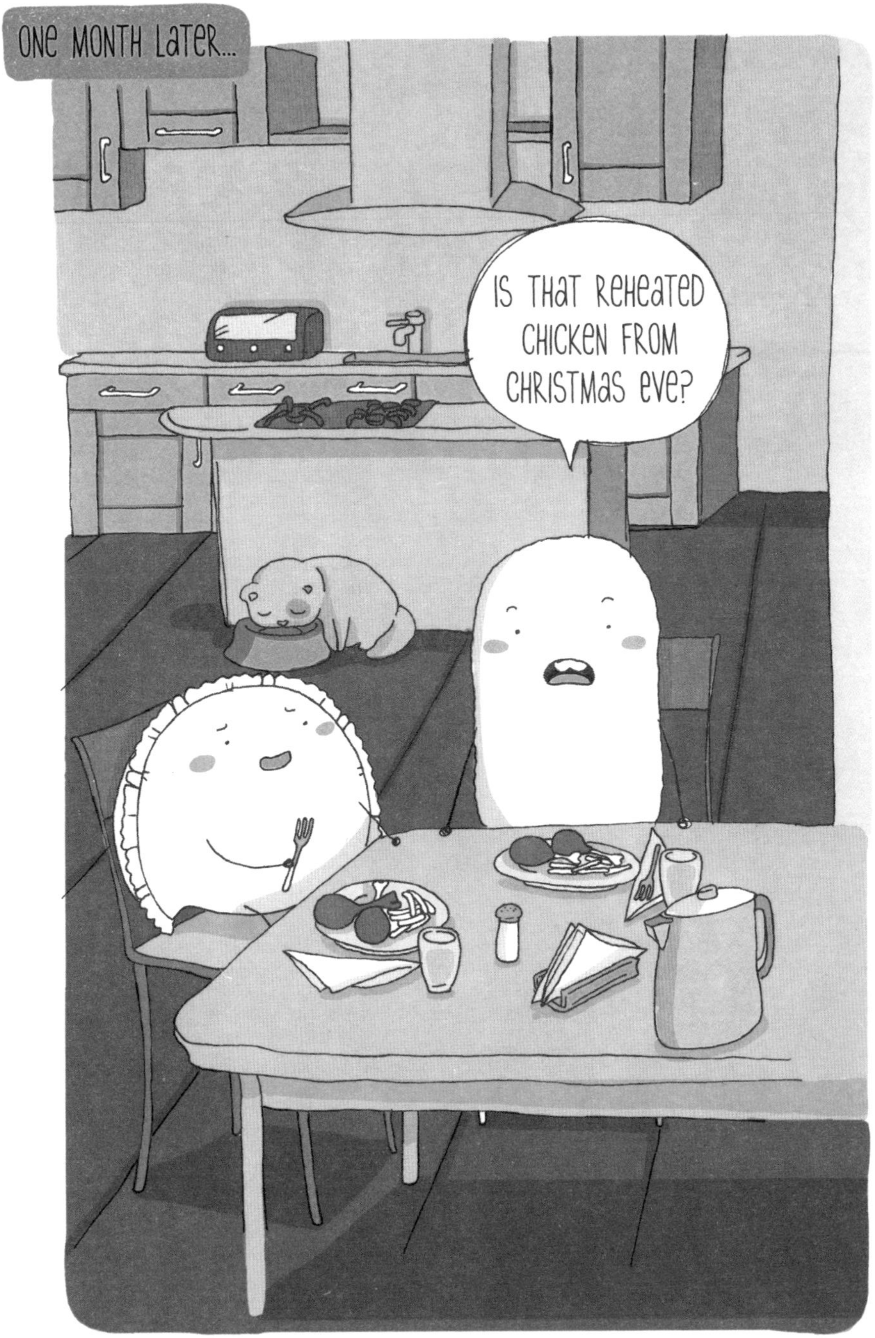
ONE MONTH LATER...
IS THAT REHEATED CHICKEN FROM CHRISTMAS EVE?

- LET'S PARTY! -

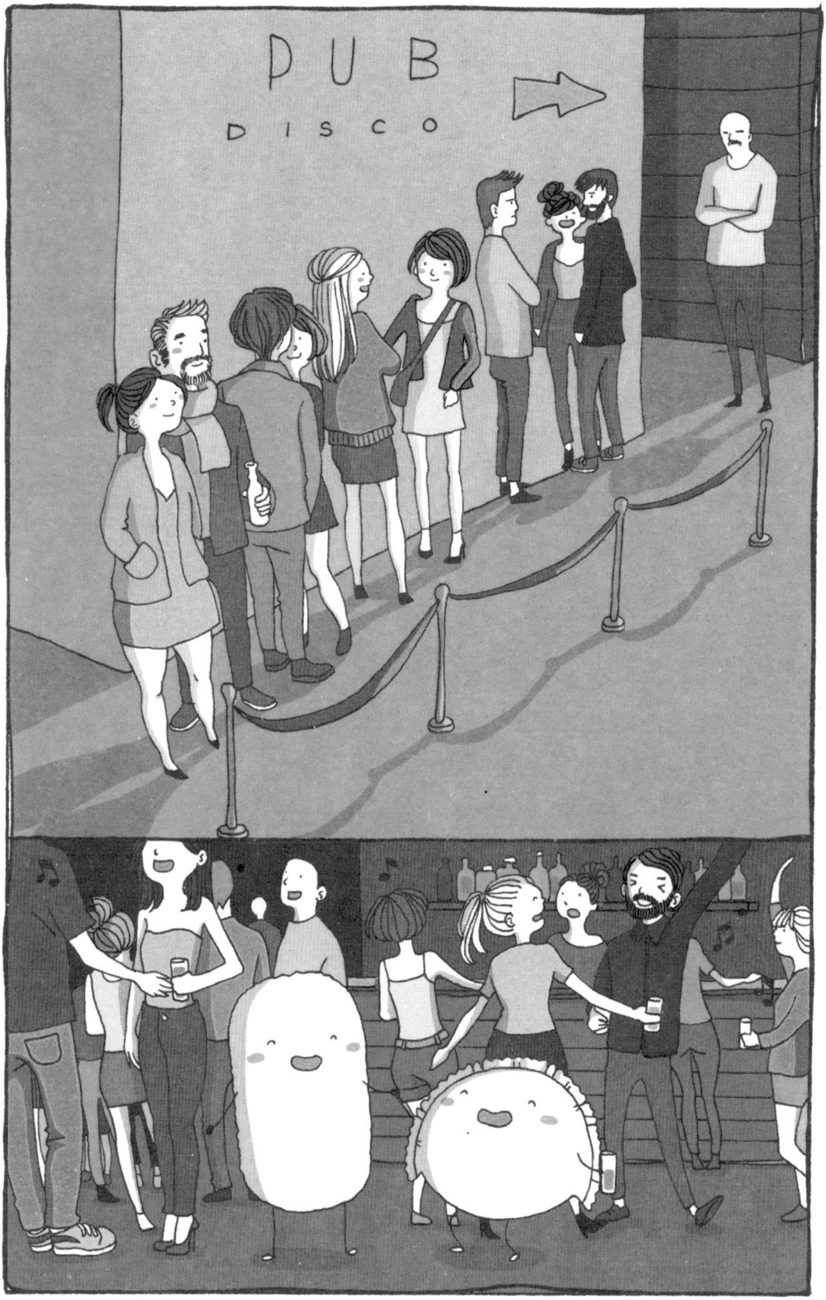
PUB
DISCO

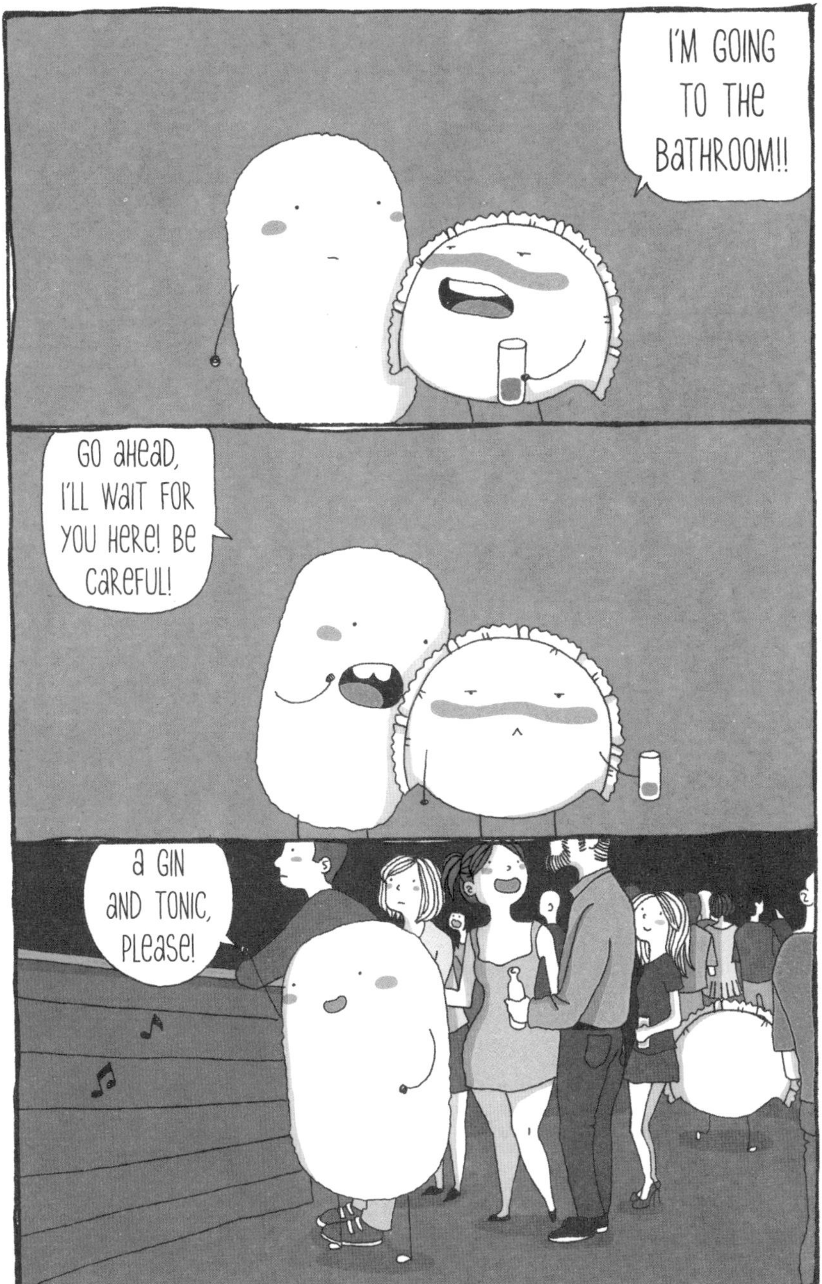
I'M GOING TO THE BATHROOM!!
GO AHEAD, I'LL WAIT FOR YOU HERE! BE CAREFUL!
A GIN AND TONIC, PLEASE!

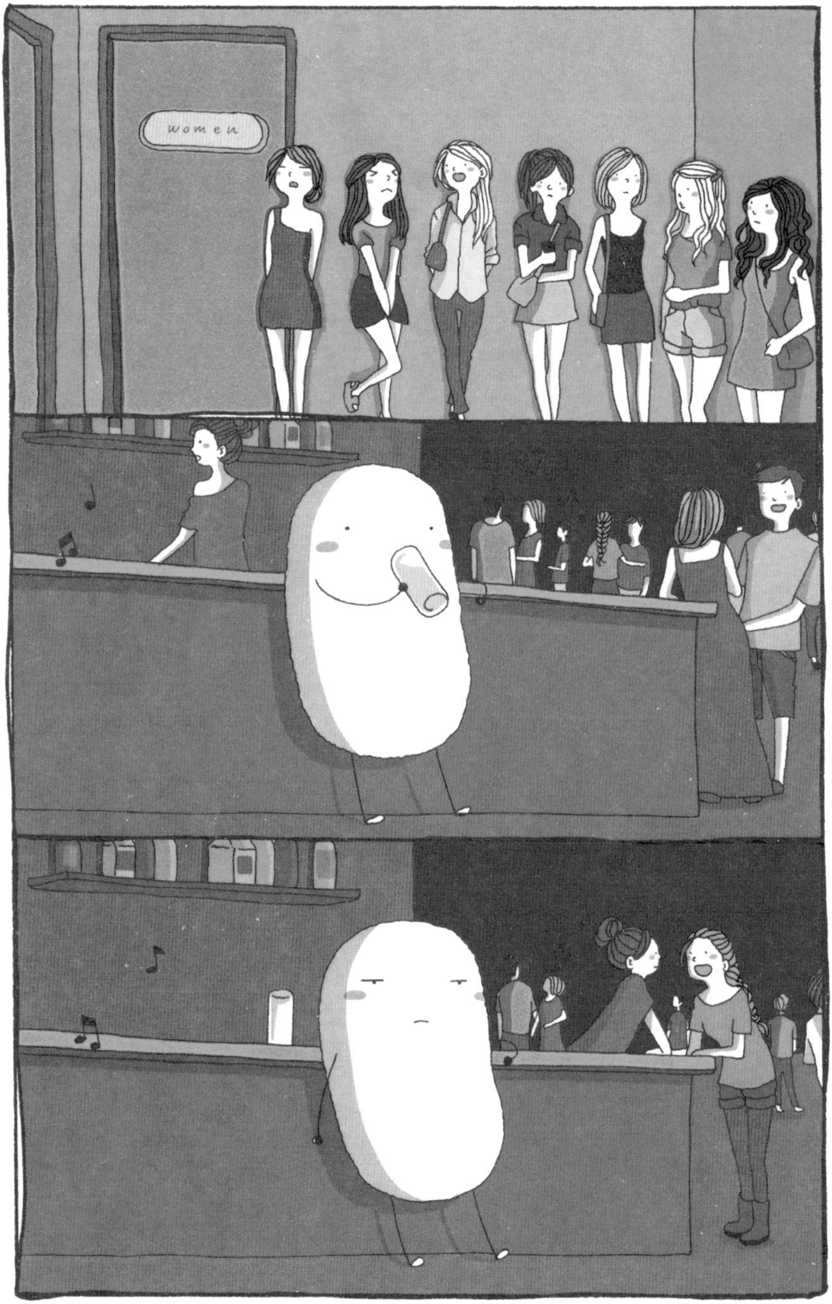
women

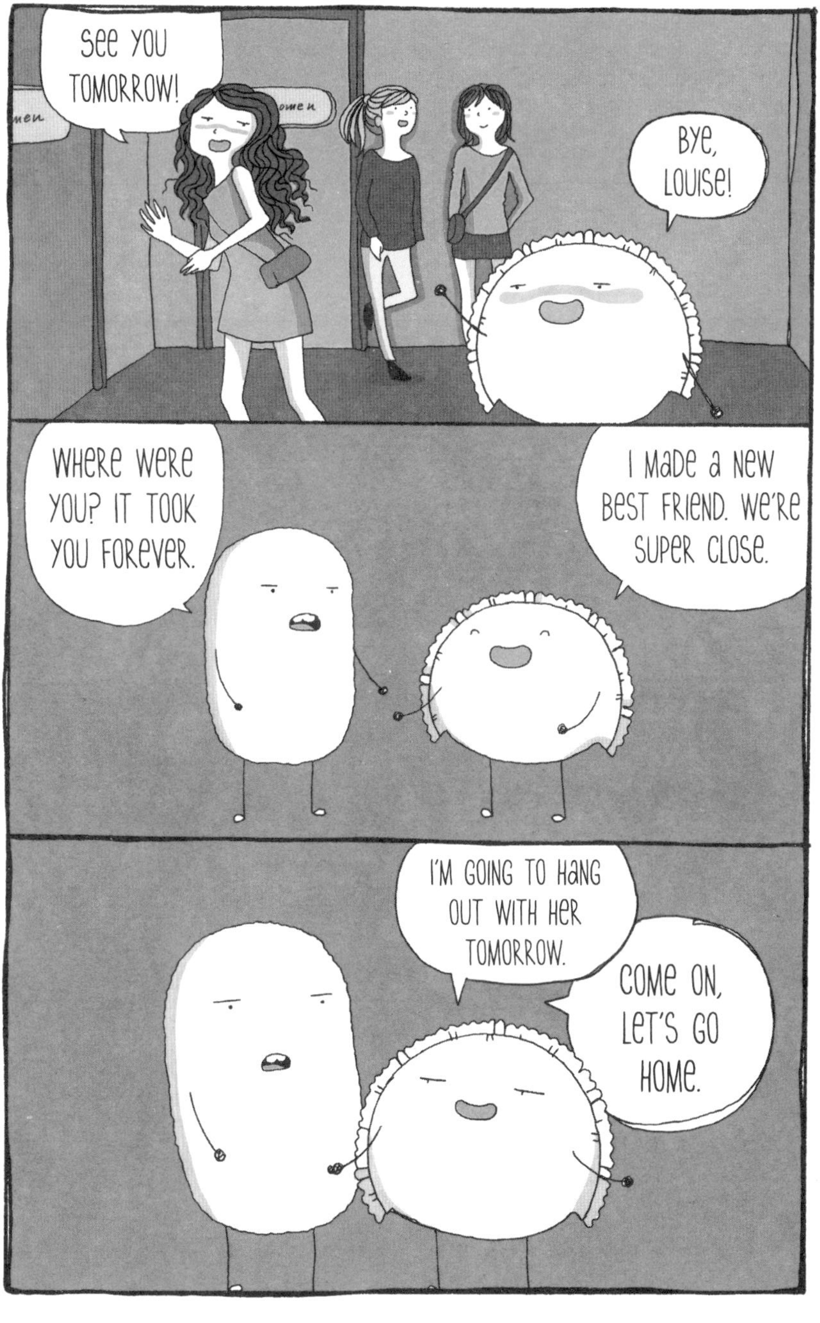
SEE YOU TOMORROW!
BYE, LOUISE!
WHERE WERE YOU? IT TOOK YOU FOREVER.
I MADE A NEW BEST FRIEND. WE'RE SUPER CLOSE.
I'M GOING TO HANG OUT WITH HER TOMORROW.
COME ON, LET'S GO HOME.

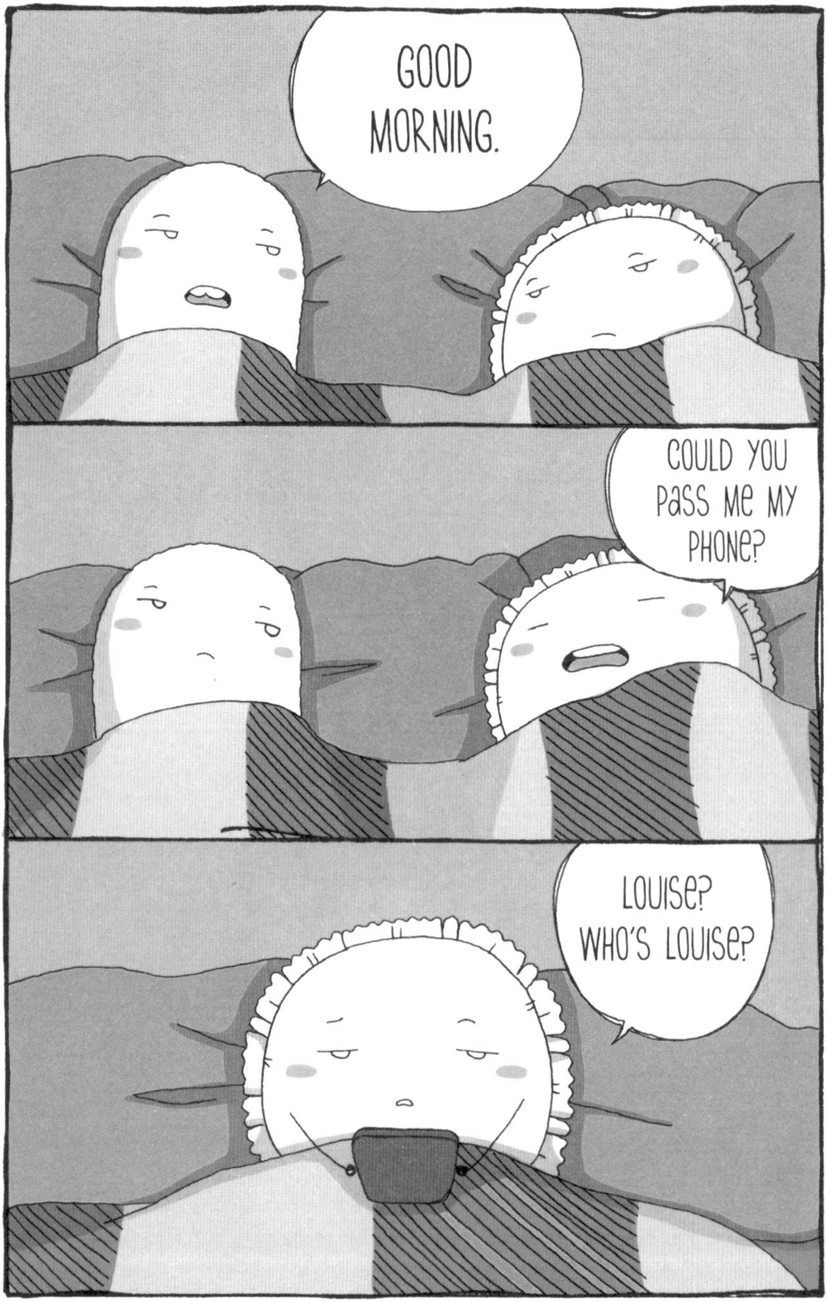
GOOD MORNING.
COULD YOU PASS ME MY PHONE?
LOUISE? WHO'S LOUISE?

- Memory Lane -

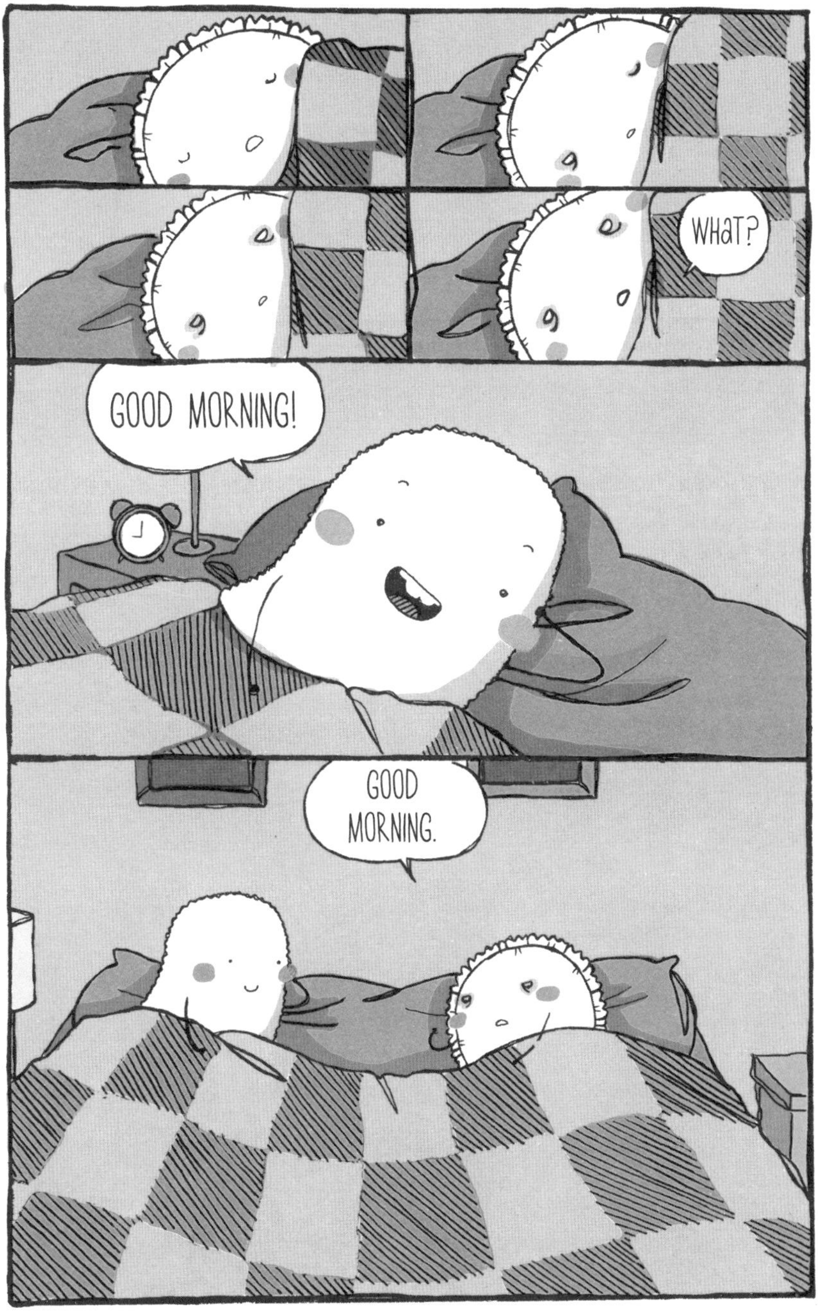
WHAT?
GOOD MORNING!
GOOD MORNING.

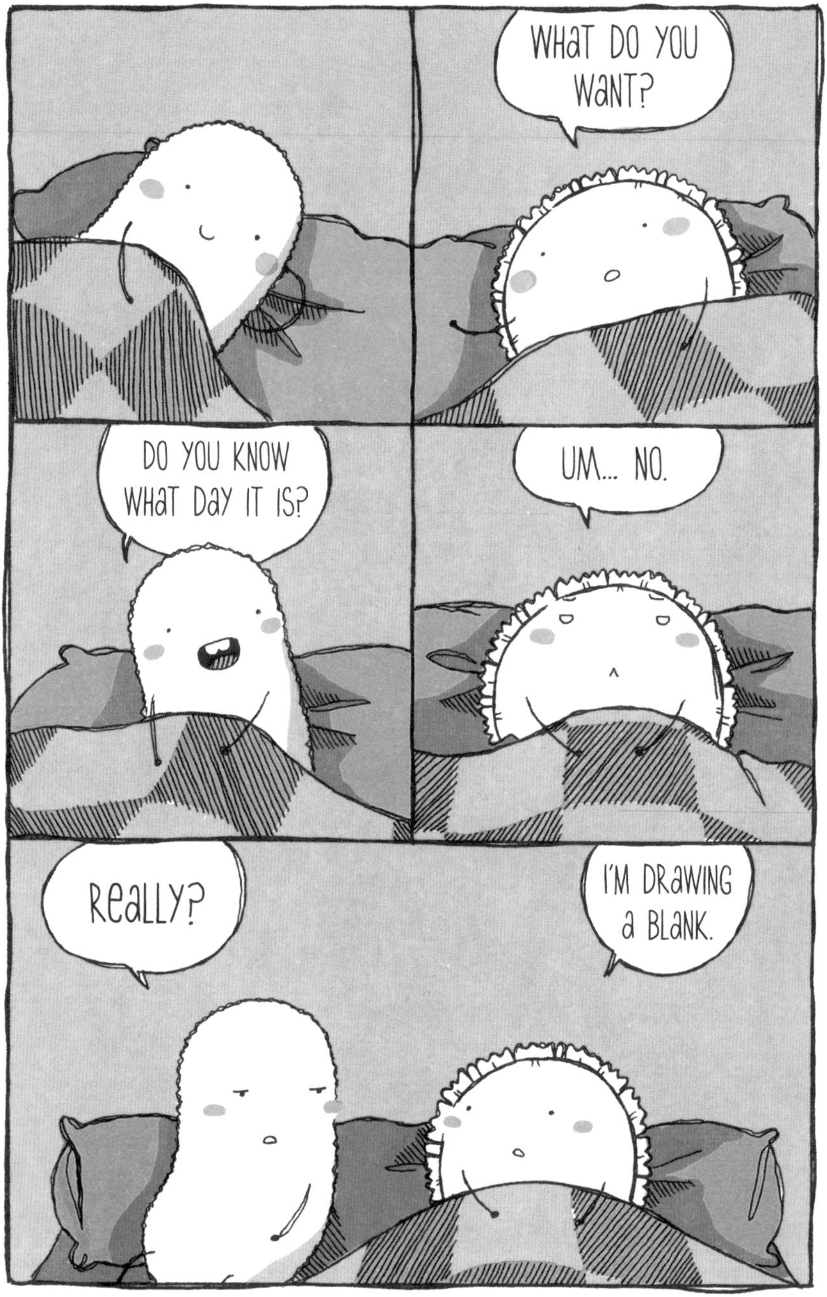
WHAT DO YOU WANT?
DO YOU KNOW WHAT DAY IT IS?
UM... NO.
REALLY?
I'M DRAWING A BLANK.

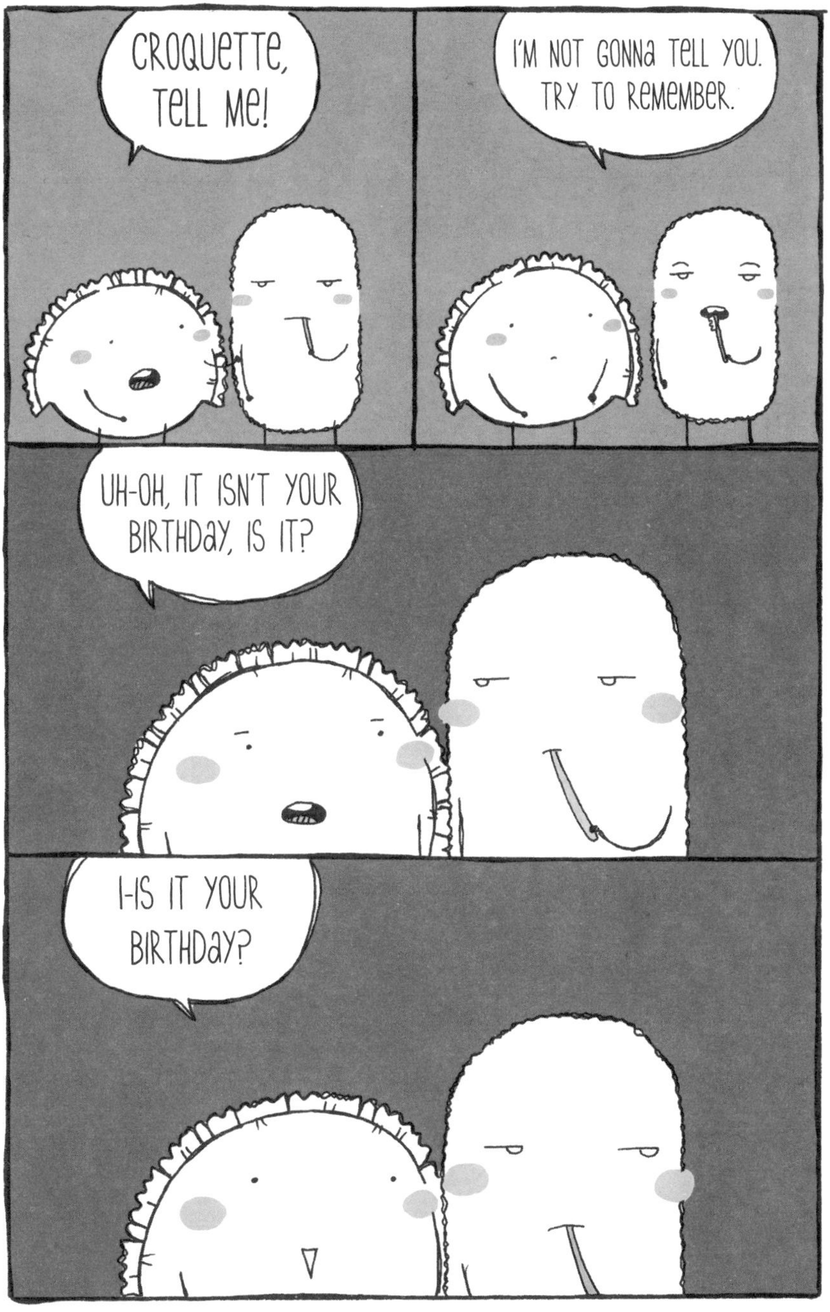
CROQUETTE, TELL ME!
I'M NOT GONNA TELL YOU. TRY TO REMEMBER.
UH-OH, IT ISN'T YOUR BIRTHDAY, IS IT?
I-IS IT YOUR BIRTHDAY?

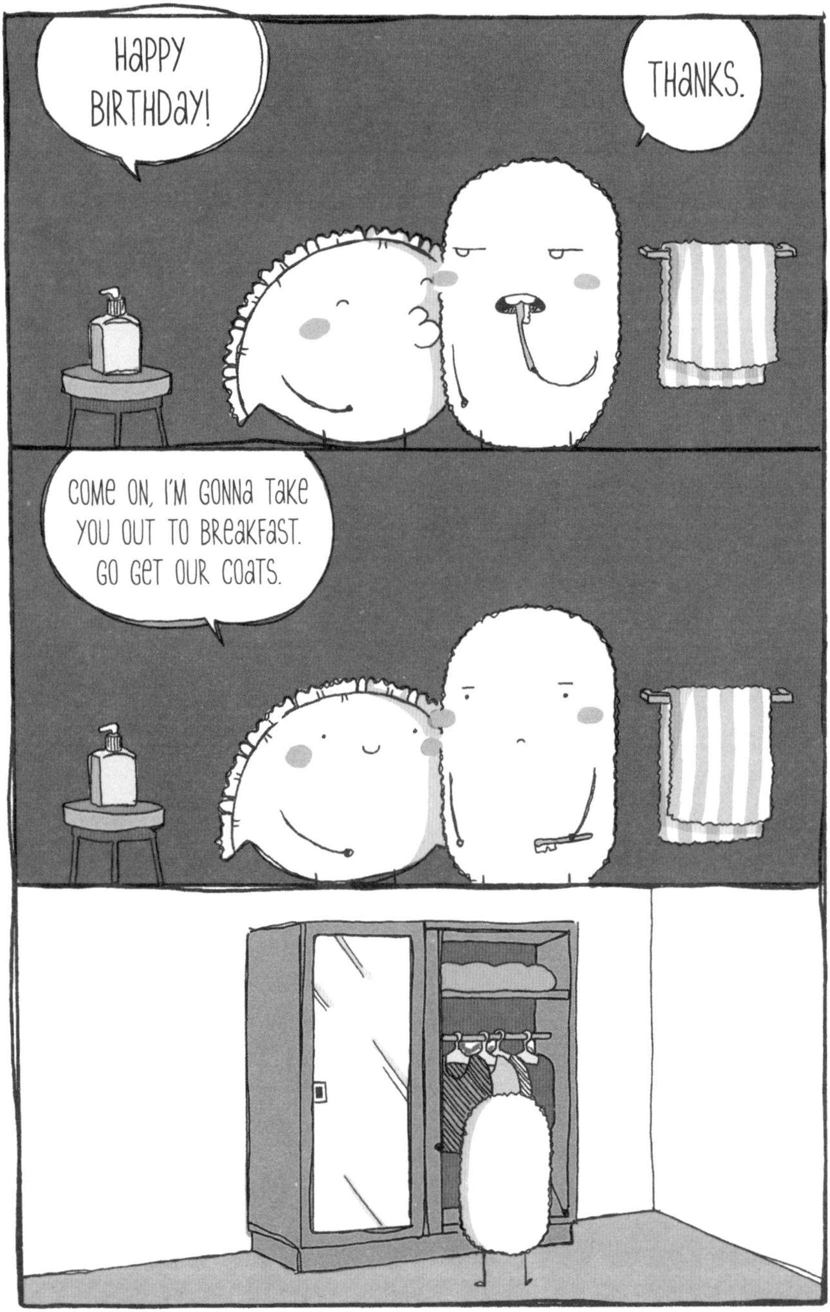
HAPPY BIRTHDAY!
THANKS.
COME ON, I'M GONNA TAKE YOU OUT TO BREAKFAST. GO GET OUR COATS.

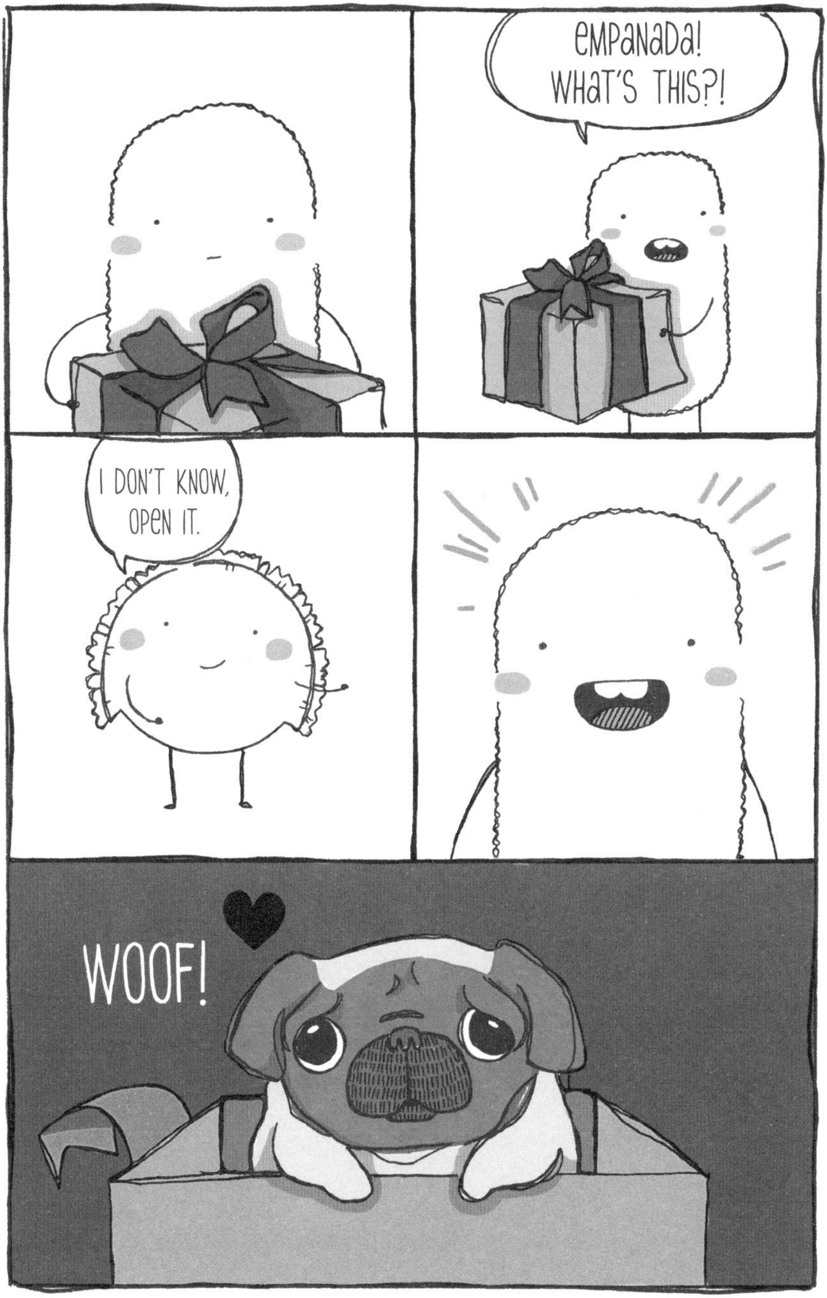
EMPANADA!
WHAT'S THIS?!
I DON'T KNOW,
OPEN IT.
WOOF!

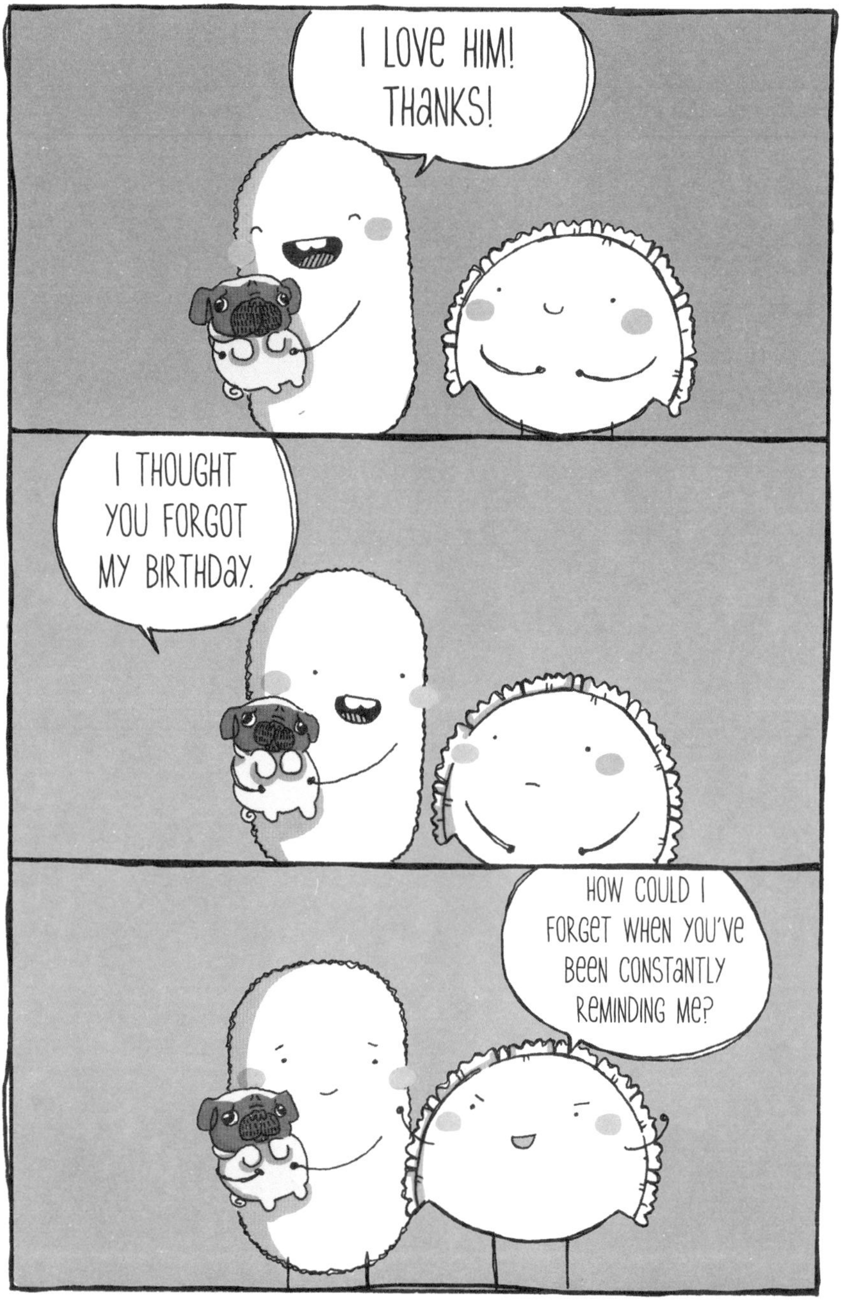
I LOVE HIM! THANKS!
I THOUGHT YOU FORGOT MY BIRTHDAY.
HOW COULD I FORGET WHEN YOU'VE BEEN CONSTANTLY REMINDING ME?

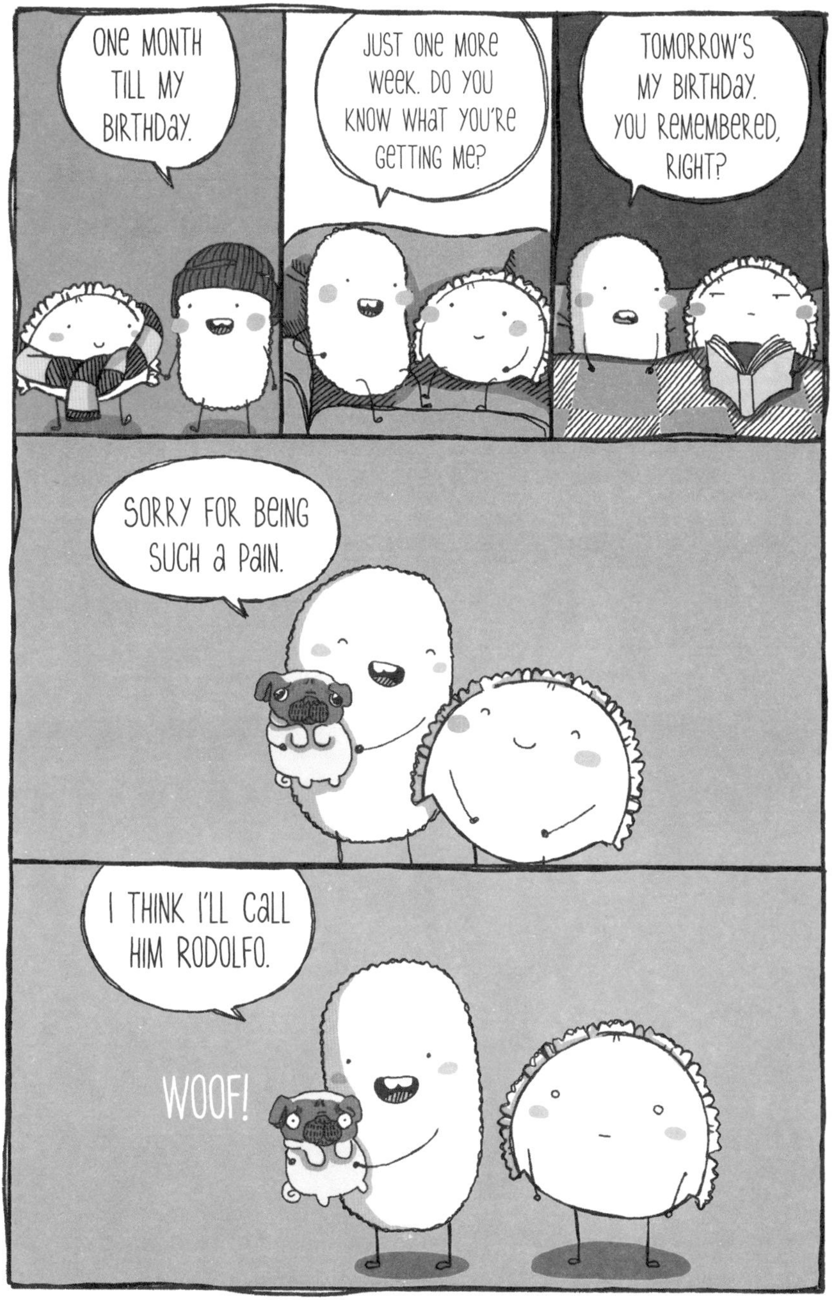
ONE MONTH TILL MY BIRTHDAY.
JUST ONE MORE WEEK. DO YOU KNOW WHAT YOU'RE GETTING ME?
TOMORROW'S MY BIRTHDAY. YOU REMEMBERED, RIGHT?
SORRY FOR BEING SUCH A PAIN.
I THINK I'LL CALL HIM RODOLFO.
WOOF!

- RODOLFO -

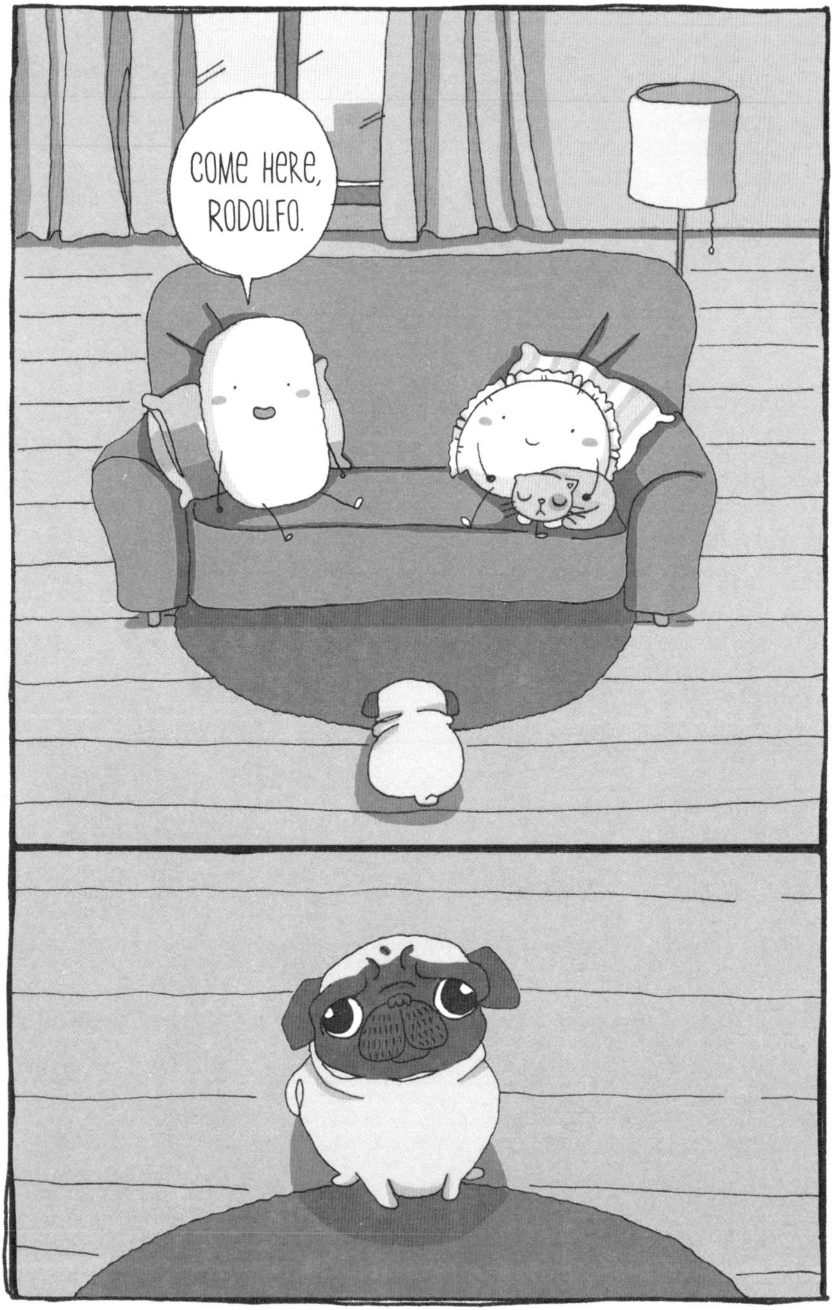
COME HERE, RODOLFO.

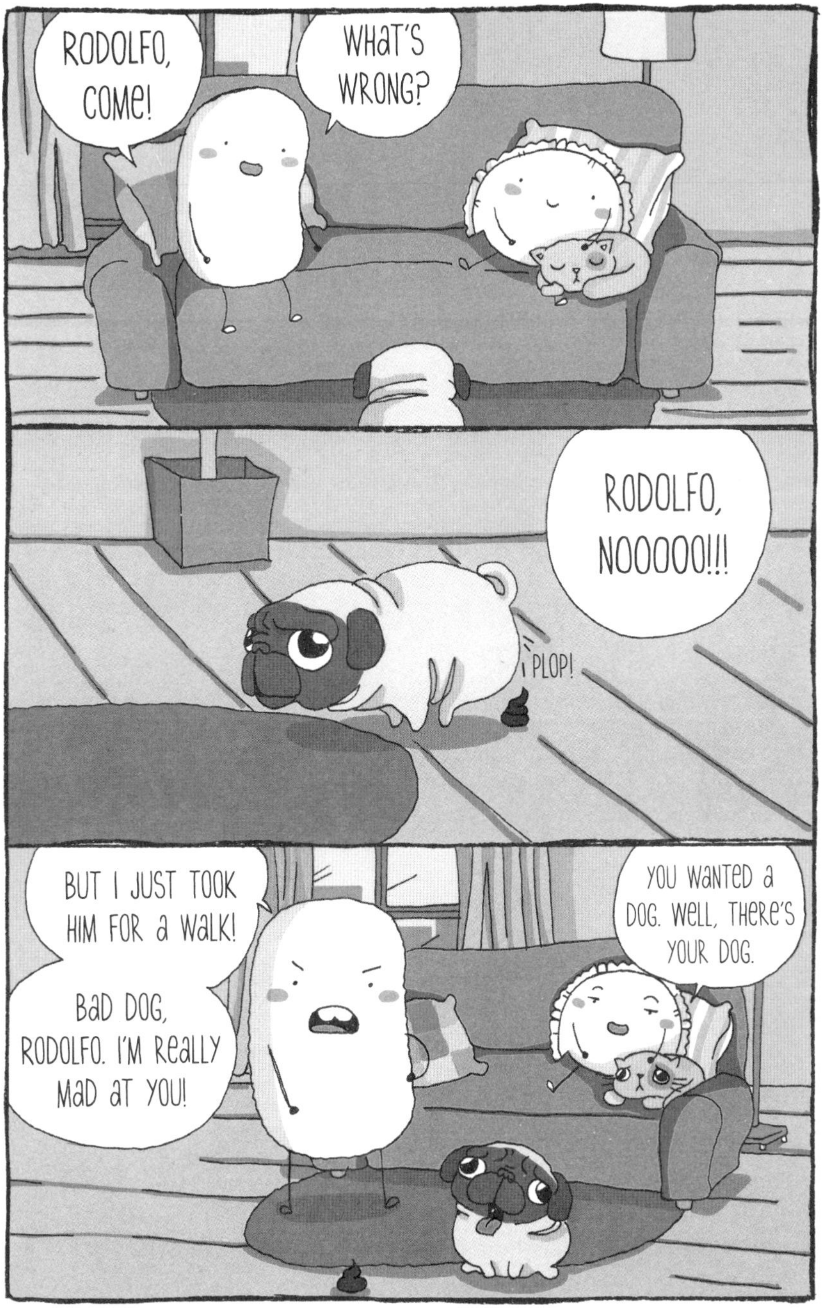
RODOLFO, COME!
WHAT'S WRONG?
RODOLFO, NOOOOO!!!
PLOP!
BUT I JUST TOOK HIM FOR A WALK!
BAD DOG, RODOLFO. I'M REALLY MAD AT YOU!
YOU WANTED A DOG. WELL, THERE'S YOUR DOG.

- BUFA -

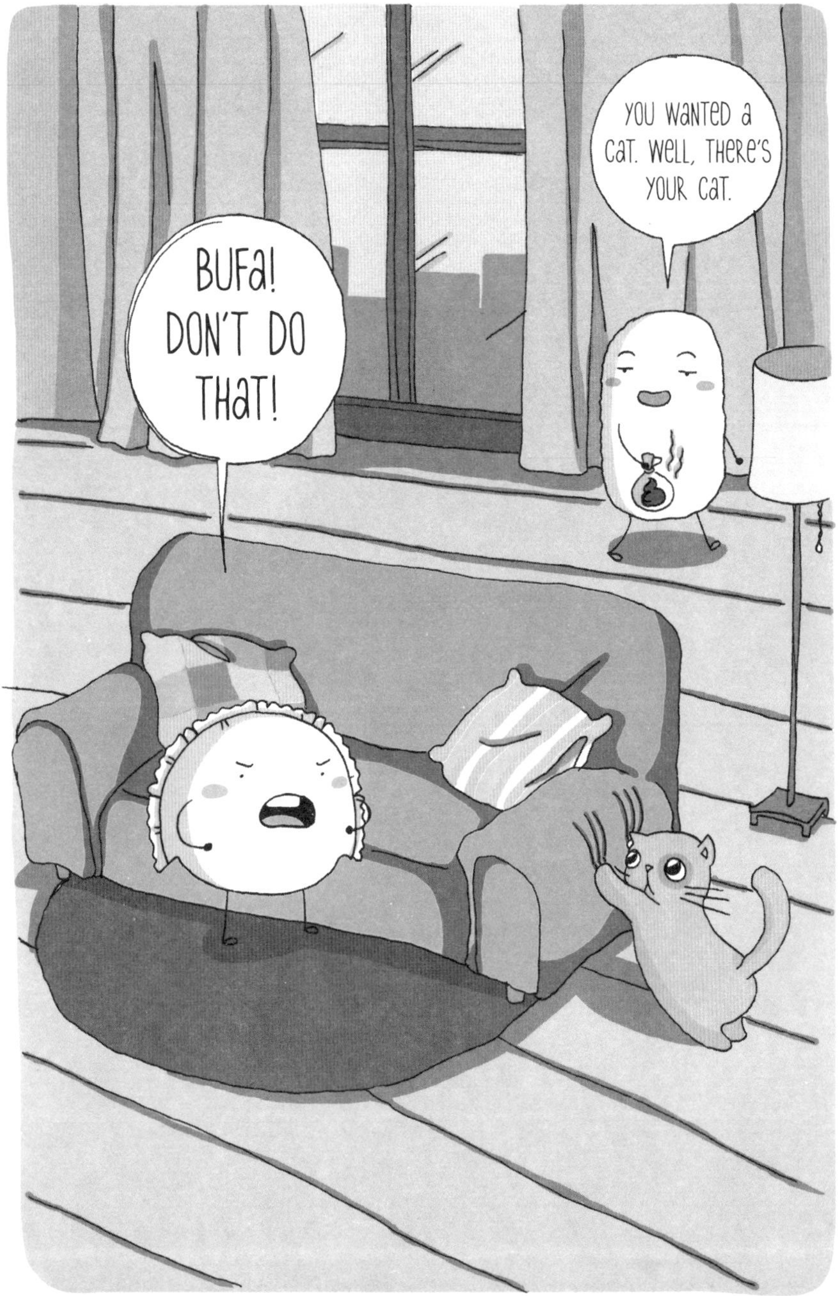
YOU WANTED A CAT. WELL, THERE'S YOUR CAT.
BUFA! DON'T DO THAT!

- TIME FOR GIRLS -

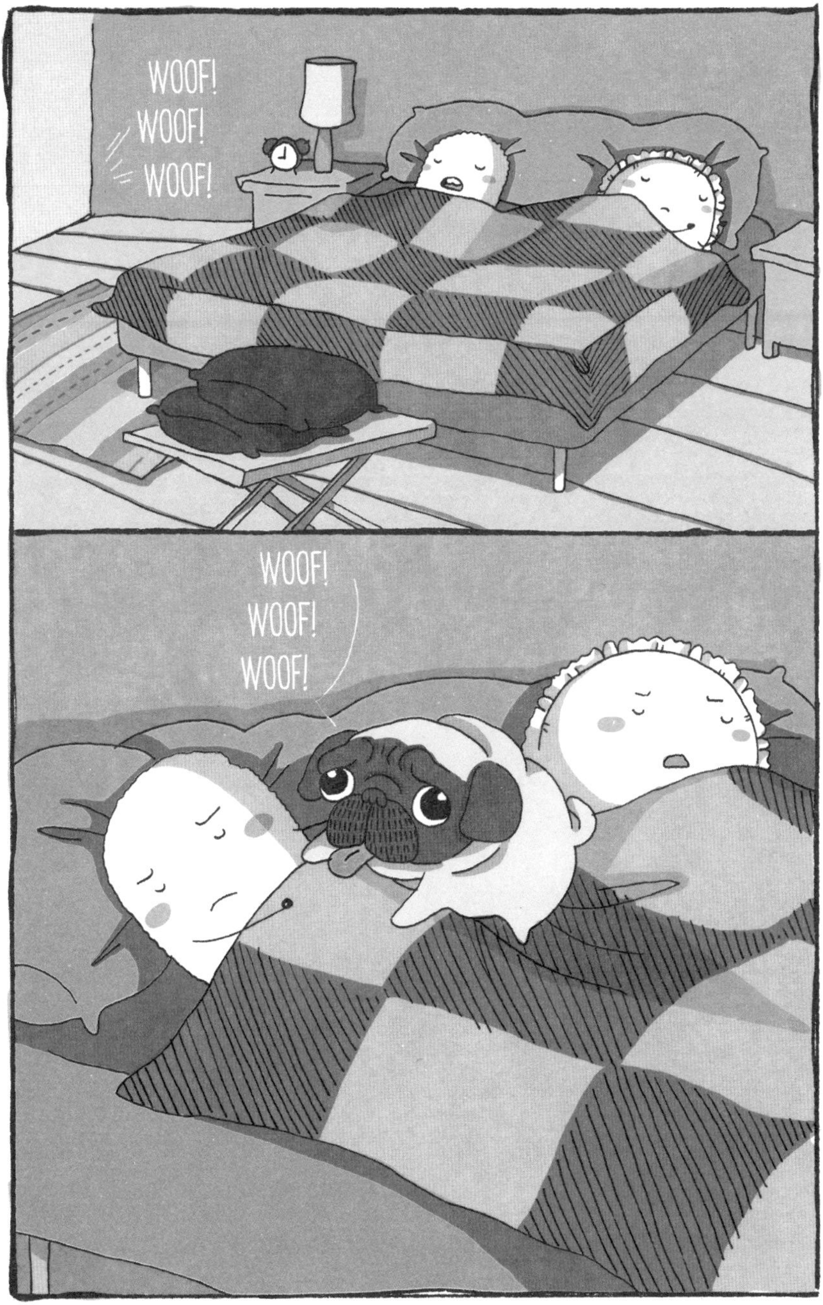
WOOF!
WOOF!
WOOF!
WOOF!
WOOF!
WOOF!

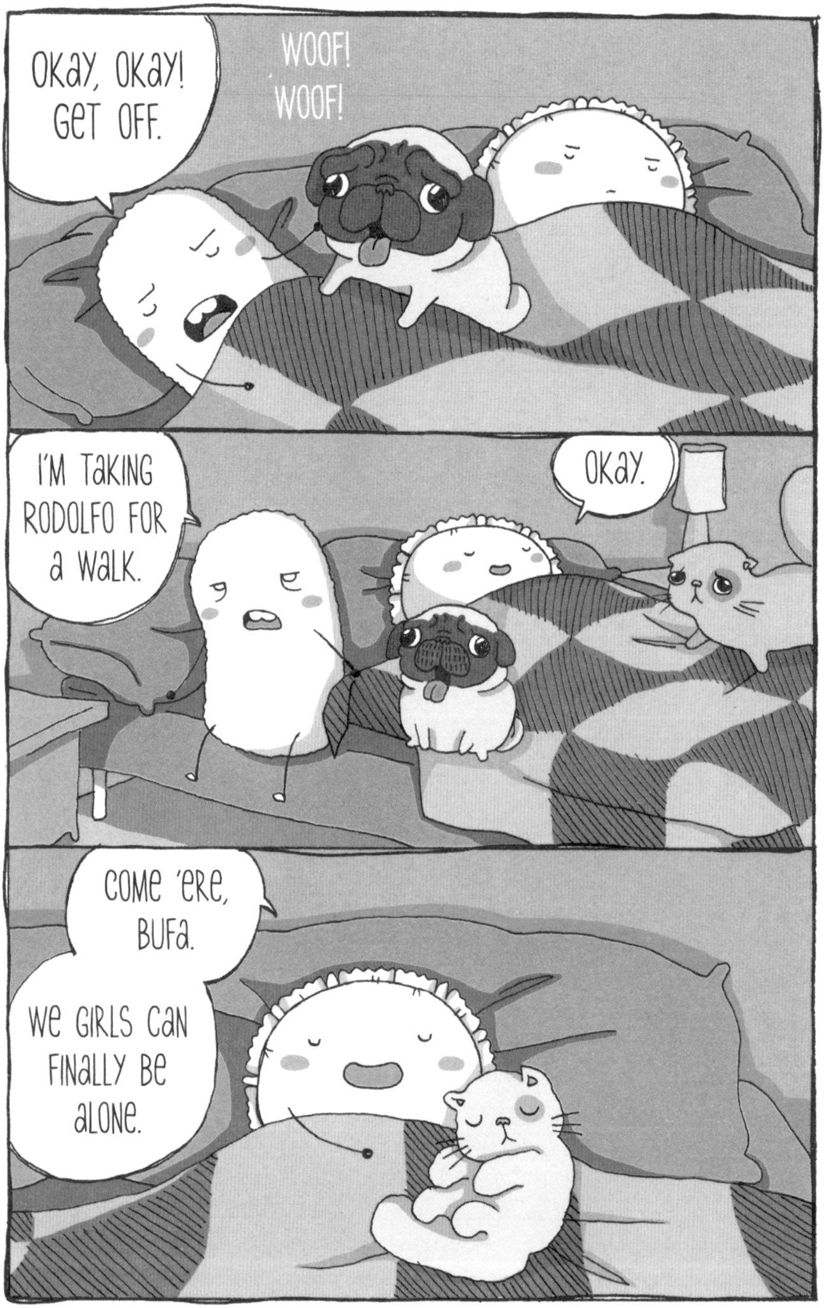
Okay, okay! Get off.
WOOF! WOOF!
I'M TAKING RODOLFO FOR a WALK.
OKay.
Come 'ere, Bufa.
We girls can finally be alone.

- DISASTER AREA -

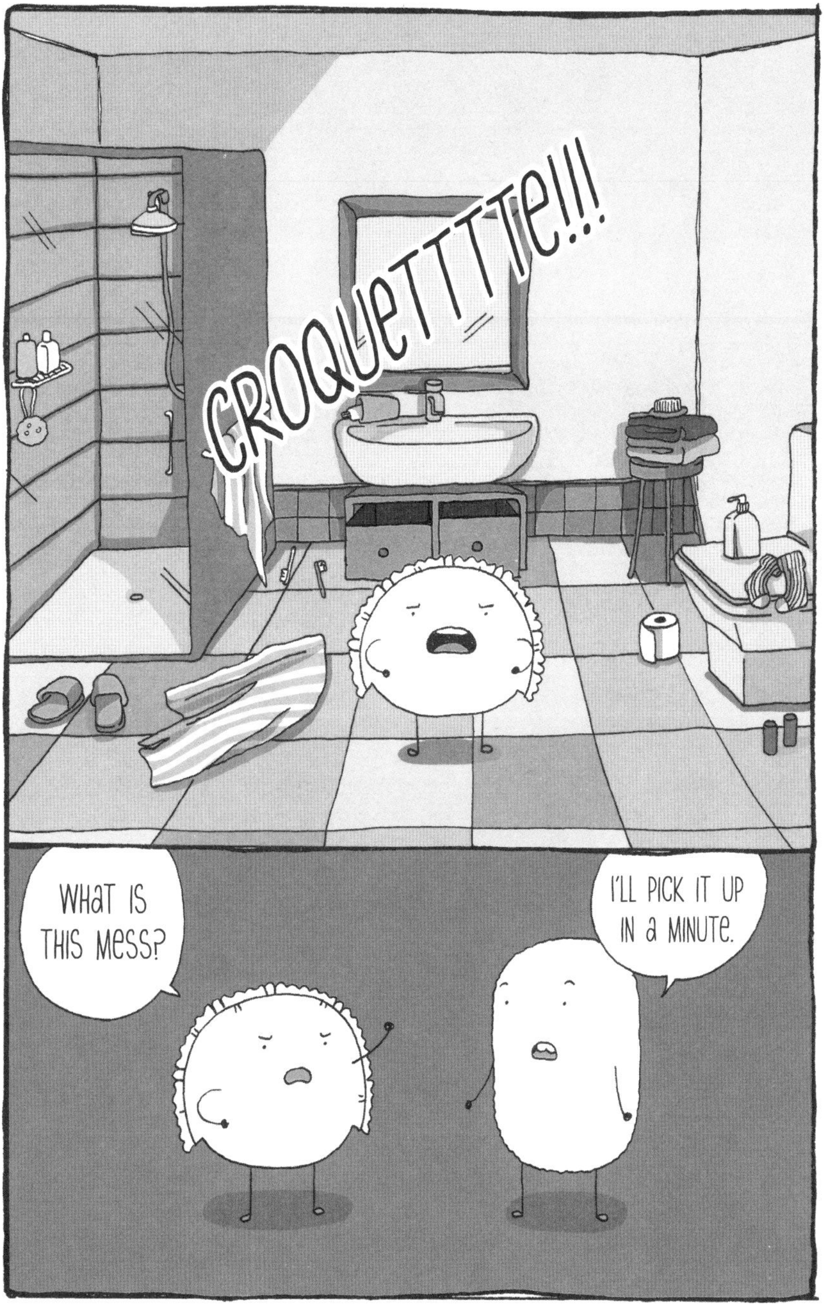
CROQUETTTTE!!!
WHAT IS THIS MESS?
I'LL PICK IT UP IN A MINUTE.

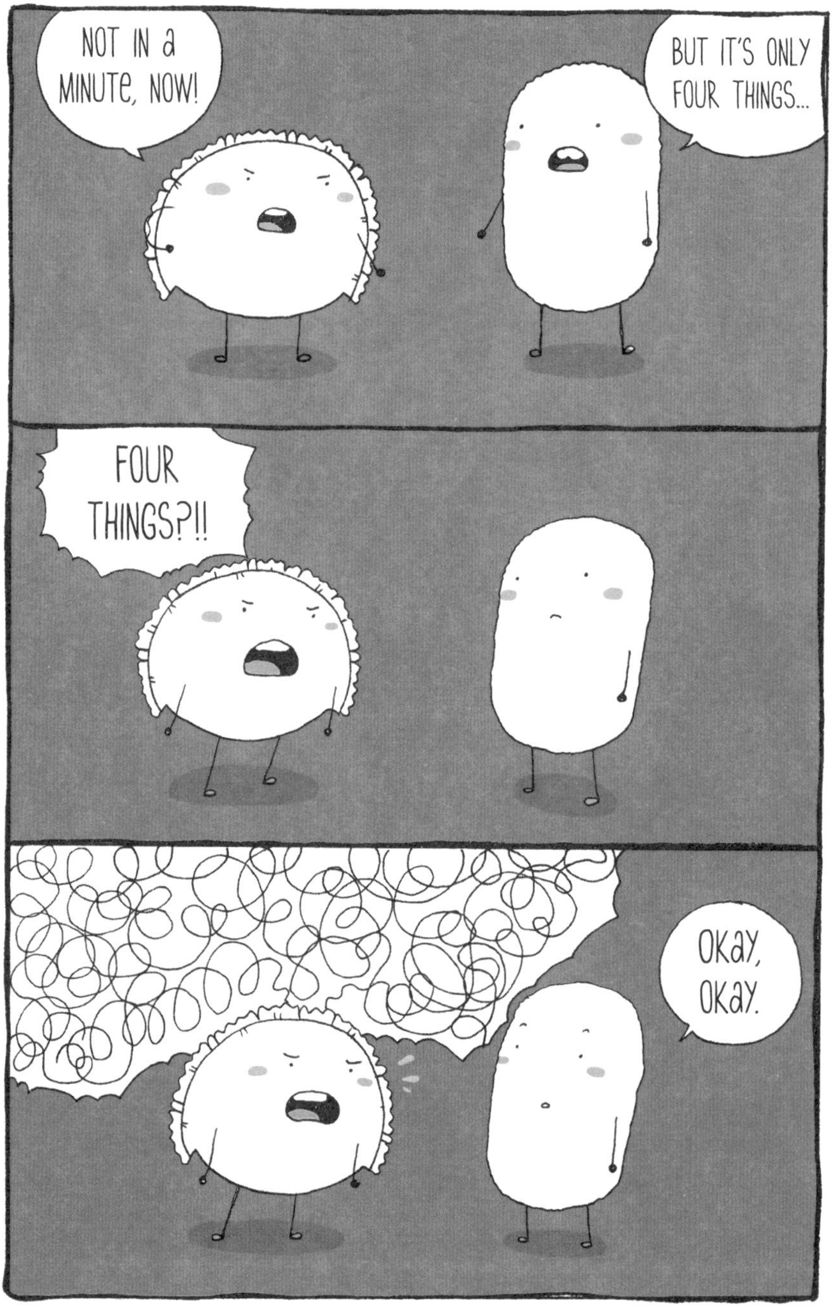
NOT IN a MINUTE, NOW!
BUT IT'S ONLY FOUR THINGS...
FOUR THINGS?!!
OKay, OKay.

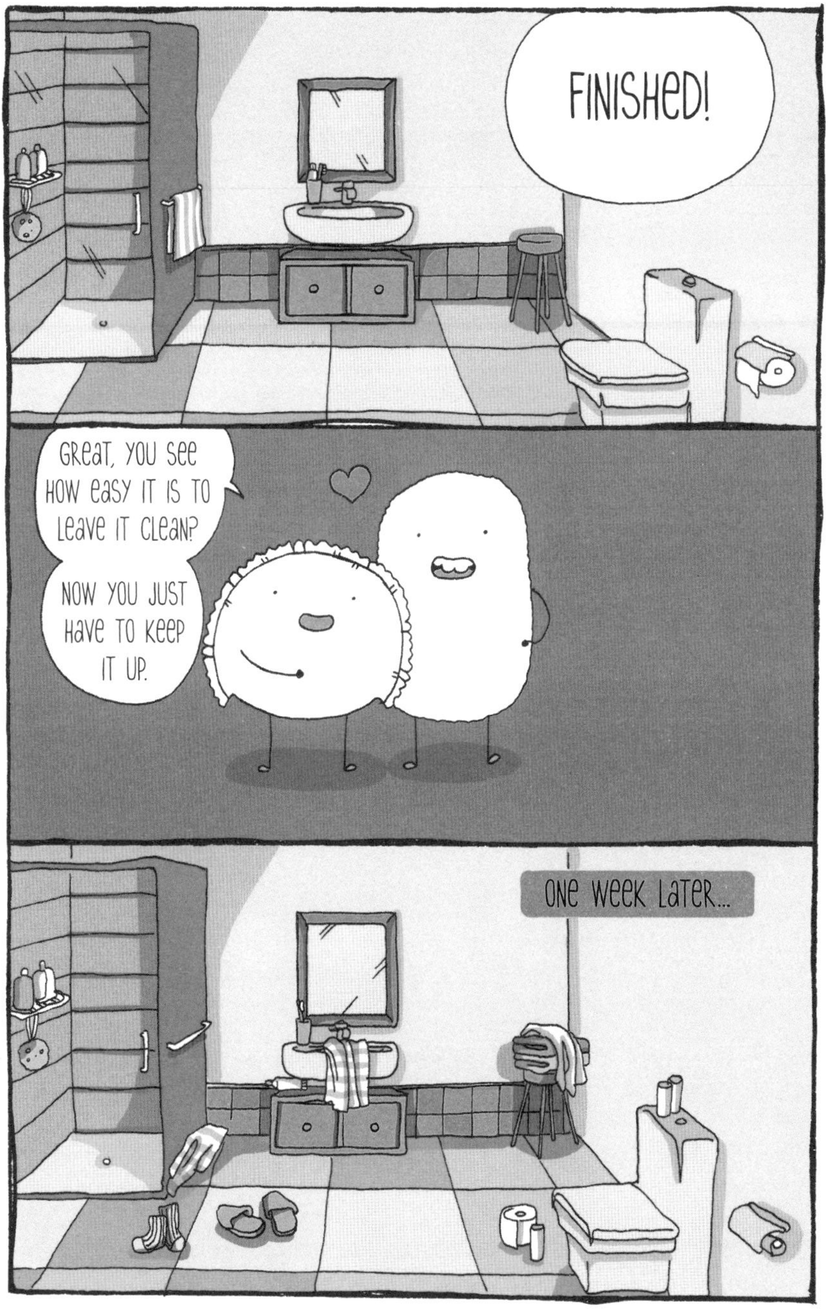
FINISHED!
GREAT, YOU SEE HOW EASY IT IS TO LEAVE IT CLEAN?
NOW YOU JUST HAVE TO KEEP IT UP.
ONE WEEK LATER...

- EMPANADA MOTIVATED -

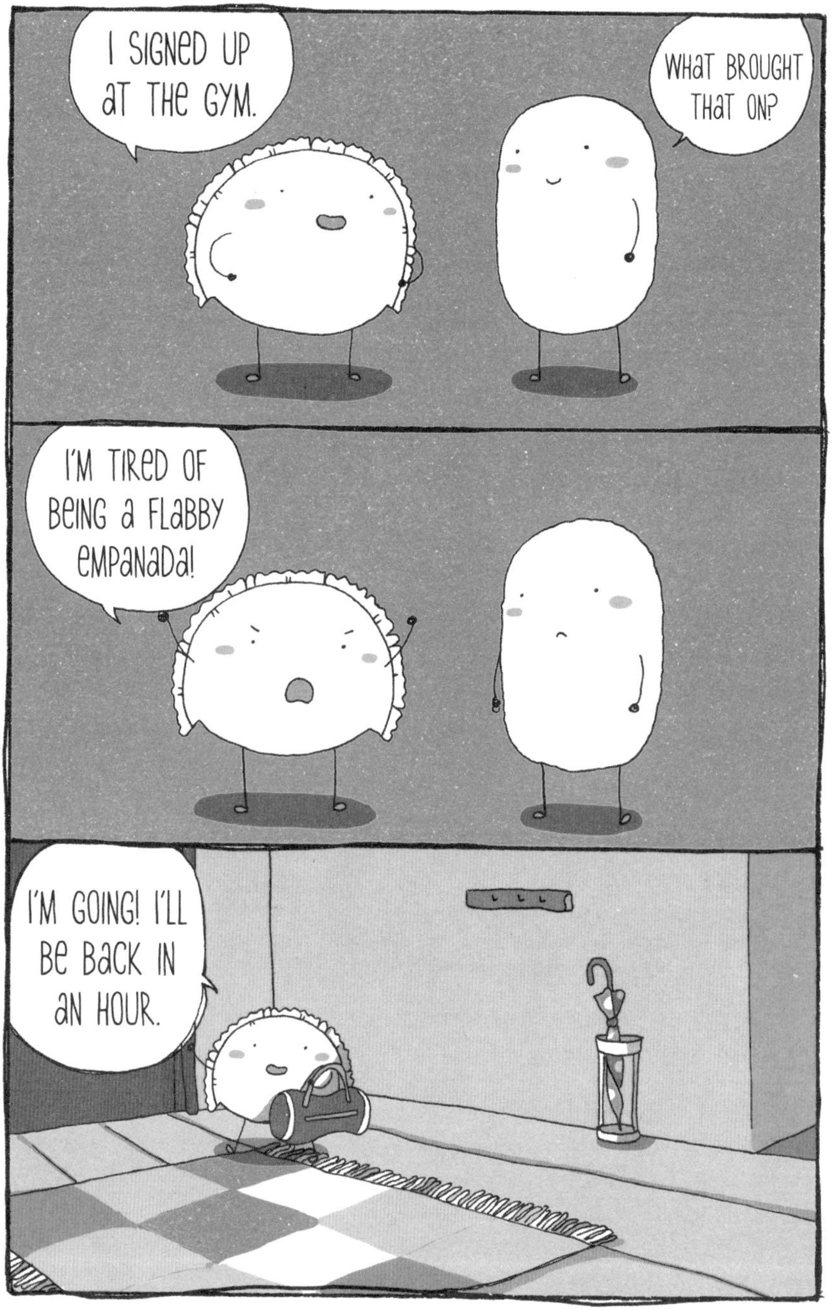
I SIGNED UP AT THE GYM.
WHAT BROUGHT THAT ON?
I'M TIRED OF BEING A FLABBY EMPANADA!
I'M GOING! I'LL BE BACK IN AN HOUR.

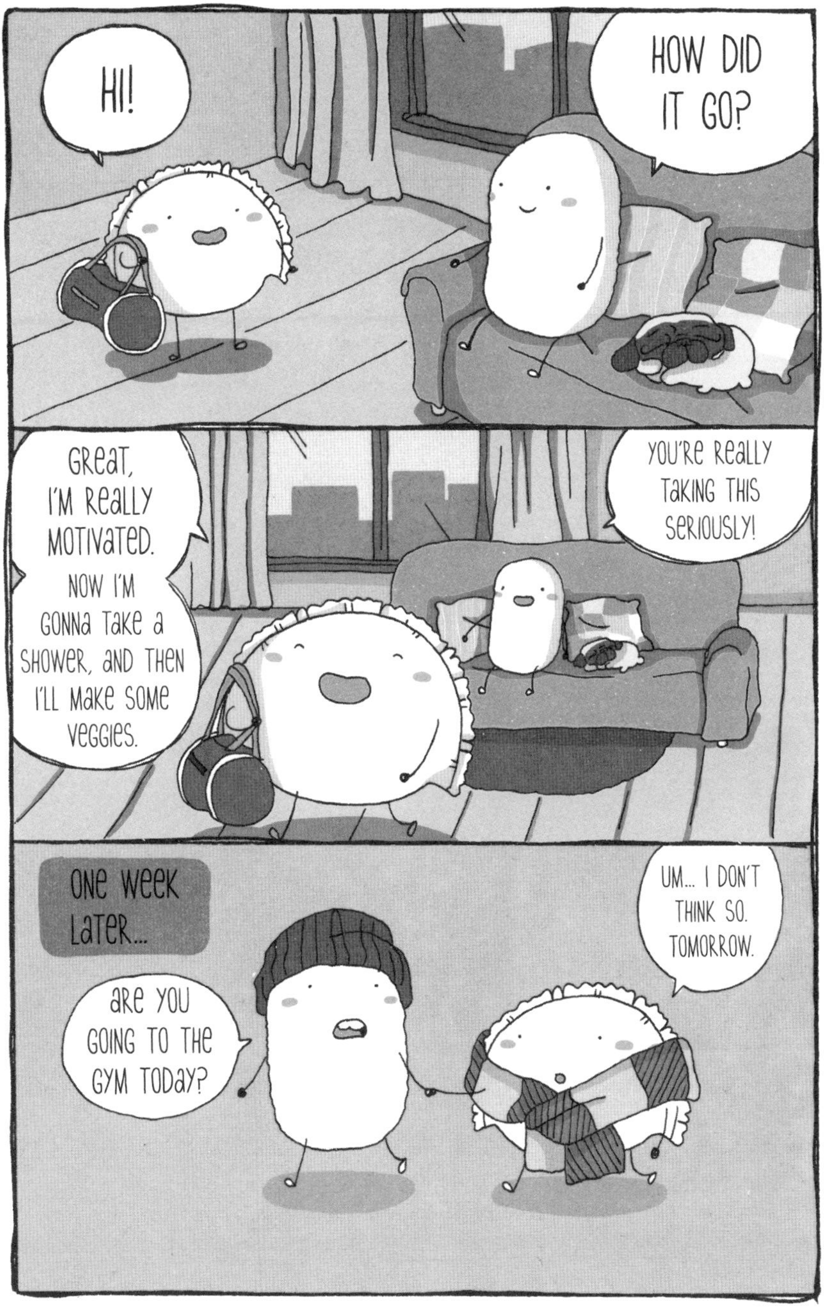
HI!
HOW DID IT GO?
GREAT, I'M REALLY MOTIVATED.
NOW I'M GONNA TAKE A SHOWER, AND THEN I'LL MAKE SOME VEGGIES.
YOU'RE REALLY TAKING THIS SERIOUSLY!
ONE WEEK LATER...
ARE YOU GOING TO THE GYM TODAY?
UM... I DON'T THINK SO. TOMORROW.

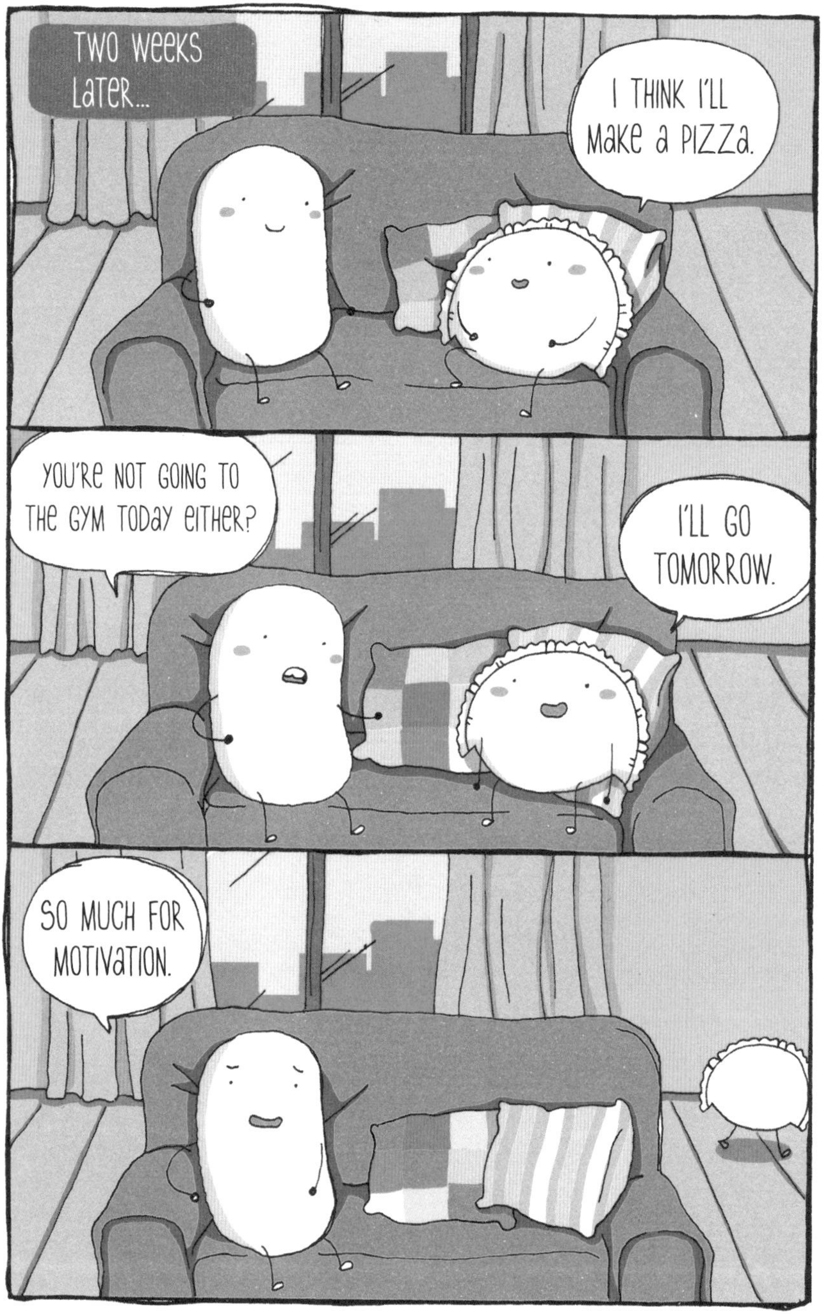
TWO WEEKS LATER...
I THINK I'LL MAKE A PIZZA.
YOU'RE NOT GOING TO THE GYM TODAY EITHER?
I'LL GO TOMORROW.
SO MUCH FOR MOTIVATION.

- THE COMFORTS OF HOME -

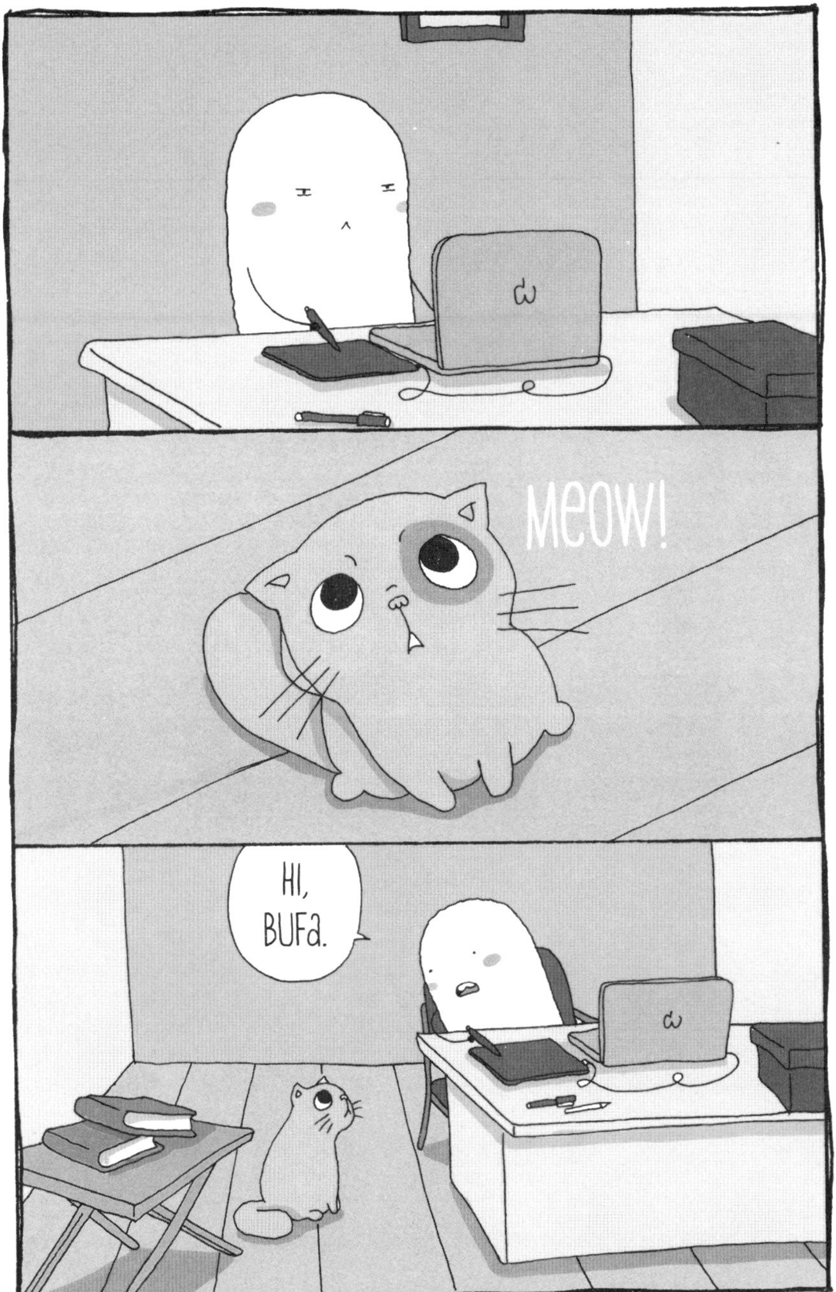
MEOW!
HI, BUFA.

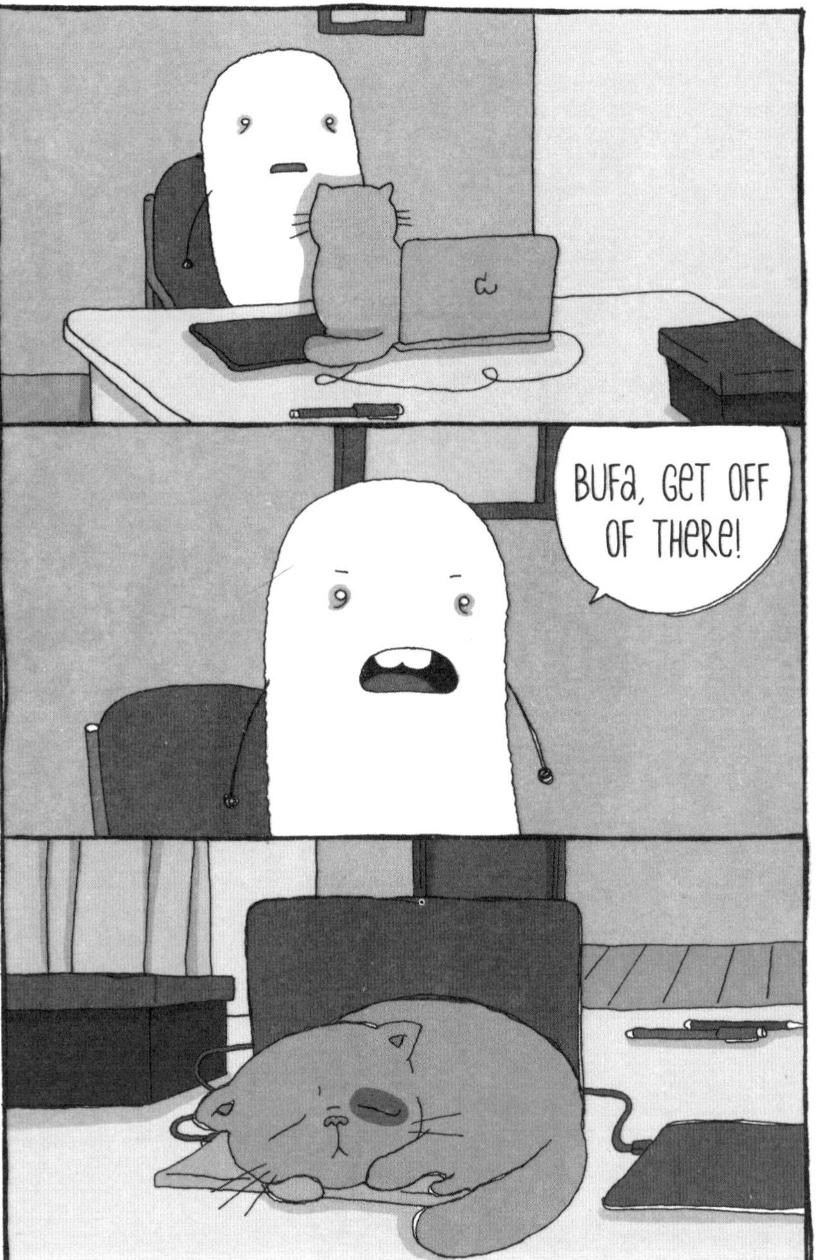
BUFa, GET OFF OF THERE!

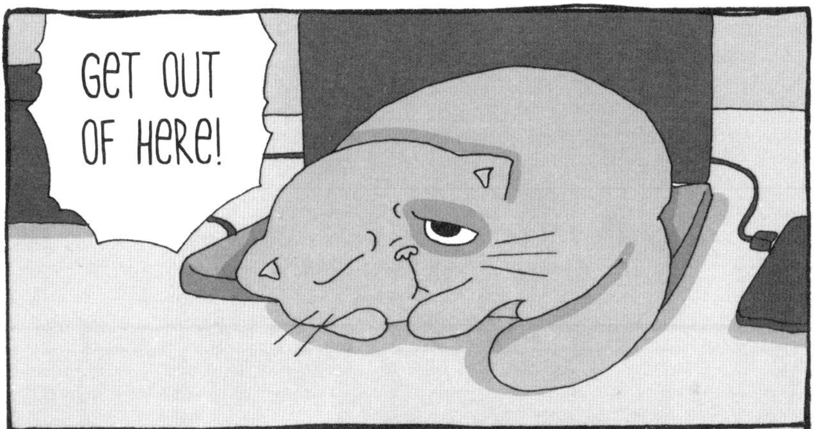
GET OUT OF HERE!

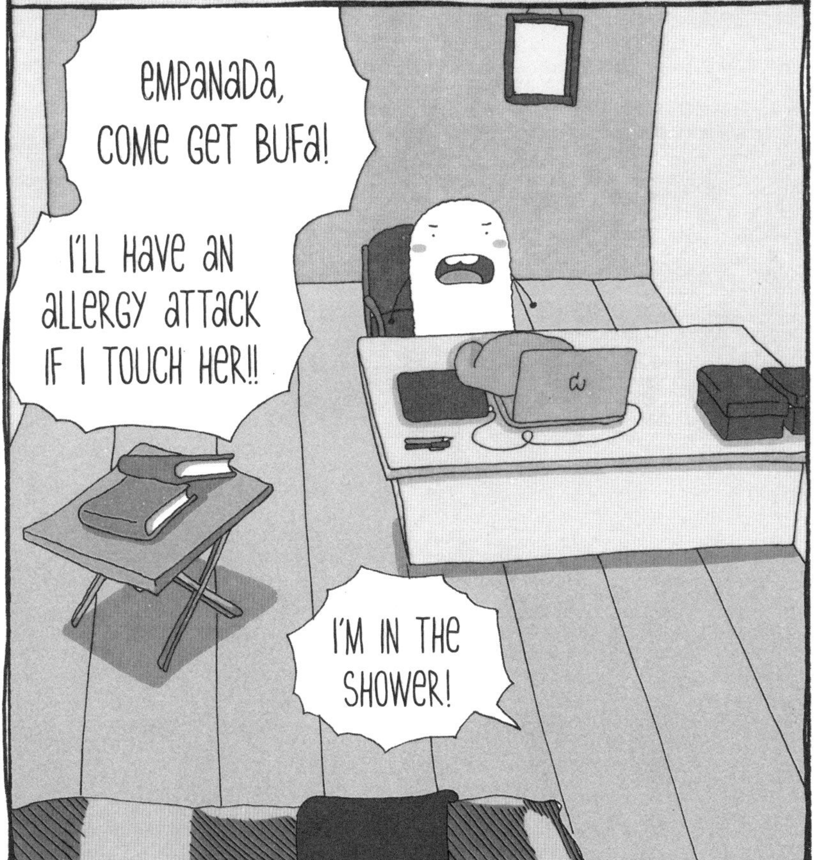
EMPANADA, COME GET BUFA!
I'LL HAVE AN ALLERGY ATTACK IF I TOUCH HER!!
I'M IN THE SHOWER!

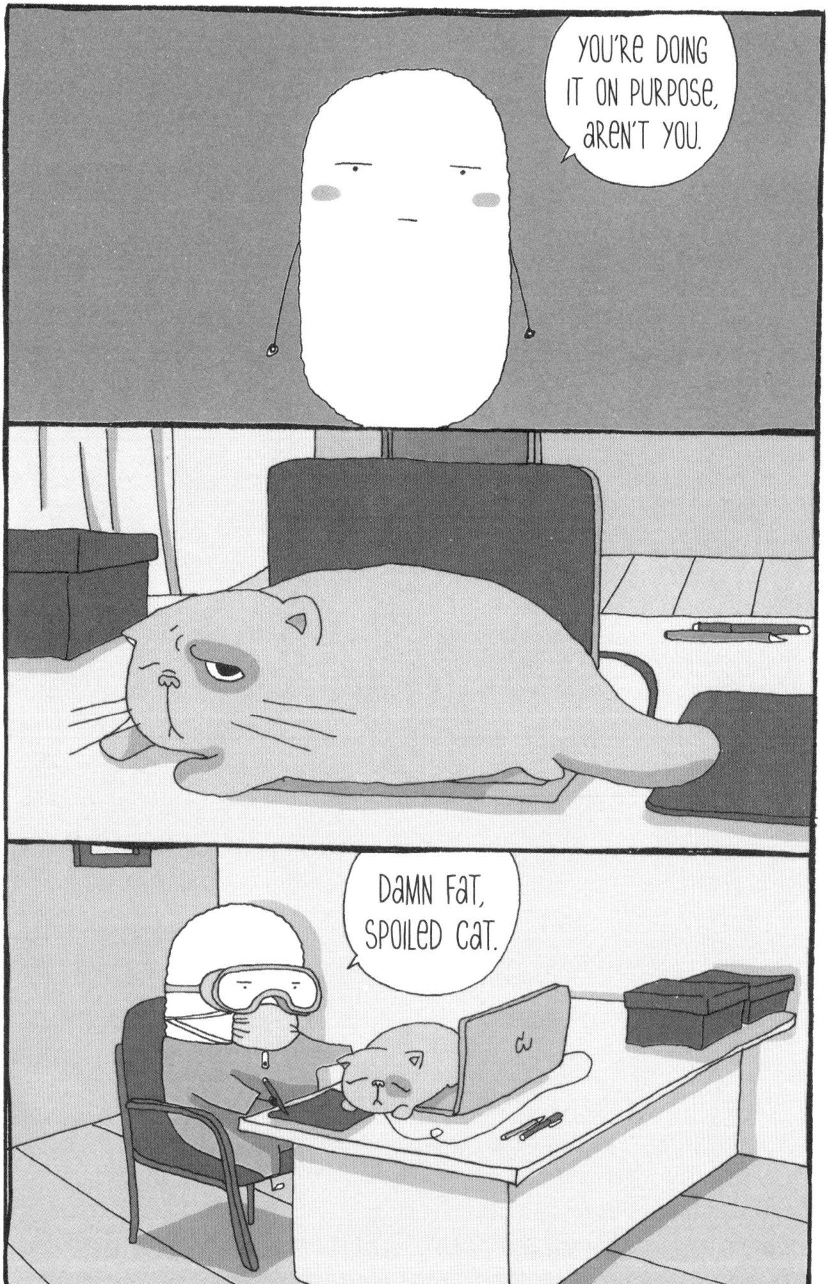
YOU'RE DOING IT ON PURPOSE, AREN'T YOU.
DAMN FAT, SPOILED CAT.

- SUPER PRODUCTIVE -

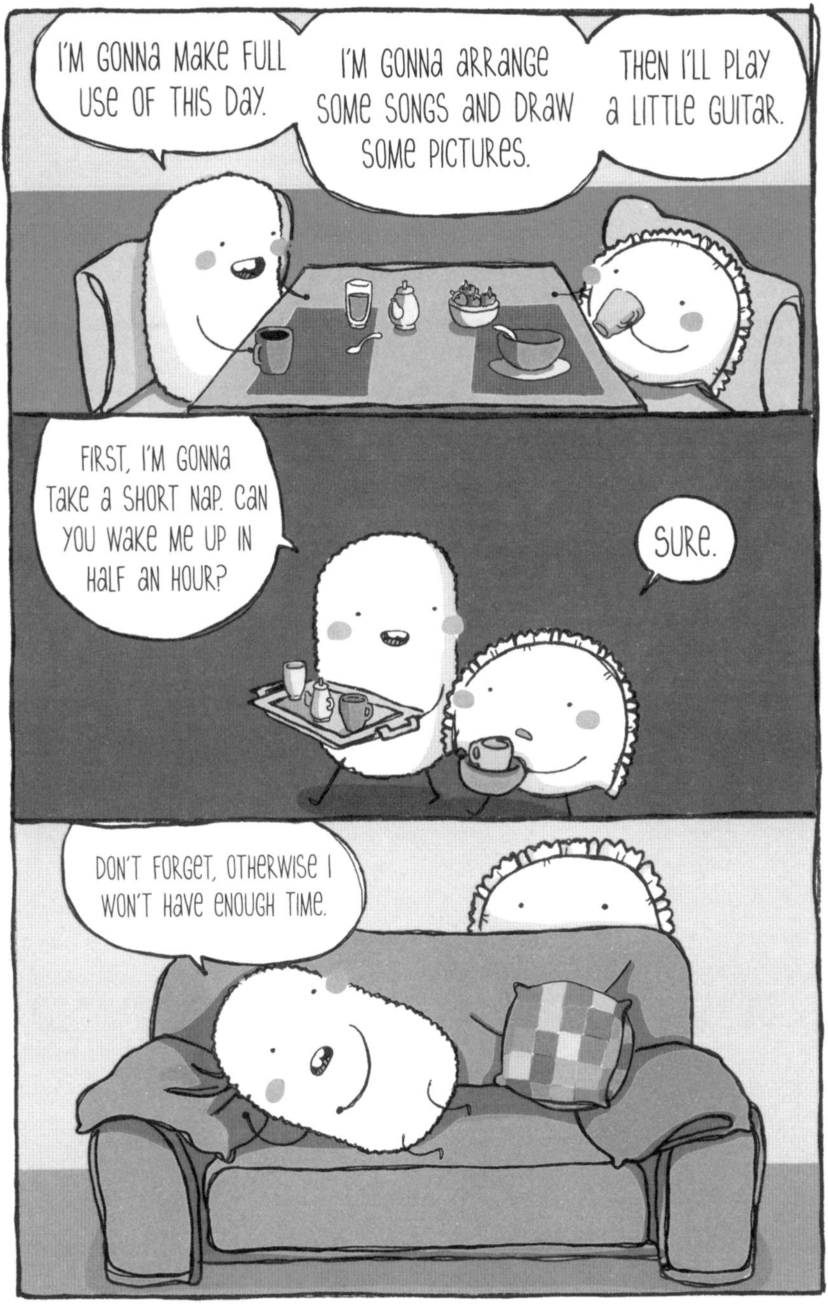
I'M GONNA MAKE FULL USE OF THIS DAY.
I'M GONNA ARRANGE SOME SONGS AND DRAW SOME PICTURES.
THEN I'LL PLAY A LITTLE GUITAR.
FIRST, I'M GONNA TAKE A SHORT NAP. CAN YOU WAKE ME UP IN HALF AN HOUR?
SURE.
DON'T FORGET, OTHERWISE I WON'T HAVE ENOUGH TIME.

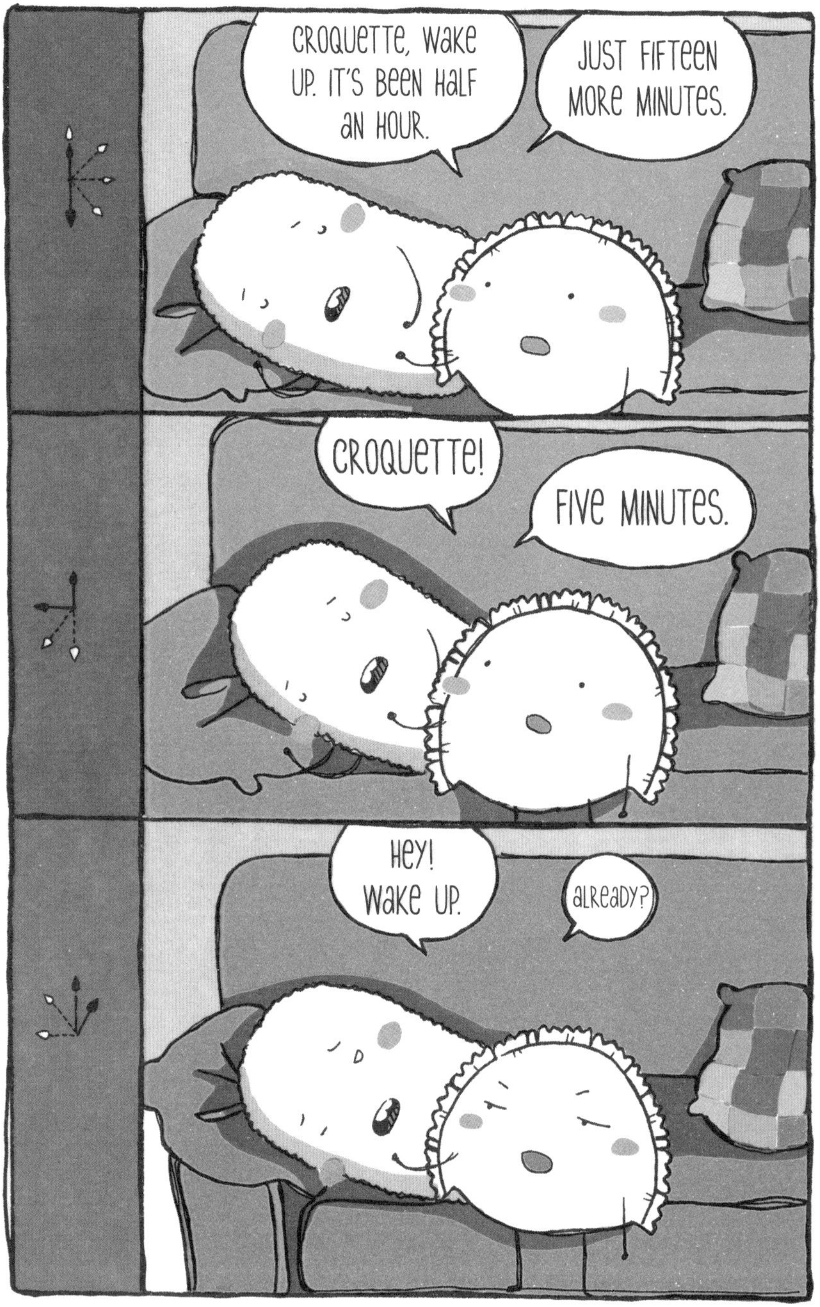
CROQUETTE, WAKE UP. IT'S BEEN HALF AN HOUR.
JUST FIFTEEN MORE MINUTES.
CROQUETTE!
FIVE MINUTES.
HEY! WAKE UP.
ALREADY?

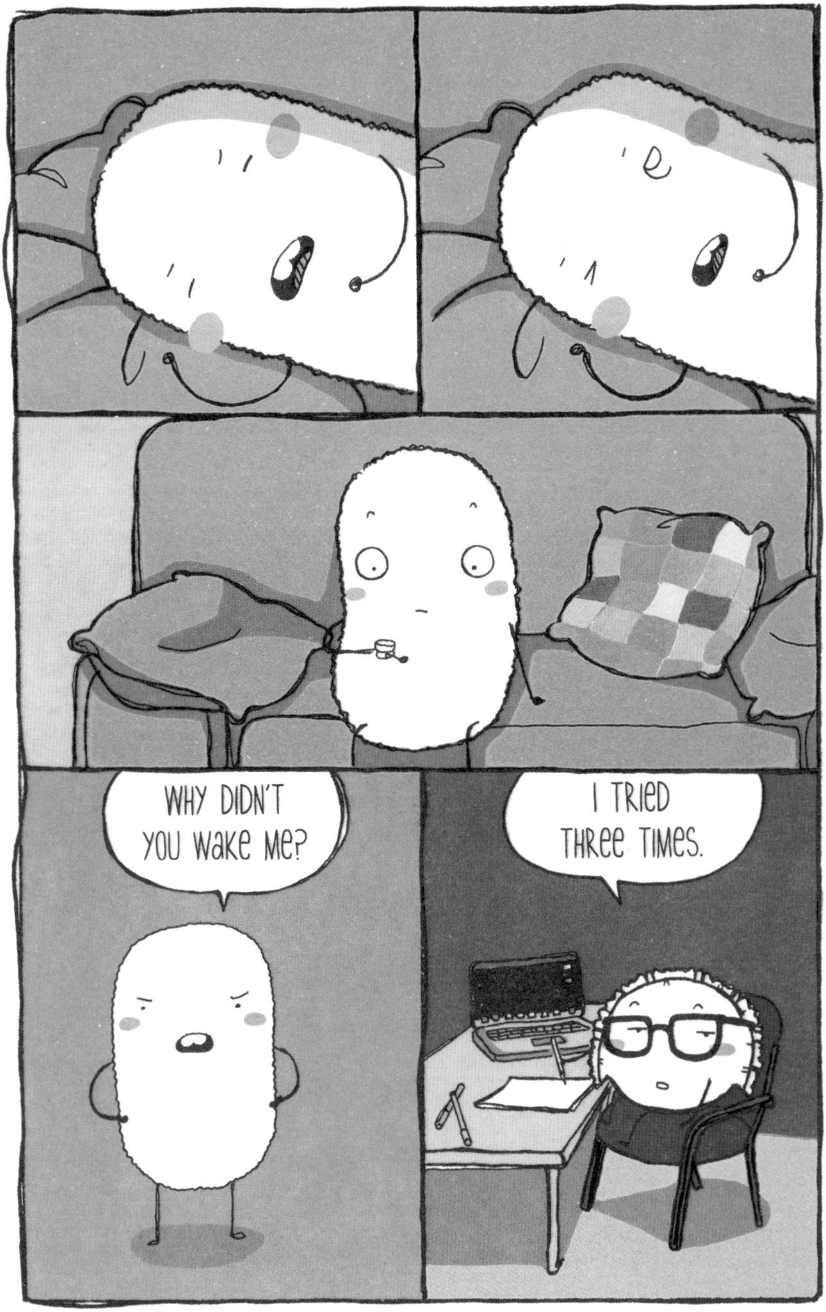
WHY DIDN'T YOU WAKE ME?
I TRIED THREE TIMES.

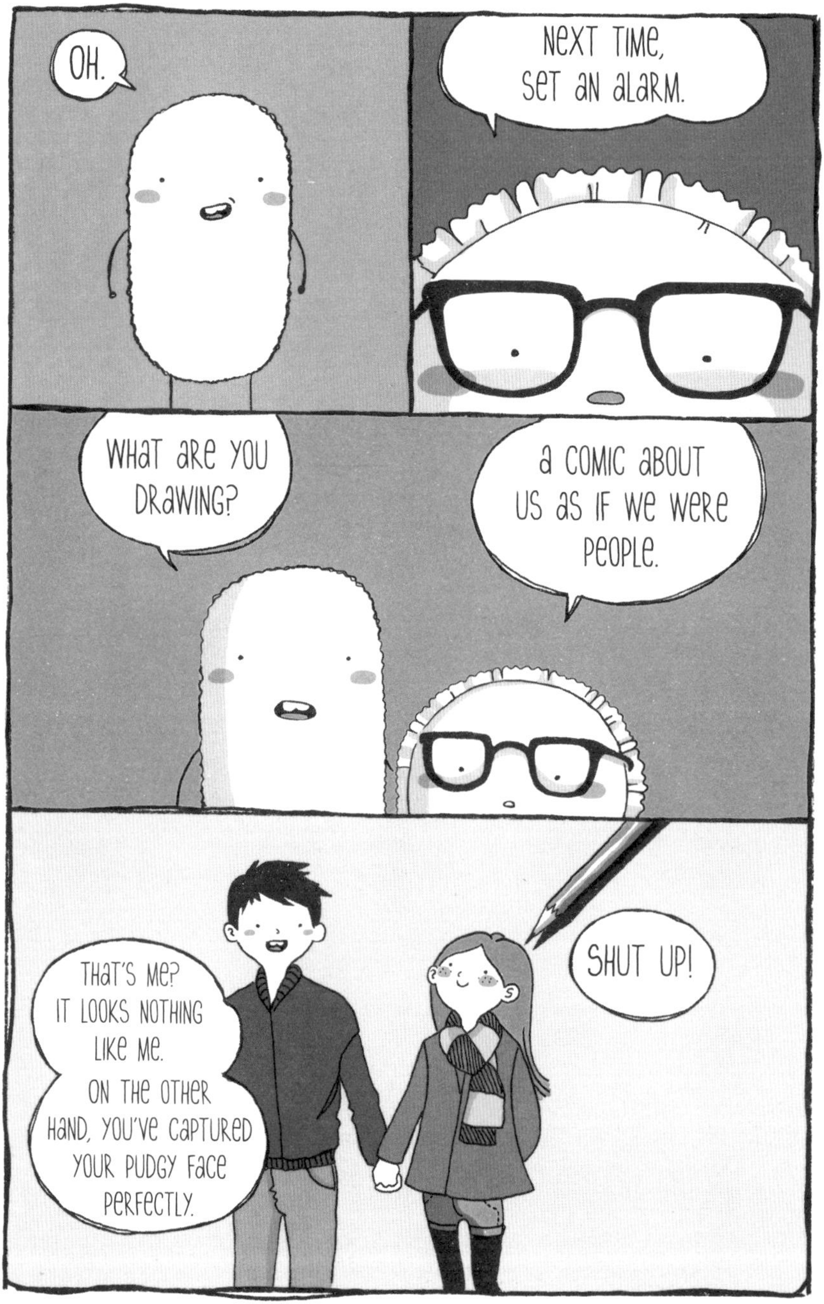
OH.
NEXT TIME, SET AN ALARM.
WHAT ARE YOU DRAWING?
A COMIC ABOUT US AS IF WE WERE PEOPLE.
THAT'S ME? IT LOOKS NOTHING LIKE ME.
ON THE OTHER HAND, YOU'VE CAPTURED YOUR PUDGY FACE PERFECTLY.
SHUT UP!

- SEE YOU LATER -

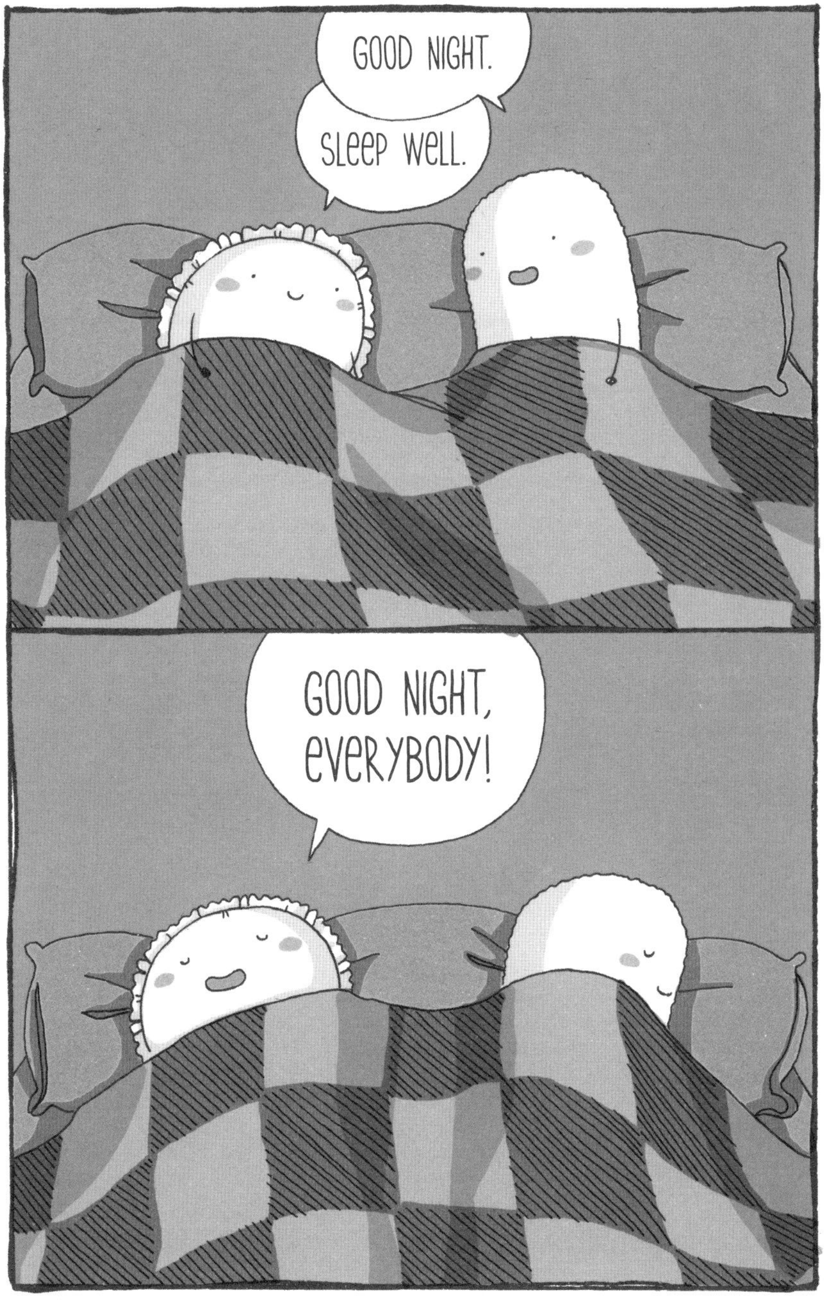
GOOD NIGHT.
SLEEP WELL.
GOOD NIGHT, EVERYBODY!

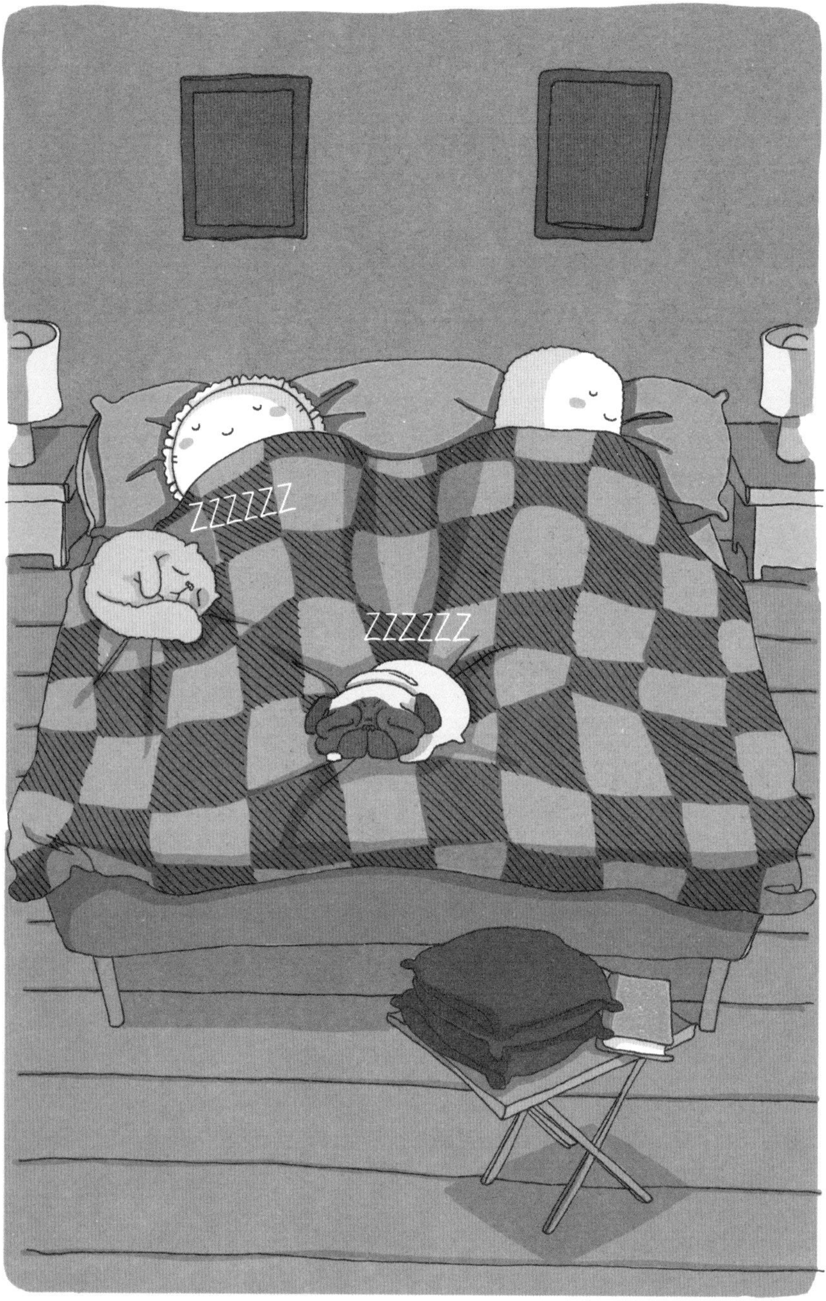
ZZZZZZ
ZZZZZZ